Mind Over Murder

Mind Over Murder

DNA and Other Forensic Adventures

JACK BATTEN

Canadian Cataloguing in Publication Data
Batten, Jack, date
    Mind over murder: DNA and other forensic adventures

ISBN 0-7710-1066-4

1. Forensic sciences – Canada. 2. Murder – Canada – Investigation.
3. Trials – Canada. I. Title.

HV8073.B37 1995   363.2'5'0971   C95-932116-0

The publishers acknowledge the support of the Canada Council and
the Ontario Arts Council for their publishing program.

Typesetting by M&S, Toronto

Printed and bound in Canada on acid-free paper.

McClelland & Stewart Inc.
The Canadian Publishers
481 University Avenue
Toronto, Ontario
M5G 2E9

1 2 3 4 5   99 98 97 96 95

To Wendy, who loves a good mystery

C O N T E N T S

ACKNOWLEDGEMENTS / ix

INTRODUCTION / xi

ONE — Ink:
The Case of the Suspect Notebook / 1

TWO — Footprints:
The Case of the Grounded Air Nikes / 62

THREE — Food:
The Case of Death's Time / 85

FOUR — Numbers:
The Case of the Man Who Took Ten Percent / 132

FIVE — Hair, Blood, Semen, DNA:
The Case of the Perfect Science / 162

EPILOGUE — DNA, the Future of Forensics? / 244

A C K N O W L E D G E M E N T S

This is a book that deals with the excitement of solving crimes from the standpoint of two disciplines, the legal and the scientific. As a graduate of the University of Toronto Law School, class of '57, I had the background to handle the legal material. But the science was another matter; my learning in that department ended with grade-twelve physics and chemistry. So I needed help and guidance, and I got them from an extremely learned, articulate, and generous collection of forensic specialists in biology, in document analysis, in hair-and-fibre analysis, in DNA, and in other exotic fields. I also found enormous help in conversations with lawyers, judges, and police officers. All of the foregoing experts are named in the course of the book's text, and I am deeply grateful to each one of them.

I'm just as grateful to the following people who assisted me, but who aren't mentioned in the text: Nick Pron (for his tour through Toronto's cocaine industry), Julian Porter (for providing me with a transcript of the Steven Truscott trial), Sylvia Barrett (for alerting me to an intriguing little corner of the Truscott case and for providing other guidance), Dennis Gruending (for his insights into Emmett Hall), Paul McLaughlin (for steering me into the material on Bob Lindquist's adventures in forensic accounting), Mary Rutherford (for her exhaustive research on the Johnny Terceira case), Joseph Wambaugh (for writing a great book, *The Blooding*, about the first DNA case), Jim Lockyer (for lending me the Terceira trial transcript), Jennifer Harris (for thinking up the apt and alliterative title for the book), Pat Kennedy (for her creative and thorough editing), and Marjorie Harris (for her love and encouragement during the writing of this book and all the others).

INTRODUCTION

When I began work on this book in the early spring of 1994, O. J. Simpson was a retired football player and nobody, except some forensic scientists and a few criminal lawyers, knew much about DNA testing. When I finished the book a year later, Simpson was the strained-looking fellow sitting at the end of the defence table in the latest Trial of the Century, and not many more people, apart from those forensic scientists and criminal lawyers, had yet got a handle on the intricacies and implications of testing for DNA. This book won't add anything to anybody's understanding of O. J. – he doesn't appear in its pages – but I hope it will wipe away some of the mystery about DNA profiling and shed light on other pieces of magic that scientists and their allies in the forensic fieldwork at the scenes of crimes and in the laboratories.

That was the point of the book when I set out to do the research for it: to apply one reasonably inquisitive and alert layperson's mind (my own) to the increasingly complex world of scientific crime solving. It wasn't all that long ago that the sleuthing of the first case by the use of fingerprints was considered a very big deal; the year was 1902, as a matter of fact, when Det.-Sgt. Charles Collins of Scotland Yard's brand-new

Fingerprint Branch nabbed a veteran break-and-enter man named Harry Jackson, who left his thumbprint on the paintwork of a house he burgled in South London. Fingerprints are still with us today, still useful in crime solving, as are such other standbys as ballistics, dental comparison, and the Identikit.

The development of all of these clever devices, indeed the development of the scientific approach to sleuthing in general, occurred in a random fashion through much of the nineteenth century and early twentieth. Policemen and scientists working alone and independently came up with splendid techniques and inventions, but it took years for anyone – principally the police departments – to bring together the techniques and inventions into a coherent system. Forensic science is defined as any science that is used in dealing with legal issues, usually *criminal* legal issues, but the organization of forensic sciences into departments that worked hand-in-glove with the police lagged far behind the mar-vellous brainstorms of the individual scientists and inventors.

So, for example, in October 1836, English chemist James Marsh, tinkering at the Royal Arsenal in Woolrich, conceived a sure-fire method of detecting the presence of the tiniest amount of arsenic in a dead body (arsenic having been for centuries the favourite means of despatching an unwanted spouse or other enemy).

It was a British civil servant in India, William Herschel, who hit on fingerprints as the bodily feature that absolutely differed from person to person and was therefore infallible in detecting a villain. That was in 1877, but, as we've seen, it wasn't until twenty-five years later that the redoubtable Detective-Sergeant Collins put the discovery to forensic use.

In 1901, Karl Landsteiner, a biologist at the University of Vienna, set the foundations for serology when he discovered that all blood fell into four main types, A, B, AB, and O.

And a few years later, it was Edmond Locard, a French scien-tist working in Lyons, who enunciated the theory upon which all forensic science is based. This is the "contact trace theory," and it says that every contact must leave a trace, that every criminal will leave some trace of himself at the scene of a crime or will carry away on himself some trace of the crime scene.

So it went, theories, inventions, ideas, techniques, all in isolation, waiting for someone to house them under one forensic roof. The someone turned out to be Edmond Locard himself. In 1910, he set up, in Lyons, the first laboratory in the world where scientists devoted themselves to analysing the physical evidence from crime scenes by using all the available forensic methods. Locard didn't waste any time putting himself and his lab on the map. Just a year later, he applied his contact trace theory to solve the case of Émile Gourbin.

Gourbin was suspected of having strangled his girlfriend in a fit of rage, but he produced what seemed to be an unshakeable alibi for the time of the murder. Locard, pursuing the notion that Gourbin would have carried with him some trace from the crime scene, took scrapings from under the suspect's fingernails. When Locard examined the scrapings under a microscope, he found flakes of skin that could have come from the dead woman's neck. That wasn't conclusive of anything, but when Locard revealed that he had also found wisps of the cosmetic powder that the girlfriend customarily patted on her face and neck, Émile Gourbin was so stunned and dazzled by Locard's forensic deductions that he confessed to the murder.

Locard's concept of a forensic laboratory spread quickly among the police forces of Europe. It spread just as rapidly to Canada, where a forensic pathologist named Wilfrid Derôme, who had done much of his studying of criminology in Paris, opened a forensic lab in Montreal in 1914. Derôme's lab was embraced by the Quebec attorney-general's office, and for almost twenty years it was the only forensic facility in North America. Even J. Edgar Hoover's FBI was left at the gate in this sleuthing area. It wasn't until the 1930s that other police organizations got into the forensic act. The FBI, after Hoover twice visited Derôme's facility, established a crime lab in Washington, D.C., in 1932. The RCMP and the Ontario attorney-general's office followed a couple of years later with their own labs. Forensic science had at last been institutionalized.

As the forensic scientists became more ingenious over the years, and as the instruments they wielded in their labs grew more sophisticated, the means they came up with to track the perpetrators of crime began to approach the kind of wonders previously known only in science fiction.

For example – for the prime example – DNA.

The route I took to investigate each piece of forensic science was by way of a Canadian trial, and, in the instance of DNA, the trial was one of the first in this country in which DNA was explored and tested, analysed and judged, and generally put on revealing display. The case, which involved a horrendous murder, began with the crime in October of 1990 and continued with a trial of fifty-six days in late 1992 and early 1993. But when I began to ask about the case, even at a remove of a year and more from the main events, the excitement of the people connected with it, the scientists from the DNA Unit at Ontario's Centre of Forensic Sciences, the scientists who studied blood and hair and semen and DNA, remained vivid and palpable. These men and one woman loved their work, thrilled to it, to this cutting-edge stuff, to going into their labs and using a new and difficult and – to their minds – certain science to catch a killer. They were excited by their jobs, and fortunately for me, the inquiring neophyte, a newcomer to this dazzling scientific world, they were keen to talk about the work. I listened and looked and, I hope, absorbed.

That was the way it was with the DNA people, and that was the way it was, in another case, with an Ontario Provincial Police forensics investigator who specialized in catching criminals through the footprints they left behind at crime scenes. This man was entranced by footprints. Even better from my standpoint as the inquiring visitor, he was happy to explain the arcane procedures – part Rube Goldberg, part Sherlock Holmes – that were involved in lifting footprints from the earth, from floors, from snow. And just as my OPP man was enthusiastic and eloquent about footprints and the satisfying results they produced, so was a chartered accountant, of all unlikely sleuth figures, keen to reveal how his brand of accounting, the forensic brand, led to the recovery of millions of dollars scammed in an international con game.

Since all of these cases reached their climax in the courtroom, defence lawyers entered into the picture, sometimes as allies of the forensic scientists, more often as their tormentors. At one trial, a defence lawyer stepped temporarily into the role of private eye and created the circumstances in which scientists who specialized in the analysis of inks could trot out their amazing tricks. But more typically, the defence lawyers were the people who put the scientists to the test. In the DNA case, for example, the counsel representing the accused murderer seemed to be the only person in the courtroom, apart from the scientists he was cross-examining, who had a firm grasp on the new science. And the lawyer, along with all the other lawyers I approached in the various cases, wasn't at all reluctant to give me his slant on forensic scientists and their work. He thought – no surprise here – that DNA profiling was an incomplete and possibly misleading science.

The most famous encounter in a Canadian courtroom between scientists and defence lawyers occurred in perhaps the most troubling murder trial in the history of this country's jurisprudence, the Steven Truscott case. It is the only case in this book that doesn't have a history as recent as the 1990s. The Truscott trial took place in 1959, and the unprecedented rehearing before the Supreme Court of Canada in 1966. Most of the principals from both trials are now dead or, in Steven Truscott's case, living in circumstances that put him beyond reach. But the written records remain very much alive, as do the memories of one of the trial's observers, and they provide a classic record of the collision between the world of forensic science and the world of defence advocacy. Scientists are certain they have answers. Lawyers know they have questions. The two points of view clashed in the Truscott case in ways that were, as courtroom drama, thrilling, and, as a search for scientific truth, perhaps more confusing than enlightening.

It was a clash — science versus the defence bar — that will continue to be repeated in trials where technical evidence becomes critical in making cases against people accused of crimes. For example, again and most compellingly, scientific advances surrounding DNA. This new science will be increasingly the tool that police and prosecutors use to go for convictions against alleged rapists and murderers. Defence lawyers will need to understand DNA profiling. So will judges, juries, reporters, all of us. That understanding, as I discovered in looking into DNA and the other forensic sciences in this book, is not easy to come by. But it is, even for a layperson, enthralling.

Ink:

The Case of the Suspect Notebook

MIKE GURMAN LOOKED LIKE a biker who'd dialled the 800 number for the Body Tech workout video. He wore hair down to his shoulders, a raggedy goatee, a black T-shirt and black jeans, and an expression on his face that said "mess with me and you die." What was missing was the biker's gut. Gurman had the testosterone, but he had muscle tone, too.

Mike Gurman was an undercover drug cop. He had joined the Metropolitan Toronto Police Force on August 29, 1977, and moved up from day one. By the late 1980s, he was an experienced member of the Narcotics Division of the Morality Squad. He was a guy who hung out in lowlife bars, made contact with the dealers, and set up buys. It was Gurman who built towards the moment when a dealer, trusting him, would get some serious drugs out in the open, a K or two of cocaine. Then half a dozen other undercover cops from Gurman's surveillance squad would erupt on the scene. They'd wave their badges and shout at the dealer, "You're busted, man!"

On this particular day, though, Thursday, June 28, 1990, working the case called Project Narrows, Gurman didn't have the limelight role. This gig belonged to Spike Glendenning. He was the cop who'd gone undercover and hooked up to the dealers. Everybody else in Project Narrows played supporting parts. They did surveillance, followed the suspects around, reported where they went, who they saw. At one point, Gurman had had to get on a plane to tail a guy to Montreal. At other times, he did protective surveillance on Spike Glendenning. He watched Spike in restaurants, in cars, rode bodyguard from a distance. It was tedious work, three months of mostly sitting on his ass, but it was part of the job. Mike Gurman was a diligent cop.

Now the job was ending; it was time for the final act of Project Narrows. At two o'clock in the afternoon of June 28, Gurman and another twenty-two people from Narcotics gathered at the Morality Bureau. Det. Ed Tymburski laid out the day's plan. Tymburski was one of the men calling the shots on this operation.

Glendenning had manipulated himself into a position of trust with the dealers. Today he was set to make a major cocaine buy from a man named Steve Warren. Glendenning had done many smaller purchases over the previous few months, but this was to be the big one. When Glendenning gave the signal, the rest of the unit would move in, arrest Warren and, better yet, arrest the man further up the drug chain of command from Warren. This guy, Warren's immediate superior, was Ulpiano Aguilera.

"The takedown is on," Ed Tymburski said at the meeting.

At 4:35 P.M., the twenty-three Narcotics guys climbed into their unmarked vehicles, or skates. (The cops call a vehicle a "skate." A vehicle they're following is the "target skate." Cop jargon can be as quirky as criminal slang. When police raid a drug operation, it's a "takedown." The cash that an undercover cop like Spike Glendenning carries to fake a drug purchase is "flash" money. Flash it for the bad guys, but don't let it out of your sight.) Gurman was driving his skate with an old buddy from Narcotics, Alby Forde. A black man, Forde was dressed undercover too, jeans, T-shirt, dreadlocks spilling down the sides of his head, a yellow baseball cap perched on top.

Forde would, if all proceeded according to script, handle much cocaine on this day, since he had been appointed the exhibits officer on the takedown. He was the cop who would keep track of everything his fellow officers scooped up by way of evidence. That ought to include three kilos of cocaine and maybe more.

If Ulpiano Aguilera and his wife, Maria, were looking for a discreet address, they had found it. The house they lived in at 46 Acacia Avenue faced south onto a small park, and was bounded in the rear and on the west by trees and thick brush that ran down an incline to the Humber River. Their only immediate neighbours lived in the house to the east, and it was cut off by leafy trees and high shrubbery planted on the Aguilera property.

Acacia Avenue is in the northwest corner of Metro, just above the old town of Weston. The postwar houses in the neighbourhood are built in a higgledy-piggledy collection of styles. Clapboard cottages sit cheek by jowl with elaborate Italian-villa mansionettes. The house at 46 Acacia is one of the more tasteful on the street. Its architecture is vaguely Tudor, and it has two stories of beige brick, a double garage, and tidy landscaping.

But while the house and its protective surroundings kept the Aguileras and their four children more or less a secret from the neighbours, the cars were a giveaway to an observant eye. Five or six vehicles usually crowded the driveway and the street out front. They included stretch limousines, a Jaguar, a slick GMC van, and a Mercedes. The limousines might be understandable since Ulpiano was supposed to drive limo for a living. But that didn't explain all those other pricey vehicles.

And what about the jewellery Ulpiano sported? A diamond-and-sapphire pinky ring, a wristwatch studded with diamonds, a necklace with a twenty-peso gold coin glittering in the middle – the man was a walking billboard for Tiffany's.

How did the Aguileras afford it all – the nice house, the cars and jewellery – this humble limo driver and his wife who'd come to Toronto from South America so recently, about a dozen years earlier, that they still spoke English with a pronounced Spanish accent?

At the time of the planned takedown on June 28, 1990, as Gurman and the other cops massed to move in, an Italian-Canadian businessman named Diego Serrano was sitting in a jail in the Calabria region near the tip of Italy's boot. He'd been there for almost fifteen months, waiting for extradition back to Toronto, where he had been charged with trafficking in cocaine. Serrano was very unhappy. He had better things to do with his time in Calabria than rot in jail. He had his Calabrian retirement project to finish, an apartment complex he was building, its $5-million penthouse designed just for him, with gold fixtures in the bathroom and a retractable roof over the swimming pool. Now he was in jail, a hard-working businessman like him wasting his time in the slammer.

Ten years earlier, in the early 1980s, Serrano was running his own furniture factory in Woodbridge on the northwest perimeter of Metro Toronto, a favourite town for prosperous Italian immigrants. But the furniture business had slumped, and Serrano owed the banks almost half a million dollars.

That's when a man whom Serrano knew slightly called on him with a proposition. The man was Bernardo Arcila, a mysterious character who always wore a panama like Sydney Greenstreet in *The Maltese Falcon*. Arcila had a bookstore on Bloor Street in the centre of Toronto. But it wasn't rare volumes that Arcila discussed with Serrano; it was a drive that Arcila wanted Serrano to take to Florida. Arcila made it sound simple: just drive the car, a Toyota Tercel, to Miami, go to a certain address, wait a couple of hours, and drive the Toyota back to Toronto. The fee was $30,000. Serrano made the trip. He made many trips in the early 1980s and collected many $30,000 fees. He paid off the bank, liberated his furniture business, and began to feel a little bit wealthy.

At the beginning, Arcila had told Serrano not to ask questions. But Serrano was no dummy. He knew, going down to Miami, that the panelling in the Toyota was lined in cash, and he knew, coming back, the panelling was lined in cocaine, good stuff, product of Colombia. Serrano also realized that his share, the $30,000 per trip, was chicken feed. This was easy to figure. Each load in the Toyota produced almost a million and a half dollars, and Arcila kept much of it. Serrano wanted his share of the big bucks, and by the late 1980s, he had quietly muscled in on Arcila, stealing away some of the customers from the man in the panama, setting up his own clientele, running his own cars to Miami.

Arcila, for his part, decided to close down his Toronto operation. It wasn't Serrano who scared him off. It was, as Arcila perceived it, the increasingly vigilant police surveillance that started to show up in 1988. A police unit called the Amigo Squad had been established with the aim of shutting down guys like Arcila and Serrano. Arcila beat it to the United States and then to Colombia. He was still there, laughing, when everybody else in Toronto was getting busted.

Serrano couldn't afford to flee, not in the late 1980s. He was earning too much money. He was also spending too much. He opened a splashy restaurant on Dufferin Street, took a million-dollar mortgage on an amusement park in Oshawa called Treasure Valley, acquired a mistress. All of these proved to be money losers. The Toronto real-estate market nosedived just at the time Serrano elected to get into it, and his stock investments weren't astute either. Serrano couldn't afford to bail out of the cocaine business. It was his only enterprise whose bottom line was written in black ink.

He took on a number-two man, Vincenzo DeBellis, another guy who came from a legit business background. DeBellis was in men's clothing; he had a shop in Toronto's chic Yorkville district.

After DeBellis entered the cocaine trade, he grew richer than he ever would have tailoring suits, although he had to admit the work was fraying on the nerves. DeBellis did much of the supervising of the fleet of cars – Mazdas became the vehicle of choice – that made the runs to Florida and back. He tended to the warehousing of the drugs in buildings in Vaughan Township, another area north of Toronto with a significant Italian population, and he handled most of the money laundering through the exchange kiosks at Union Station. It was risky stuff, but DeBellis accumulated $1.3 million in personal wealth in just three years in the late 1980s. He lavished the money on his lovely house in the expensive Thornhill neighbourhood, furnishing the place in antiques, a $15,000 chandelier, Louis Quinze chairs at $10,000 a pop. Life for Vincenzo was good, if dangerous.

The coke business needed plenty of manpower, guys to drive the cars, to retail the cocaine, to do the courier work. Serrano seems to have been mainly responsible for recruiting bodies. Certainly it was Serrano who approached his buddy Ulpiano Aguilera and proposed an opportunity for the limousine driver to earn some drug money. Ulpiano thought it over. He considered, well, with four kids to raise on a chauffeur's salary and tips, why not? It seemed safe enough, this cocaine business, if a man was careful. Look at Diego, he was walking the streets, and he had much, much money. Ulpiano declared that he was in and that he and his wife were a team. And the Aguileras stayed in even after Diego Serrano departed for Calabria.

(Serrano would be extradited from Italy in 1993 on the charges of drug trafficking laid by the Amigo Squad. He waited in the Don Jail for a year while his lawyer, Glenn Orr, a former provincial Crown attorney with an impressive record of convictions, negotiated with the Crown's office over a deal. It would turn out to be a sweetheart of a deal for Serrano. In return for a guilty plea on two counts of importing and trafficking in drugs, he would receive a sentence of ten years in prison and a fine of $50,000. Since Serrano had already served almost three years in jails in Calabria and Toronto, and since such pre-trial imprisonment – dead time, it's called – usually counts for double the time of sentencing, Serrano could expect to get day parole towards the end of 1997. That wasn't bad for a man who had been the biggest cocaine importer in eastern Canada, when the sentence was compared with the time handed out at trial to other people busted by the Amigo Squad. These were guys who worked *under* Serrano, guys like Joe Sevillano (twenty years in jail), Joe DeFrancesca (fifteen years), Domenic Condello (fourteen years). On the other hand, by pleading guilty, Serrano was saving the heavy costs to the government of a long trial and subsequent appeals. So, all in all, everybody was happy when Serrano went into court in Toronto on November 1, 1994, and heard Mr. Justice John Hamilton of the Ontario Court's General Division approve the deal, a guilty plea in exchange for ten years and a $50,000 fine.)

On takedown day, June 28, 1990, while Diego Serrano still twitched in his Calabrian cell, the car that Mike Gurman drove, with Alby Forde in the passenger seat, was one of three surveillance vehicles assigned to cover Spike Glendenning at a double remove.

Glendenning, as the undercover man, went equipped with two crucial items: $160,000 in flash money to show the coke dealers he meant business and a bodypack strapped under his shirt to link him with his surveillance team. At the receiving end of the bodypack was the number-one surveillance car. When Glendenning signalled that the deal for the cocaine was going down, number one would flash the word by radio to Gurman and the other backup car. The three would speed to whatever destination the first car indicated.

That was the first part of the takedown operation.

Then there were the two cop cars on Ulpiano Aguilera's tail. This was a relatively soft assignment, since Aguilera, at the wheel of a limo and all duded up in a sharp suit, dress shirt, and silk tie, was himself on a fun run. He was happily chauffeuring two teenage couples in formal wear who had rented his services for the drive to their high-school prom.

More police vehicles staked out the Aguilera neighbourhood, including one stationed on Lilac Avenue, directly across a small park from Ulpiano and Maria's house. The Aguilera Mercedes sat in the Acacia driveway. That told the watching cops that the lady of the house was at home.

It was 5:45 P.M. Everybody waited.

Spike Glendenning arrived at 8 Jasmine Road shortly after six.

He had met with Steven Warren an hour earlier at another address a few miles away. Warren had checked the flash money, the whole $160,000 of it, and had driven Glendenning in Aguilera's brown GMC van to 8 Jasmine. That, Warren said, was where the exchange would be made, cocaine for cash.

The house at 8 Jasmine was another piece of Aguilera real estate, two and a half blocks from 46 Acacia, only a minute away by car. The Jasmine house was much more modest than the one on Acacia; it measured no more than twenty-five square feet, stood a storey and a half high, and was made of clapboard with a bit of stone at the front for show. The Aguileras owned it and, so it seemed, used it to consummate drug deals.

The surveillance cars fanned out in the Jasmine–Acacia neighbourhood. Mike Gurman, in his car with Alby Forde, parked on a side street. It was 6:20 P.M.

Back at 46 Acacia, Maria Aguilera had a visitor. He was none other than Vincenzo DeBellis, Yorkville clothier, drug smuggler, cocaine boss. As the cops watched, DeBellis arrived, lightly swinging a black gym bag in one hand. He and Maria chatted, not long, but pleasantly, easily, as if it was a nice day like all nice days. The two got into DeBellis's car, the black gym bag accompanying them. DeBellis set off on the short trip to 8 Jasmine.

People cooking barbecues in the neighbourhood, people mowing lawns, drinking beer on their patios, all of them stopped for a moment, listening. What was it with the car engines, all erupting at once? What was happening around here?

It was 6:35 P.M. Close to TD, to takedown. The surveillance skates revved up. The Narcotics cops knew they were almost there, so near to the bust, just this far from nailing the dealers with the coke.

Mike Gurman started his car.

Spike Glendenning and Steve Warren stood on the lawn at 8 Jasmine watching as Vincenzo DeBellis pulled up on the road in front of the house and let Maria Aguilera out. She was now carrying the black gym bag. She crossed the lawn and handed the bag to Warren. He unzipped it to give Glendenning a peek inside, a look at kilos of cocaine.

"It's party time," Glendenning said.

As signals go, "it's party time" doesn't match "don't fire until you see the whites of their eyes" for dramatic flair, but they were the words the cops in the cars were keyed to react to. When Spike Glendenning spoke them into his bodypack, the takedown was on.

Now the racket in the neighbourhood really caught the attention of the barbecuers, the lawn mowers, and the beer drinkers on their patios. The cars with the idling engines took off all at the same instant, shattering the air, roaring down the narrow streets between Weston Road and the Humber River, down Flindon, down Bradmore, down Flaxman, down Jasmine.

Mike Gurman hit 8 Jasmine twenty or thirty seconds behind the first cop cars on the scene. He ripped his car across the lawn and braked within a yard or two of the small porch. Other cops on foot were trotting down each side of the house. Alby Forde, flying out of the car, headed for Glendenning and the gym bag of coke. Gurman swung from the driver's side and, reaching for the gun tucked in the back of his jeans, he took the front door.

For Gurman and the other invading cops, the sweep through the tiny house was quick and anticlimactic. The rooms were clean of anything suspicious. There were no people, no cocaine, in sight, none of the paraphernalia for cutting and measuring the drug.

Back outside, in the rush of the bust, Gurman had only a minute to absorb some of what was going on. Ed Tymburski, one of the senior guys, had arrived. He and Glendenning were talking to Steve Warren. Gurman noticed them. Alby Forde, as exhibits officer, was taking charge of the coke in the black gym bag. Other guys from Narcotics moved around, Payne, Durling, Alfonso, Manuel, everybody looking purposeful about something.

Manuel asked Gurman to drive him and Maria Aguilera over to 46 Acacia.

"No problem," Gurman said.

At the Acacia house, more cops were getting themselves set for a rush into the place. The manpower was even thicker here. One cop carried a videocamera to record the event. Another cop, who bore a name familiar from another kind of theatre, Cary Grant, controlled his special charge on a leash – this was Morgan, the drug-sniffing wonder dog.

Gurman's assignment at Acacia was to cover the basement, to search for plastic bags, weigh scales, cutting agents, anything that pointed to the fact that the inhabitants dealt in cocaine. Gurman poked around the basement for ten minutes. He turned up nothing incriminating. He checked the backyard. Nothing. Gurman wasn't having a particularly productive evening.

He *heard* about lots of productive activities that went on in other parts of the house.

He *heard* that Maria Aguilera directed the cops to a stash of coke in the master bedroom.

He *heard* that Ulpiano Aguilera arrived home from his drive to the high-school prom, backed the limo up to the Acacia garage, and stepped out of the car smack into a wave of cops. They slammed Aguilera in his spiffy suit face down into the driveway's concrete while an officer named Chase shouted words of arrest into his ear. That done, the cops led the prisoner into his own kitchen, where Det. Gus Selemedis took charge.

That's what Mike Gurman heard. He heard that Selemedis gave Aguilera his caution. Selemedis said in the kitchen, "You are charged with trafficking in cocaine. Do you wish to say anything in answer to the charge? You are not obliged to say anything unless you wish to do so, but whatever you say may be given in evidence. If you have spoken to a police officer or anyone with authority, or if any such person has spoken to you in connection with this case, I want it clearly understood that I do not want it to influence you in making a statement." Selemedis told Aguilera that he had a right to instruct counsel without delay, that a legal-aid lawyer was available to him, and that, if Aguilera wanted the legal-aid phone number, it was his for the asking.

Mike Gurman heard all about these events.

Vincenzo DeBellis seemed to have slipped through the take-down. Or maybe the cops purposely let him go and tailed him. Either way, a few months later, DeBellis would surface and cut a deal with the police and the Crown attorneys. In return for his testimony against his old associates in the cocaine business – against Ulpiano and Maria Aguilera for starters – he would be granted immunity from prosecution, and entered into the witness-protection program, which gave him a new name and a new address in a different city.

And what about the former Vincenzo DeBellis's lovingly collected antiques?

He sold them for a song.

"Everything was bought with drug profits," the reformed cocaine dealer testified piously at one trial. "I couldn't stand the sight of them. I wanted to start fresh."

As he spoke, three armed bodyguards kept an eye on everyone else in the courtroom.

But back on the evening of the takedown, Mike Gurman left 46 Acacia at 7:40 P.M. Alone, he drove across the top of the city to Metro Police 32 Division, where the people on Project Narrows would process the masses of paper the takedown now required. Thirty-two Division is on a side street near the corner of Yonge Street and Sheppard Avenue, and, inside, the Narcotics cops worked in the CIB office – CIB for Criminal Investigations Bureau – a long, open, rectangular area lined with identical desks.

When Gurman reached 32, Ulpiano and Maria Aguilera were already locked in separate interview rooms off the CIB main office. Each room was a stark cell, about the size of a walk-in closet, furnished with one chair and one table, both bolted to the floor. Gurman's instructions at 32 were to prepare and type up the documents for the Aguileras' show-cause hearing the next morning. At the hearing, a judge would read the documents, listen to the lawyers, and decide whether the Aguileras should be let out on bail pending further court hearings. There was nothing complex or thrilling about the chore given to Gurman, just a matter of obtaining basic data from the Aguileras – age, nationality, family – and entering it in quintuplicate on a form called the Supplementary Record of Arrest. But to Gurman, after his ho–hum evening, a lot of rushing from one house to another in pursuit of evidence that wasn't there, it might have seemed that, at last, he had something mildly meaningful to do on takedown day.

∼

A Metro Toronto police officer's notebook, enclosed in a black vinyl cover, holds fifty sheets of paper, 100 numbered pages.

Police officers write constantly in their notebooks. They record each significant event that takes place during their working day. That's the law. The law says that, when police officers testify in court, they can use these notes to refresh their memory, *but* the notes must have been made at the very time, or immediately after, an officer did, saw, heard, or said the things he or she is testifying to.

So, at 8:50 P.M. on June 28, when Mike Gurman entered the interview room where Maria Aguilera waited, he carried his notebook and a ballpoint pen that wrote in black ink.

Gurman found Maria cooperative enough. In fact, he wrote, "This accused when arrested was polite and offered no resistance." But Maria told Gurman that one thing really bothered her. It was her kids, four of them, none older than fourteen. She was worried about them. Gurman allowed Maria to make phone calls from the main CIB office to her relatives. They lived in the Acacia neighbourhood. The relatives would take care of the kids for the time being.

"I don't want go to jail," Maria said to Gurman. "I don't want be away from children for long time."

Gurman didn't like the sound of that. It made Maria sound like a lousy risk for bail, like she'd take her kids and flee. He told Maria he was recommending that she be held in custody until her trial.

Gurman wrote everything down.

At 9:50, Gurman let himself into the interview room on the opposite side of the CIB, the one where Ulpiano Aguilera was nursing the troubles that had come at him this evening, so swiftly and, it seemed to him, so stunningly.

"I need information for your court appearance tomorrow," Gurman said to Aguilera. "You know what the charges are?"

"Yeah." Aguilera still wore his smart business suit, the dress shirt, without the tie now. A cop had taken it, officially so the prisoner couldn't do harm to himself. "Yeah. Traffic cocaine," Aguilera said. His voice was calm, though there may have been something else in the sound – resignation? "It's bad thing, I know."

"You understand your rights about a lawyer?"

"Everybody been telling me about I get a lawyer. I know maybe I go to jail long time, but I don't want my wife to go, you know?"

Gurman shrugged. "Your wife's been charged with the same thing, with trafficking. I don't control these things."

Gurman, writing in his notebook, began to take Aguilera's particulars for the show-cause hearing. His date of birth? November 28, 1946. Place of birth? Ecuador. Present occupation? Limousine driver.

Gurman asked the questions and wrote the answers in his notebook. And after a while, Aguilera began to ask questions of his own. Innocuous stuff, just being curious and friendly, two guys isolated in a small room together. You a special policeman, Ulpiano asked, a narcotics man? In those clothes, you do, like what? Undercover? How long you been policeman?

Right about there, as Gurman and Aguilera exchanged questions and answers, Gurman must have decided he felt something yielding in the other man. Maybe this was wishful thinking on Gurman's part. Maybe, after putting in eight routine hours on takedown day, he was experiencing an emotion close to anxiety, just to score *some* small triumph. Whatever, Gurman may have thought, he saw an opening in Aguilera. Why not go for it? If Aguilera really had confidences he wanted to unload, Gurman might be able to "roll him over," as the cops say, to turn Aguilera into an informer, cajole him into giving up people in the cocaine trade further up the line. Wouldn't *that* be a game breaker?

At this point, according to Gurman, he wrote on page 62 of his notebook, "Ulpiano want to talk."

Then, Gurman said later, he read Aguilera the full caution all over again, the same one Gus Selemedis had read earlier in the evening at 46 Acacia. "You are charged with trafficking in cocaine. Do you wish to say anything in answer to the charges? You are not obliged to say anything . . . "

Gurman later said he wrote in his notebook, still on page 62, "2nd caution read & understood."

Gurman and Aguilera got back into the conversation.

Aguilera spoke first. What he said sounded to Gurman like a glimpse of very interesting stuff. "I think was big mistake to get in this business," he said. "Is bad thing now. I start because friend say is good thing, I make good money."

"A friend?" Gurman coaxed, writing in his notebook as Aguilera talked.

"Yeah, my friend Diego say is good. I don't deal with him long time now. Then he tell me Vincenzo will deal with me."

"What happened to Diego?"

"He travel now a lot. That's all I know." Aguilera paused, gave Gurman a look, and apparently arrived at a decision. "I maybe talk to other officer, Gus, about him, about Diego."

Gus Selemedis? Was he already rolling Aguilera over? Gurman made a decision of his own right then. Better leave this guy alone. Even though he seemed to be getting incriminating stuff from Aguilera, it was better to leave him to Gus.

"Suit yourself," Gurman said to Aguilera.

He left the interview room and locked it. It was 10:10 P.M. He'd been with Ulpiano Aguilera for twenty minutes.

The mood in the CIB turned giddy that night. People got their work done, filled out the forms, made the paper ready for next day in court. But, riding on the success of the takedown, knowing the Aguileras were out of business, guys bobbed and bounced at the desks. Somebody went out for hamburgers all round. Det. Burt Durling snapped colour photos of the happy crew. One shot

showed Alby Forde, exhibits officer, sitting behind a desk piled
with the cocaine that had been seized. Alby in his dreadlocks,
goofy grin on his face. And behind him, standing off to the side,
looking tentative, maybe forcing it a little, was Mike Gurman.

Over the next three years, the justice system ground slowly. The
Aguileras hired lawyers, Paul Bennett for Ulpiano, Tony Bryant
for Maria. Bennett and Bryant, during all the proceedings that
followed, would work closely in the many areas where their
clients' interests intersected. Both of the Aguileras were released
on bail, but, at their preliminary hearing, both were committed
to trial on the charges of trafficking in cocaine. Finally, in the first
week of April 1993, in Courtroom 7-6 of the Toronto Courthouse on University Avenue, the trial opened.

Judge George Adams kept apologizing.
    "Sorry," he'd say, "but what was the question again?"
    The people to whom he was directing his apology and plea
were the lawyers in the Aguilera trial. Sometimes it was to one
of the two Crown attorneys, other times to one of the two
defence counsel. Always the judge wanted the lawyer, please, to
repeat once more, maybe a third time, whatever it was he'd asked.
    "Sorry," George Adams would say, "question again?"
    Judges at trials make notes. They take down lawyers' ques-
tions and witnesses' answers almost verbatim. They need the
notes for instant reference. They need them for backup if they
are called on during a trial to make a legal ruling about the evidence. They need them at the end of the trial for guidance in
making their charge to the jury. So, for judges, a trial is scribble,
scribble, scribble.
    That was what was giving George Adams fits. He raced to keep
up with the Qs and As, and especially when the testimony dodged
into tricky technical terrain, as it did frequently in the Aguilera
trial, he fell a few steps off pace.

"Hold on just for a second," Judge Adams would say, often a couple of times within a minute or two. "What was that term again?"

George Adams was by no means slow on the uptake. Far from it. Paul Bennett, Ulpiano's lawyer, assessed Adams as "a very bright man." The judge's problem lay in his background. He had only recently been appointed to the bench, and almost all of his previous career as a lawyer had been in labour law. He had risen high, to the chairmanship of the Ontario Labour Relations Board. Now he was presiding over not just a criminal trial but his *first* criminal trial. And not just any old routine criminal trial, but one that lasted almost eighty days, that produced exceedingly intricate evidence of a forensic sort, that involved hair-splitting points of law over statements to the police by an accused person. Small wonder that Judge Adams, new kid on the block, kept asking for repeats on the questions.

As it happened, George Adams's next big case was a non-criminal monster. In January 1994, the Ontario government would apply to the Ontario Court, General Division, Judge Adams sitting, for an injunction to bar picketing within five hundred feet of twenty-three locations that had some connection to doctors who performed abortions. The locations included clinics and hospitals where the doctors operated, the offices they worked in, the houses they and their families lived in.

Judge Adams would ponder the matter for almost six months. On August 31, 1994, he would produce a ruling that had the ebb and flow and readability of a Dickens novel and, at 548 pages, was almost as long. The ruling permitted exclusionary picketing zones at eighteen of the locations but left public hospitals off the list; it reduced the zone from five hundred feet to sixty feet at some clinics, but accepted the five-hundred-foot-zone at homes of nine doctors; it observed that "there is something fundamentally disturbing about 'capturing' women at the threshold of a medical facility and doing so immediately before they undergo a serious medical procedure," but recognized that anti-abortion advocates have the right to speak their piece, too. Most people in the legal community thought Judge Adams had been Socratic as well as Dickensian.

Right out of the box, on the first day of the Aguilera trial, George Adams was faced with a doozy of a dilemma.

Tony Bryant, the lawyer for Maria Aguilera, brought a motion to have Damien Frost, the lead counsel for the Crown, kicked off the case.

Why? Because, by coincidence, Frost's office happened to lie directly across the hall from the office of Paul Bennett. The two offices faced one another at a distance of five or six feet on the third floor of an elderly mansion at 81 Wellesley Street East in midtown Toronto that had been converted into quarters for criminal lawyers. Damien Frost practised criminal law, alone, in private practice, but he also worked as a part-time Department of Justice prosecutor. The Crown had named him the number-one man on the Aguilera case; Kofi Barnes was in the second chair, a full-time Department of Justice lawyer, but he was young, new on the job, ready to learn from Frost.

"It's potentially threatening, Your Honour," Bryant argued. "Mr. Frost might inadvertently become privy to Mr. Bennett's confidential strategies in the case."

Adams wondered why it was Frost who had to go. Why not Bennett?

"Mr. Bennett was *first* on the case, Your Honour. He was retained by Mr. Aguilera *before* the Department of Justice appointed Mr. Frost to prosecute."

There wasn't a precedent in the case books.

Adams ruled that Frost could remain on the case, but the judge tried to set up a kind of Chinese wall in the corridors of 81 Wellesley. Frost and Bennett had to keep their office doors shut. Neither could be summoned on the office pager. Their secretaries would not be permitted to do relief work on the reception desk inside the first-floor door. That ought to keep each lawyer from catching an improper whiff of what the opposition was up to.

Frost shrugged. Bennett did too. They'd live with it. But wait a minute, the secretaries for the other lawyers in the building said. What about us? If Bennett's secretary and Frost's were banned from the reception desk, the others would have to put in extra time on reception. Thanks a lot.

Once Adams settled the counsel matter, the trial went immediately into a *voir dire* and stayed there for forty days.

A *voir dire* is a hearing within a trial, with the jury excluded, during which the judge decides whether the jury may hear certain pieces of contested evidence. Usually it's the defence that does the contesting, and that was the case in the Aguilera trial. Paul Bennett and Tony Bryant found plenty of evidence in the Crown's case to challenge. They argued over the admissibility of statements Ulpiano Aguilera made to the police, over the authority of the search warrant that got the police into 46 Acacia, over the admissibility of statements the police took from other people accused in the cocaine bust, Steve Warren and Vincenzo DeBellis. The two defence counsel turned the hearing into one huge, all-encompassing, omnibus *voir dire*, a *voir dire* that ate up more than half of the entire trial.

In the course of it, the Crown paraded into the courtroom most of the twenty-three men from Narcotics who participated in the big takedown of June 28, 1990. Each cop took the witness stand, notebook in hand, and described his part in the day's events. Each cop, questioned by one of the two Crown attorneys, gave his evidence in chief, and each found himself vigorously cross-examined by Bennett and Bryant. It consumed time, this marathon of interrogation, and it wasn't until May 18, far down the list, almost six weeks after the trial began, that Mike Gurman appeared on the witness stand.

~

Gurman had changed from three years earlier. No more goatee, no long hair, no biker's gear. Gurman had been promoted out of Morality and now worked in Metro Police's Court Services Department. He was attached to the College Park Courts, where he supervised cases and organized officers to give their testimony. He looked and dressed the part, good suit, short hair, an overall trimness, and somehow, with his new makeover, he radiated an almost boyish air.

Kofi Barnes, the junior Crown, led Gurman through his examination-in-chief. Gurman told the story of his day and night on that June 28. He covered the hours of waiting in his unmarked surveillance car, the descent on 8 Jasmine, his fruitless search through the basement and backyard at 46 Acacia, his questioning of Maria Aguilera and then of her husband for the show-cause hearing. He read from his notebook to refresh his memory.

"When did you make your notes?" Barnes asked Gurman.

"I made the notes during the investigation and specifically on the evening of the takedown of this drug project. I made them during my investigation on that night."

Tony Bryant, Maria Aguilera's counsel, went first in cross-examining Gurman. He conducted Gurman once more through the account of his moves on takedown day. He pressed Gurman for details, pushing him for elaboration. This was standard stuff for a defence lawyer, probing for inconsistencies, for facts that didn't match up.

Gurman's response to Bryant's tactics fell into two general categories: One, he stuck to the bare-bones recital from his notebook for June 28, 1990. And, two, he said, "I don't recall."

That was the line he invoked in answer to Bryant's requests for simple details.

"Was Alby Forde wearing a hat?" Bryant asked.

"I don't recall," Gurman answered.

"Did you ever recall him wearing a baseball-type cap, some sort of cap with, at least, a brim?"

"I don't recall."

"Doesn't ring any bells?"

"No."

And Gurman invoked the line when Bryant waded into possibly crucial areas of evidence. At one point, Bryant wanted to know about the conversation in Gurman's car on June 28 when Gurman drove Maria Aguilera and Detective Manuel from 8 Jasmine to 46 Acacia. Gurman granted that Manuel and Maria talked to one another. But what did they talk about? That seemed to be another, more mysterious, matter.

"Just give us a word," Bryant said, "any word that you remember hearing either of them saying while they were in the car with you."

"I don't recall what words were spoken."

"Did you hear the word 'stash'?"

"No."

"Did you hear 'cocaine'?"

"I don't recall that word."

"Did you hear the word 'stuff'?"

"I don't recall that word."

"Did you hear 'know'?"

"I don't recall it."

"Did you hear the word 'lawyer'?"

"I don't recall that."

"Did you hear the word 'silent'?"

"I don't recall that word."

"Did you hear the word 'right' or 'rights'?"

"Well, I made a right turn onto the street. Somebody might have said it. I don't know."

"Did you hear the word 'warrant'?"

" 'Warren'?"

" 'Warrant.' W-a-r-r-a-n-t. Or 'search warrant'?"

"I don't recall that word or those words."

Altogether, in about three and a half hours of Bryant's cross-examination, Mike Gurman answered "I don't recall" 124 times.

Paul Bennett, Ulpiano Aguilera's lawyer, listened to Gurman and began to wonder, was something fishy here?

Paul Bennett is in some inconsequential ways an unorthodox sort of lawyer. For one thing, he never went to university. In fact, he never finished high school. He was one credit shy of passing his grade thirteen at Jarvis Collegiate in Toronto in the 1960s when he got bored and dropped out to do 1960s things, leaving a gap in his résumé for a few years. He re-emerged in the early 1970s, working as an assistant to two left-wing members of Toronto City Council. He held a couple of other jobs – such as executive director of the walkathon for Miles for Millions – and then entered Osgoode Hall Law School as a mature student. The minute he got his call to the bar in 1984, he went into practice on his own as a criminal lawyer.

He loves defence work. He relishes it, glories in it. So do other criminal lawyers, but Bennett looks positively merry when he's in courtroom action, when he's anticipating future courtroom action, when he's reliving past courtroom action. In personality, he's direct, generous, and funny. In appearance, he's slim and wiry, which is perverse rather than unorthodox, since he smokes, drinks beer, and gets his major athletic activity around the billiards table in his basement at home. He also wears a moustache of the impenetrably bushy sort that is otherwise seen only on the labels of rum bottles.

Bennett began his cross-examination of Mike Gurman shortly after three o'clock on the afternoon of Wednesday, May 19, and he plunged straight into Gurman's seemingly elusive way with an answer.

"After the takedown on the twenty-eighth," Bennett asked, "when did you first see Mr. Aguilera? Perhaps I will break it down. Did you see him at 8 Jasmine?"

"No."

"Did you see him at 46 Acacia?"

"I don't recall seeing him there."

Bennett speeded up his delivery. "I am somewhat troubled, Detective Gurman, because you use a phrase I am not sure is a habit of speech. What do you mean by the phrase 'I don't recall'?"

"It means I don't recall. It means that —"

Bennett interrupted. "It could have and it could not have?"

"It means that three years ago I could have seen him there. I don't recall seeing him there."

"So it is a neutral phrase." Bennett pounced. "It encompasses everything. If I said 'Was the sun shining?' and you said 'I don't recall,' that could mean the sun was shining, the sun wasn't shining, the sun was hidden by a cloud, or it was night-time. When you use a phrase like 'I don't recall,' it is absolutely meaningless."

That established, Bennett having shown Gurman he intended to play hardball, that it was way past fooling-around time in the courtroom, he hit on Gurman's notebook. Bennett's focus was still on Gurman's handling of Ulpiano Aguilera — where did Gurman first see Aguilera? Who said what to whom? — but this time, the unrelenting reference point for Bennett was the series of entries about Aguilera that Gurman had made in his notebook.

"Now," Bennett asked, "can you take me to where in your notes on the twenty-eighth your first involvement with Mr. Aguilera is, if you would be so kind?"

"That is at 9:50 P.M."

"Nine-fifty."

Bennett, standing at the counsel's lectern next to the defence table, asked questions. Gurman, on the witness stand a few yards away, slowly turning the pages in his notebook, answered.

"The note of your dealings with Maria Aguilera would be in your book before 9:50," Bennett went on. "Then you would go into Mr. Aguilera's room?"

"Yes."

As Bennett continued his questioning, out of some instinct, some faint, nagging suspicion, a feeling that maybe there *was* something fishy here, a kind of Rumpolian sensitivity, he left the lectern, strolled across the courtroom to the witness stand, and looked into the notebook Gurman was holding.

At the top of page 61 of the notebook, Gurman's entry read:

"I require some information
from you for your court
appearance tomorrow."

Bennett, still asking about Gurman's first words to Ulpiano Aguilera, looked at the notebook more closely. Half his mind was on the questioning, half was on the notebook. But even with his concentration divided, Bennett saw patterns in Gurman's style of note making.

Gurman habitually wrote just four or five words per line, with generous space between words. The four or five words never filled out a full line across the page. Bennett also noticed that Gurman had a custom of using plus signs in the middle of blank spaces between lines as a device to mark the end of a subject or thought. The plus signs often came in pairs, though sometimes it was just a single sign, and sometimes, probably when Gurman was rushing, the plus signs looked more like minus signs. The signs, pluses or minuses, could appear as often as three times per page. Bennett noticed all of that, too.

Gurman turned to page 62 of the notebook. The top three lines read:

"Info taken for
s/c. Ulpiano want to talk. 2nd
caution read & understood."

Now the tumblers started clicking into place in Bennett's head. Those second two lines on page 62, starting after s/c (for "show-cause"), didn't seem to match up with the rest of the page. It was as if the words were squeezed into place, tighter than the other lines, with a slightly different slant. And Bennett's antennae really began to quiver when he studied the second word in the third line.

"It appears the word 'read' on the third line has something written underneath it," Bennett said to Gurman. "Can you tell me what that would be? See the 'r' in 'read'?"

"Yes."

"It appears to be a lot thicker in ink."

"It is thicker in ink."

"Than any other word on the page, correct?"

"I have to look," Gurman said, just a cop trying to be a helpful witness. "It is thicker than any other word and in some cases twice as thick."

"And the 'r' in 'read' lines up with the little plus signs that you have on the same page?"

"Yes, pretty close."

"I'm not an expert in these sorts of things, but as I look at it, [the writing under the 'r'] sort of looks like the little marks you put on blank lines. There's a certain similarity to your blank line marks in what is underneath the 'r'."

"I disagree," Gurman said, starting to pull back.

Bennett said, "Would you be content to have your book scientifically checked to see whether or not there is anything underneath that letter 'r'?"

"Would I be content?"

"To have this page filed as an exhibit so that it can be released for scientific testing to see whether there is an ink mark under the letter 'r' in the word 'read'?"

If Gurman was rattled by the proposal that Bennett zinged at him, he quickly rallied. "I have no problem with that at all," he said.

At about this point, or perhaps a little earlier – Bennett couldn't recall later – as he picked at page 62 of Gurman's notebook, another penny dropped.

In criminal cases, the Crown is obliged to provide defence counsel with a Disclosure Brief, a document that outlines the nature of the Crown's case and contains a list of witnesses the Crown expects to call, together with a précis of what each witness is likely to testify to. A witness statement in the Disclosure Brief is called a "will say," as in "this is what the witness will say." A police officer prepares his own will say by dictating a statement that is almost invariably a word-for-word copy of his relevant notebook. Then the policeman's statement is incorporated in the Disclosure Brief and delivered to the defence counsel.

In the Aguilera case, Mike Gurman's will say covered pages 115 to 156 of the Disclosure Brief. It was, in the usual custom, just about exactly a verbatim transcription of the notebook he'd kept during Project Narrows. Except – and here is where the penny made its rattling sound – Bennett realized that Gurman's will say did not include the lines "Ulpiano want to talk. 2nd/ caution read & understood."

Kofi Barnes, the junior Crown, tried to shield his witness. He asked Judge Adams to exclude Gurman from the courtroom while he and Bennett debated just what it was that Bennett was up to. Gurman stepped outside, and Bennett unloaded his suspicions.

He said that the thick "r" might indicate that Gurman had written the word "read" over top of one of his plus or minus signs. And not just the single word "read," but Gurman had written two complete lines – "Ulpiano want to talk. 2nd/ caution read & understood" – some time after he'd written the rest of the notes on page 62. Then Bennett revealed to the judge that the two lines in question didn't appear in Gurman's will say. Wasn't *that* curious? If some sort of scientific testing showed that the two lines *were* written later, maybe much later, Bennett went on, it might be enough to put the statement Gurman claimed he got from Ulpiano Aguilera in question. Hell, Bennett continued, going slightly overboard, knowing it was a long shot, it might even put into question "the bona fides of this *entire* investigation."

Kofi Barnes argued that Bennett was making a mountain out of a molehill. And Judge Adams, while granting that Bennett might have a point of some sort, wondered if it was all "worth the candle, so to speak." But Bennett insisted on his contentions that the notebook, if something was wrong with it, might indicate a completely flawed investigation, and in the end, Judge Adams ruled that, okay, Gurman's notebook would be made an exhibit and, yes, it would be delivered to the Centre of Forensic Sciences where someone would put page 62 to whatever testing the centre thought appropriate.

When Gurman returned to the courtroom, Bennett broke the news to him in the resumption of the cross-examination that the notebook had been taken out of his control and made an exhibit of the court.

"At that moment," Bennett remembered, "if Gurman's eyes could shoot bullets, I was a dead man."

Bennett's cross-examination of Gurman continued over the rest of the afternoon of Wednesday, May 19, and through much of the next day. For most of it, Bennett danced Gurman over his will say. He got Gurman to concede that the two key lines – "Ulpiano want to talk. 2nd/ caution read & understood" – weren't in the will say. And towards the end of the cross-examination, Bennett put in the open in the most in-your-face language his notion of Gurman's perfidy.

"I am going to suggest to you," he said, "that your notebook of your involvement that evening is a fabrication. I just want to put that on the record so you understand where I am coming from because you know I have hinted at this for a while."

"If you are suggesting my notebook is a fabrication," Gurman

countered, "you are not only wrong, you are suggesting something that is wrong, and it upsets me."

The two men batted that one back and forth in an exchange
that reached a climax when Bennett supplied a reason, as he saw
it, for Gurman to have messed with the notebook.

"You were trying to entice Aguilera into squealing," Bennett
said, "into being a rat, an informer. You were trying to entice him
to give up someone a little higher [in the drug ring]."

This was Bennett's theory: Gurman, anxious to make a few
yards with Aguilera, hadn't first given him the caution, and later,
possibly months later or years later, realizing that failure, had
written the caution into his notebook. Or perhaps Gurman had
given the caution but not noted it in his book when he first wrote
up the encounter with Aguilera, then added the notation later.
Beyond that, Bennett figured that Gurman had pulled some sort
of stunt – the scientific testing of page 62 might reveal exactly
what sort of stunt – that threw doubt on everything he'd sworn
to in court.

Gurman held fast in his denial of hanky-panky, and the cross-
examination came to an angry end just before three o'clock on
May 20. Gurman left the courtroom, but his notebook stayed
behind. It had been handed to the court registrar for delivery to
the Centre of Forensic Sciences.

In Greg Boyd's line of work, he's on the lookout for anything
on the written or printed page that might be phony. Faked
lottery tickets, counterfeit documents, altered cheques – any
slippery stuff done to a piece of paper with the intent of fooling
someone is right up Greg Boyd's alley. Boyd is an examiner in
the Documents Section at the Centre of Forensic Sciences in
Toronto, and it was to him that Mike Gurman's notebook, under
court seal in a plastic evidence bag, was handed on Monday,
May 31, 1993.

A man in his mid-thirties, Boyd wears a clipped moustache

and goatee, has a long, serious face, and approaches his work with a gently earnest manner. His section occupies part of the third floor in the George Drew Building on Grosvenor Street, not far from all the other buildings in mid-Toronto that house employees, both high and low, of the Ontario government (the forensic centre is part of the Ministry of the Solicitor General).

Boyd could choose from several rooms of machines and apparatuses on the third floor to plumb the possible mysteries of page 62 in Mike Gurman's notebook, but he knew from experience that this was a job for the video spectral comparator, or VSC for short. Actually, Boyd's first testing of the page was by plain old eyeball. He held a bright light close to page 62 and looked at the colour and impression of the ink in which the words were written. To anybody else's eye, the whole page was written in black ink. To Greg Boyd's practised eye, some words on some lines were written in a darker ink. Specifically, the darker words were "Ulpiano" in the second line and "read" in the third line. Nothing conclusive, as far as Boyd was concerned, but interesting.

Now it was on to the video spectral comparator.

The Documents Section had been working with this particular VSC for two years. It cost $70,000, and it sits on a table in one of the third floor's very clean, very still rooms, and, at first glance, it doesn't appear to be capable of performing any special magic. It's so mundane looking, this VSC, just a collection of four sleek, rectangular metal containers stacked on top of one another. By far the largest container, the one at the bottom of the stack, holds the working guts of the VSC; the other containers include such things as a video monitor for seeing what's going on inside the main apparatus and a thermal printer that provides hard copies of the images shown on the video. All of this looks ordinary enough, but as it turns out, it's capable of working small wonders.

The VSC works by bombarding a page of writing or printing

with assorted types of light that reveal secrets on the page that are invisible to the naked eye. The document is slid into an area of the VSC's main container, called the stage, which is closed off from the outside by a small hood. Once on the stage, the page is zapped by one of three different lights, infrared, ultraviolet, or infrared luminescence. These three lights, in turn, draw different reactions of possibly great revelation from the inks on the page.

The principle behind all of this finagling with lights relates to the optical properties of ink. For starters, different-coloured inks register to the normal eye as those different colours because the components of the inks reflect light at varying wavelengths. So the ordinary unencumbered eye looks at a piece of writing in ink and advises the brain that the ink in question is black or mauve or emerald. The VSC, by striking the ink with wavelengths of light that the eye cannot take in, extends the perception of the inks into realms the eye is incapable of reaching on its own.

As the wavelengths do their work, the ink on the page, as seen in the VSC's video monitor and as printed on the thermal printer, can react in a variety of ways. For example, the ink can absorb the light and become darker. Or it can reflect the light and grow much dimmer. Or, yet again, it can transmit the light and vanish altogether.

Greg Boyd likes to display an amusing little bogus document, a sort of forensic party game, to demonstrate a tiny aspect of the VSC's powers. The document is a cheque drawn on a Royal Bank branch in Kingston, Ontario. Wild Bill Hickok purported to sign the cheque after making it out to Wyatt Earp. Every written part of the cheque is in black ink, and to the eye, the amount, in both numerals and letters, is "70" and "seventy" dollars. But, when it is placed in the VSC and hit with infrared light, the "0" in "70" and the "ty" in "seventy" fade entirely away. Thus it's revealed that sneaky Wyatt was trying to take Wild Bill for sixty-three dollars by doctoring a seven-dollar cheque into one for seventy bucks.

⁓

Boyd placed page 62 of Gurman's notebook in the stage of the VSC and treated it with ultraviolet light. Nothing instructive happened. No lines, in comparison with other lines, faded or brightened or disappeared. All of the writing on the page appeared to be the same. So much for ultraviolet.

Next, infrared luminescence. Precisely, technically, Boyd applied to page 62 infrared luminescence at a wavelength of 735 nanometres (a nanometre is one-billionth of a metre) using an F.S. 1(a) filter. This time, jackpot. The second and third lines of the page, beginning with the period after "s/c" and continuing through the words "Ulpiano want to talk. 2nd/ caution read & understood" came out black, while all the rest of the writing on the page showed white. The two lines had reacted differently to the infrared luminescence, and, for Boyd, this established that a different ink had been used for those two lines.

Boyd tried one more test, this time with the infrared light at a wavelength of 645 nanometres. The result? The same as in test two with the infrared luminescence: the two questioned lines showed black, while the other lines showed white. Confirmed and reconfirmed.

And, there was one more thing he had to look into: the possibility of something under the word "read" in line three. This was the point Paul Bennett had pressed Gurman about, the notion that, as Bennett surmised, there was one of Gurman's characteristic plus or minus signs below the letter "r."

Greg Boyd applied a high-powered white light to the word and examined it under a microscope at fairly high magnification. He came to two conclusions. First, the mark under the "r" was, in Boyd's words, "just a tiny dash, a horizontal dash" that resembled the dashes or minus signs farther down on page 62 in the blank spaces between sections of Gurman's notes. And, second, the ink in the tiny dash was "consistent with the ink in the main body of page 62." In other words, the different ink in the lines

"Ulpiano want to talk. 2nd/ caution read & understood" was probably written over the ink in the dash.

Greg Boyd had completed his assignment.

Four days later, on the morning of Friday, June 4, Boyd appeared on the witness stand in Judge George Adams's courtroom. Paul Bennett conducted him through an examination-in-chief that took not much more than thirty minutes. Boyd described his procedures with the VSC and laid out in plain language what the machine had established.

"It demonstrates that there are two different inks present here," Boyd testified. "The second and third lines are very obviously written in different ink than the remaining portion of the page."

Tony Bryant, on behalf of Maria Aguilera, questioned Boyd for another half hour, mostly underlining points that Bennett had made in his examination. But Bryant also wondered about the possibility that Boyd might be able to take his testing a little further.

"Does the Centre of Forensic Sciences," Bryant asked, "possess the capability for determining the age of ink?"

"No, sir."

"Are there facilities in the Western world where the age of ink can be determined?"

"Yes, sir, there are."

"Where are they located?"

"The Secret Service in the United States has an ink library and is doing ink testing. An officer by the name of Larry Stewart, I believe, is in charge of that."

When Damien Frost, the lead Crown attorney, cross-examined Boyd, he had on his mind the very point that Bryant had raised. What about the age of the inks? If Boyd couldn't determine how long *any* ink had been on any page – specifically, if he couldn't tell how long each of the two inks had been on page 62 of the notebook – then, Frost suggested, one might imagine all sorts of hypotheses to explain Gurman's two-inked writing on page 62. And Frost proceeded to raise one of those hypotheses with Boyd.

"You can't tell us," Frost began, "whether or not the ink which is different from the vast majority of the page was entered at a different time from the rest of the page?"

"No, sir."

"Okay, if I was to give you a hypothetical that the writer started out with a police-issued black pen and made the entries at the top of the page, and when he got to the second line, he had difficulty with his pen and changed the pen and then [after two lines] picked up the *original* pen for some reason, you couldn't disagree with that?"

Boyd thought about it. "Yes, sir, that's possible."

"I mean," Frost said, "the bottom line here is that all you can tell us is that the ink on lines two and three appears to be different than the ink on what preceded it and followed it?"

"Yes, that's right."

Later that afternoon, after court finished for the day, Bennett and Bryant talked over the possibility that Frost had put in play.

All right, they told one another, it was crazy, the idea that Gurman was writing away in his notebook in the witness room with Ulpiano Aguilera, switched pens to write a couple of lines, then switched back to the first pen for the rest of the page. It was nuts. Everybody must realize by now that Gurman had written those two lines with another pen long after he'd written the rest of the page. Those two lines *looked* wrong on the page, and one of the words in the two lines, "read," was written *over* one of Gurman's little plus signs. It was all so obvious in the view of Bennett and Bryant.

On the other hand, the two lawyers wondered, could they take the chance of riding on Greg Boyd's testimony alone? Could they make the assumption that Judge Adams read the evidence the same way they read it? Adams *was* inexperienced in criminal law. Who knew what he was thinking? Maybe, as far as Adams was concerned, Frost's hypothesis held water.

By the end of the conversation, Bennett and Bryant had decided they needed another witness. They needed an expert who knew about the age of inks, who could do his tests and tell the court that, yeah, the two suspect lines were written sometime after the rest of the page. They needed someone like this Larry Stewart, the Secret Service guy Greg Boyd had mentioned on the witness stand. Not a guy *like* Larry Stewart. If he really was the genius of inks, they needed Larry Stewart.

Tony Bryant made a phone call to Internal Affairs, the branch of Metro Police that looks into cops who may have done something wrong, who may even have committed a criminal offence. Bryant suggested that Internal Affairs might be interested in the issue that had come up over Mike Gurman in the Aguilera trial. There might be a cop here, Bryant said, who has doctored his notebook. Internal Affairs said they were very interested. In fact, they were so interested when they heard everything Bryant had to say about the ink in the notebook and about the tests it should undergo that they arranged for Sgt. Tony Corrie of Internal Affairs to take personal possession of the notebook and deliver it for testing to Larry Stewart at the U.S. Department of the Treasury, in Washington, D.C.

The U.S. Bureau of Alcohol, Tobacco and Firearms started collecting inks in 1929. At first, the collection came together in a haphazard fashion, but, by the 1970s, people in the bureau got serious about their inks. After all, the analysis of inks could help uncover forgers and cheats of every description, and a library of inks would be a major aid in identifying counterfeit money and faked documents. So the bureau asked other law-enforcement agencies – the CIA, the FBI, the Secret Service, the IRS, the police in European countries – to send it all the inks they'd run across in their investigations. The bureau also canvassed ink manufacturers around the world for samples of the inks they produced. More than that, the bureau requested that the ink manufacturers add a unique component to their new inks each year so that the bureau would be able to identify which inks came from which manufacturers in which years. Some companies obliged the bureau, some didn't. Many of those that went along with the idea still tag their inks to this day.

In the early 1980s, responsibility for the ink library passed to the Secret Service, part of the Department of the Treasury, which became just as indefatigable about rounding up all the inks of the world. By 1993, the library had on its shelves some seven thousand inks. Each of these had been tested in various ways, catalogued, and kept available for comparisons against the inks that appeared on a great range of documents – fifty-dollar bills, accounting ledgers, love letters – that might not be what they represented themselves to be. (Counterfeit money keeps the ink-comparison people at the Secret Service particularly busy, and, at any one time, the vault in the ink laboratory holds $200 million in currency, all, alas, phony.)

Other agencies in other countries – the German federal police, the Russian federal forensic lab, one lone RCMP officer in Ottawa – have the training or facilities to do intricate ink testing, but the Secret Service in Washington, with its magnificent store of inks, is way out in front of the rest of the ink establishment. That may qualify the number-one man in the Secret Service's Documents Department as the universe's great wizard of inks. The man in question is Larry Stewart, whose official title is senior documents examiner for the Instrument Analysis Section of the U.S. Secret Service, Department of the Treasury.

Larry Stewart is the perfect scientific bureaucrat. A man of about forty years of age, Stewart appears normal, almost anonymous in every way, medium height, medium build, regular features, speaking voice of moderate range. But there's nothing

conventional or restrained about his approach to life on the job.
In that department, he's passionate, sharing, and self-assured. He's
proud of the ink collection that is under his jurisdiction, and he
regards it as his duty to make it, and everything he's learned from
it, available to anyone who comes asking. That includes law-
enforcement agencies, foreign governments, and a couple of
criminal lawyers from Toronto who were trying to prove that a
cop was pulling a fast one.

Tony Corrie of Metro Police's Internal Affairs delivered the notebook to Stewart on June 9, and, for much of each day over the
following week, Stewart gave the notebook's inks the sort of
ratiocinative scrutiny that would have sent Sherlock Holmes to
his violin – or his cocaine pipe – in envy.

Stewart began by examining all one hundred pages under a
microscope. To him, it appeared that there were two inks used
throughout the notebook – not just two inks on page 62, but two
inks scattered across the whole body of the book. These two, as
far as Stewart could judge in his first pass through the pages,
occurred about equally often in the notes.

Next, Stewart repeated the test that Greg Boyd had run at the
Centre of Forensic Sciences. That is, he checked the notebook
under a video spectral comparator. Actually, it was under the
Secret Service's equivalent of a VSC since, as Stewart modestly
confessed, "our particular machine was produced by us out of
spare parts."

A major difference separated Stewart's VSC study from Boyd's.
Where Boyd concentrated on page 62, Stewart ran the entire one
hundred pages through his VSC. What he found confirmed the
impression he had from his examination by microscope: Gurman
had used two inks in writing the notes, and there were about the
same number of notes in each ink.

These two tests, helpful as they were in pointing the direction, were mere preliminaries to the fancy stuff. Now Stewart

moved on to the means of exploration that would answer the big questions, questions about the identity of each ink, about the age of each, about the length of time each had been in the notebook, and about – here was the really big one – the length of time each had been on page 62.

In step number one on this voyage of discovery, Stewart took samples of the ink off the pages, samples he would submit to his testing. The removal work required two things: a devilishly clever little instrument and an awfully steady hand. Stewart had both: he perfected the instrument and he possessed the hand.

The basis of the instrument was an ordinary hypodermic needle, which Stewart had modified. First, he filed off the end of the needle to make it flat. Then he inserted a very tiny syringe tip through the flattened end of the needle. The tip projected microscopically from the hypodermic needle, just enough to dig into the surface of a page or, more precisely, into the ink on the surface of the page.

Which is where the steady hand came in.

What Stewart did next was turn through Mike Gurman's notebook and select lines from which he would remove pinholes of ink. The process, with hand kept solid as a rock, was this: choose the spot on the page – say, a loop in a letter in a particular word – plunge in the modified hypodermic needle, remove a pinhole of ink, and drop the pinhole into a glass vial.

But before Stewart performed this delicate operation, he took two precautions. First, he checked the back of the page in question to ensure there was no ink on the back of the small spot where he was going to remove the pinhole. Otherwise the sample might mix two inks. And, second, he placed a piece of cardboard between the page he was working on and the next page over. Otherwise there might be a transfer of ink from the second page. With those two precautions, Stewart guaranteed himself uncontaminated samples.

Altogether, Stewart wielded his hypodermic needle to remove

five hundred samples of ink from the notebook. They came in
clusters. From each entry he selected for sampling, he took ten
pinholes of ink, and he settled for an even fifty entries. Page 62
came in for the most attention. On it, Stewart took tests from lines
one, two, three, four, six, eleven, fourteen, twenty-two, and
twenty-four. Nine entries at ten pinholes per entry. Ninety
samples from page 62.

The inks in the Secret Service ink library aren't kept as inks *per
se*. Not vats of the stuff, not in ink wells, not in pure liquid form
at all. Rather, they're stored in dry form on small rectangular
glass or plastic plates, after the inks have been put through a
process called thin-layer chromatography. The inks on the plates
look like pretty little ribbons. These narrow ribbons are the separated dyes of the inks, and since every ink in the world has a
distinct type, quantity, and/or combination of dyes, the nature
of the ribbons provides a point of ink identification. And there's
another identifying characteristic on the plates. This is the retardation factor, which is the distance the dyes have travelled along
the plates. The two features – colour of dyes plus retardation
factor – combine to provide an absolutely sure-fire lock on ink
identification.

So, in order to match up the two inks in Gurman's notebook
to inks in the library, Stewart had to perform thin-layer chromatography on both of the Gurman inks. Needless to say, this
was another excruciatingly intricate operation.

First, Stewart had to turn the little pinholes of ink back into
liquid form. This was no big deal, though the work was necessarily picky.

Operating on a metal lab table, Stewart removed one pinhole
of ink from its glass vial and placed it on the metal surface. Then
he applied a minuscule amount of solvent to the pinhole. A
solvent is a liquid mixture used for dissolving a material or substance. The particular solvent Stewart used was of moderate

strength, not too harsh, not too weak. Carefully applied, it returned the pinhole to its original liquid form.

Next, Stewart picked up this wee droplet of ink with a micropipette. A pipette is a slender tube for transferring small quantities of liquid; a micropipette is an even-more-slender tube, used for transferring even-smaller quantities of liquid; Stewart was working in ultra-miniatures here. He and his micropipette transferred the droplet of ink to a circular spot on a rectangular chromatographic plate, a plate that had previously been treated with a silica gel, which is a powdery substance. The spot on the plate where the droplet of ink was placed, in the silica gel, was approximately two centimetres from the plate's edge.

Then Stewart left the ink to dry on the plate, which didn't take long. Once the ink was dry, Stewart inserted the plate vertically in a small tank that was partly filled with more solvent. He positioned the plate so that the solvent was about one centimetre above the bottom of the plate, meaning that it was also one centimetre below the fixed droplet of ink.

In the tank, as Stewart watched, the solvent travelled up the plate.

How? By capillary action, tugged along by the silica gel.

When the solvent, in capillary crawl, reached the droplet of ink – and this was the magic moment – it began the process of concentrating the dye components of the ink. The dyes separated, their colours emerged, and they travelled various lengths, depending on their retardation factors, along the surface of the plate – in effect, bleeding towards the edge.

Stewart now had a plate with a pretty design. He also had a plate he could compare with plates in the library of seven thousand inks to determine which of the seven thousand exactly matched this particular ink from Mike Gurman's notebook.

Of course Stewart didn't perform this process of thin layer chromatography on just one pinhole of ink. He performed the same operation on dozens of pinholes selected from all the pinhole clusters he had taken out of Gurman's notebook. He divided the inks into two general groups, according to the two inks that he had already determined to exist in the notebook. Each group, with all the subsamples from the various clusters, were now at last ready for the next step: comparison with inks in the library and identification of the two subject inks by name.

For a man like Stewart, an old hand in the ink game, the matter of handling the library's inks, comparing, and identifying, depended largely on eye and experience — *Stewart's* eye and *Stewart's* experience. He went to the black-ink section of the library, a sample of one of the inks in hand, and he knew from long practice what areas to scout in. He sorted through the library's black inks and decided, out of his memory bank, out of an intuition built over years of examining inks the way other people study baseball statistics or Lepidoptera, that there were six inks in the library that were close to the subject ink as revealed by the chromatographic plates.

Well, that narrowed things down, but it was far from definitive. What next?

What was next was another round of thin-layer chromatography on this first Gurman ink. The second time around, though, Stewart did the job with a system — using different solvents, for one thing — that provided a higher grade of result, that gave a better resolution among dye components, that made it easier to detect the subtle differences in ink formulas.

With this superior chromatography plate, Stewart marched back to the ink library and unhesitatingly nailed down the single ink out of seven thousand that precisely matched the Gurman ink on the plate. The ink — no mistaking it — was a popular but particular Bic black ballpoint ink. The clincher as to which Bic it was, in Stewart's words, lay in "a unique yellow dye that no other black ballpoint ink matches."

That accomplished, one ink detected, Stewart went through the same long process with the second ink from the Gurman notebook. This one, Stewart concluded, no question, was of German manufacture. It was an I.F.K. ink, formula M38 PG3, created in 1974 and identifiable by its distinctive methyl violet dye. Two inks, two names.

Now Stewart was ready to focus on the writing in the notebook that had generated all the commotion, the writing on lines two and three of page 62. Since Stewart already knew which inks he was dealing with, this aspect of his work didn't take much time. In short order, he determined that all of page 62, apart from most of line two and all of line three, was written in the Bic ballpoint ink. The rest, starting with the period after "s/c" in line two and including all of "Ulpiano want to talk. 2nd/ caution read & understood" was written in I.F.K. black ink. As for the mark underneath the letter "r" in "read," it was sufficiently blurred and hidden that Stewart wouldn't say to an absolute certainty what ink it was written in, but he concluded it was "consistent with" the Bic ballpoint ink. In scientific circles, "consistent with" is right next door to damned positive.

Age determination came next. How long had the two inks been on page 62? The same period of time? Or had the ink in the suspect two lines been on the page a shorter time than the ink on the rest of the page?

Actually, to come up with an answer to that last question, an answer that could prove Mike Gurman to be untruthful, Larry Stewart didn't bother comparing the two inks on page 62. Instead, he did something apparently more ingenious. He set out to compare the I.F.K. ink in the two lines on page 62 with I.F.K. ink in other parts of the notebook. So the question now became, was the I.F.K. ink on page 62, which was supposed to have been written on June 28, 1990, approximately the same age as the I.F.K. inks that appeared on earlier and later pages, which were written in May, June, and July of 1990?

To get at the answer, Stewart adopted one of the major

methods by which he customarily targeted the age of inks. This
is by looking at the rate of extraction of various samples of ink,
by discovering how hard it is to make the inks liquid again. The
more difficult it is to turn ink back to liquid form, the older is
the ink. This is the principle, a basic one at that, that guided Larry
Stewart's next moves.

He began by selecting from the notebook two samples of
I.F.K. ink that weren't in question, inks from entries that nobody
considered to have been written on dates other than the dates
indicated. These two were I.F.K. inks for sure, and they came from
the opposite ends of the notebook. One sample appeared on page
7, which Gurman had written on May 31, 1990, and the other
sample originated from page 97, which Gurman had written on
July 19, 1990. These two pieces of writing would have been
among the first and last entries Gurman put in his notebook, and
they occurred about equidistant on each side of the I.F.K. writing
in the two lines of June 28, 1990, on page 62.

Stewart got under way on these two samples of ink by treat-
ing each with two kinds of solvent. One solvent, butanol, was
soft, and would take a relatively longer time to extract the ink
and make it liquid again. The other solvent, pyridine, was stronger
than butanol, and would do the same job more quickly. Stewart
allowed each solvent to work on the ink samples for exactly one
minute per sample. Then, using his trusty micropipette, he transferred all the samples to chromatography plates and let them
form their pretty little patterns of dye.

What Stewart had at this point were plates with samples of ink
from pages 7 and 97 that had been treated for one minute with
a hard and with a soft solvent. What he was looking for was the
rate that the ink extracted in each sample in that one minute using
those two solvents. How did he measure such rates for such solvents? By recording the densities of the inks on the chromatographic plates. What device provided this measurement? The
densitometer.

For something with such a fancy name, a densitometer is a dis-concertingly straightforward piece of work. It's a smallish flat-bed machine with a head that contains an intense little light-bulb that gives off a very accurate light that probes the density of the sample. It also comes equipped with a calibrated system that provides a numerical reading of the density of the inks it's measuring.

As Stewart passed the light over the ink samples, over the sep-arated dyes on the chromatography plates, the light registered peaks or raised spots in each sample. The size of the peaks was in direct proportion to the concentration of the sample: the more concentrated the ink sample, the more dense the sample, then the higher the peak. The light recorded different peaks for the ink from May 31 as it had been treated with the weak solvent and as it had been treated with the strong solvent. It did the same for the July 19 ink. That is to say, the heights of the peaks created numbers, one for the weak solvent, one for the strong solvent. Stewart took these numbers and ratioed them to give him one final number for each ink. The number reflected the degree of difficulty in turning the inks on the written pages back into liquid, which, in turn, pro-vided a comment on the ages of the inks.

Here is the way the ratioed numbers came out: 1.82 for the May 31 entry on page 7, and 1.77 for the July 19 entry on page 97.

The numbers were much of the sort Stewart expected. They were close together, which indicated that the writing had been done on the two pages in the same general time frame. And it was proper for the later entry, July 19, to have a slightly lower number, since it would be marginally easier to turn the ink in it back to liquid form than it would for the ink in the May 31 entry, which was older by almost two months. The differences were small but meaningful.

Still, the numbers in isolation meant nothing. How did the numbers stack up against a number for the ink in the two lines from page 62 dated June 28 that was obtained in the same way?

So Stewart put samples of ink from the suspect two lines

through the densitometer process. He gave the samples a treatment with butanol and pyridine, transferred them via micropipette to chromatography plates, let the densitometer light play over them, took down the numbers, ratioed them, and produced a final figure for comparison.

If everything about the two lines from page 62, the two lines in I.F.K. ink amidst a sea of Bic ballpoint, two lines dated June 28 being compared with ink from lines dated May 31 and July 19, was straight and above-board, then the number that Stewart arrived at would be somewhere between 1.82 and 1.77.

It was nowhere close.

The number was 1.11.

Hmm, Stewart said, this is way off. This is an ink, the so-called June 28 ink, that's just at the *beginning* of its ageing cycle. This isn't an old ink at all. It isn't three years old. It definitely isn't a 1990 ink.

Stewart was finished his lab work. He was ready to fly to Toronto and tell the court what he had discovered.

Larry Stewart was called to the witness stand on the morning of Tuesday, June 22, 1993. Paul Bennett on examination-in-chief and Tony Bryant with some mop-up questioning were finished with him at one o'clock the same day. The examination, especially by Bennett, was succinct, sharp, and elicited just about what the defence was looking for.

"With regard to the questioned entry of June 28," Bennett asked Stewart, "is it consistent or inconsistent with having been written on June 28, 1990?"

The question came after Bennett had led Stewart through a description in précis form of his tests with the chromatographic plates, the densitometer, and the other gizmos in his Washington laboratory, and the arrival at the numbers, 1.82, 1.77, and 1.11.

"It's inconsistent," Stewart answered, "based on the results of the other entries."

"Is it consistent or inconsistent with being written any time between the sample entries of May 31 and July 19?"

"It is not consistent with that."

"Are you in a position to plot out, within some range, when the putative entry of June 28 would have been written?"

"Based on my experience and the test results, the entry is testing as if it were written very recently, within the past few months."

In Bennett's fondest dreams, he was hoping that Stewart would say Gurman had written the two suspect lines on May 18, 1993, which was the day before Bennett started cross-examining him. But it was way too much to ask that Gurman had doctored his notebook on the very eve of his testimony. Still, "written very recently" wasn't bad, though "within the past few months" took some edge off it. Bennett nudged Stewart for something a bit more specific.

"Are you indicating three, four months, that kind of range?" Bennett asked. "What are you happy with in terms of the past few months? Would you like to pinpoint this down to an exact date?"

The scientist in Stewart began to show itself in a hesitant way. He got cautious. "I cannot pinpoint it down to an exact date," he said, "based on the limitations of the dates within this notebook."

"Within a range of a few months, would you be content to pin it down to that range?"

"The questioned entry," Stewart answered, "is consistent with having been placed in the notebook within the past year."

Bennett knew this was a conservative answer. He recognized that Stewart wouldn't allow himself to budge any further from his cautious scientist's reply. But it was more than enough. Stewart had just testified that Gurman had written the two crucial lines at least two years after he'd written the rest of the notebook. Stewart was saying that Gurman had faked his book and had been untruthful in court.

"Thank you, sir," Bennett said to Stewart.

~

This wasn't the first time Larry Stewart had given evidence in a Canadian courtroom. It was the second. The first had come three and a half years earlier, in the case of a man named Imre Finta. Finta was seventy-seven and frail when he went on trial at the Toronto Courthouse in late 1989 on charges of unlawful confinement, robbery, kidnapping, and manslaughter. The crimes, so the Crown alleged, had taken place almost forty-six years earlier, in June 1944, in the Hungarian city of Szeged. At the time, Finta served as an officer in the Hungarian Gendarmerie. And it was the Gendarmerie, acting on instructions from their Nazi masters, who had herded 8,617 Jews into the Szeged brickyard, stripped them of money and jewellery, packed them into boxcars, and waved the trains down the tracks to death camps.

A year later, the Nazis defeated, the war over, Finta embarked on a long, arduous flight. It landed him in Toronto in 1951. He became a Canadian citizen in 1956 and made a career as a glad-handing restaurateur in establishments that featured goulash on the menu and displayed framed photographs of a smiling Imre and smiling celebrity patrons on the walls. Finta prospered, and he was enjoying the rewards of a comfortable retirement in the mid-1980s when Nazi hunters fingered him as the monster of Szeged. He, they said, was the senior officer at the brickyards, the man responsible for escorting eight thousand Jews from their homes to humiliation to death.

At Finta's trial, which lasted eight months, the Crown called nineteen elderly survivors of the brickyard who identified Finta as their chief tormentor. But the defence presented three witnesses, also survivors, who were sceptical that Finta, though he was possibly present at the brickyard, was the officer who issued the deadly commands. If Finta was there, he was an underling. The testimony of the three defence witnesses was sufficient to raise a reasonable doubt in the minds of the jury. They acquitted Finta, and the acquittal was upheld by the Supreme Court of Canada. Finta slipped back to retirement in his Toronto apartment.

The Department of Justice had laboured diligently to build a case against Imre Finta. It had rounded up forty-eight witnesses in all, hunted down some of them in obscure Hungarian villages, tried to overlook no detail in wrapping a cloak of guilt around Finta. The Justice people were particularly proud of the documents expert they brought in from the U.S. Secret Service. This man was essential in persuading the court of the veracity of papers that placed Finta as a captain of the Gendarmerie at Szeged in June 1944. The Secret Service expert performed brilliantly, albeit in an ultimately losing cause, and the Justice Department praised him as a star witness for the Crown.

The expert was Larry Stewart.

And now Damien Frost, acting for the same Department of Justice, was setting out in his cross-examination on the afternoon of June 22, 1993, to make the same Larry Stewart look like a bit of an eccentric who practised hocus-pocus on inks.

Damien Frost is a tall, slender, balding man in his early forties. He sports a black beard, salted with grey, and, as he was about to demonstrate, he has a style in cross-examination that can be resourceful and hectoring.

With Larry Stewart, he began at ground zero. He asked Stewart to take the courtroom through the entire testing operation he'd performed in Washington once more. Frost wanted it all again, and he wanted it in detail.

And as Stewart plodded over the familiar terrain, Frost nipped at his heels with questions that had a scoffing edge to them. Wasn't there another testing method Stewart could have used? A better method? Did he conform to the highest standards of testing? Shouldn't there have been backup tests to confirm Stewart's findings?

"Has this ever happened?" Frost asked halfway through the

afternoon. "Have you ever had a phone call from somebody who says, 'I've read the papers you've written on ink samples, and I've tried to reproduce your results, and I've had problems'?"

"I'm not aware of that ever happening," Stewart answered.

Stewart bore Frost's bombardment with poise, but Paul Bennett, never a fellow to suffer gladly someone he perceives as acting foolishly, got monumentally fed up.

"Your Honour, I *object!*" he snapped. "This is getting repetitive, the same questions being asked seventy times. He *got* the same answer seventy times. There comes a point where Mr. Frost should move on."

Judge Adams, who perhaps hadn't made up his mind about suffering foolish behaviour gladly or otherwise, or even if the behaviour *was* foolish, sighed and said, "Just carry on, Mr. Frost."

Bennett's objection came shortly before court adjourned for the day. The judge told Stewart to return next morning for Frost's further cross-examination. This drew a flashing glance of exasperation from Stewart. He'd expected to be in and out of Toronto in a day.

"How about a ball game tonight?" Bennett asked in the corridor outside the courtroom, trying to cheer Stewart up. "You like baseball? Blue Jays at the SkyDome?"

"Sure, that'd be nice," Stewart said.

Bennett had to do prep work on the trial that night. His wife took Stewart to the ball game. Bennett's wife is Alison Gordon, a bright and witty former *Toronto Star* baseball-beat writer and the author of crime novels featuring Kate Henry, ace baseball journalist.

Stewart said later he'd had a great night at the ball game.

Next morning, Frost put Stewart through more hoops. Frost had a theory. What, he asked Stewart, if this happened? What if Mike Gurman left his notebook under the windshield in the front of his car? What if the notebook sat in the sun all day long for many days? Wouldn't the book get hot? Wouldn't the heat dry the inks? Wouldn't *that* affect Stewart's testing of the inks? Especially the inks on page 62?

Stewart thought definitely not. "Any external source of heat," he said, "is going to affect the whole document approximately the same, unless a particular page is opened to the cause of the heat."

Frost let that notion pass. The possibility that Gurman had left page 62 out in the sun for days and weeks was too far-out, even for Frost. But he wouldn't let go of his theory that heat leaking through the front of the notebook would eventually dry out the inks all the way down to page 62.

Stewart answered that he'd tested for that. "The changes from an external heat greatly diminish with each page that you go down. The effect is almost non-existent as you go four or five pages down."

Frost gave up on the heat theory, but he kept on for several more runs at Stewart's testing methods. By now, Stewart's body language was definitely registering impatience.

"I know you have *places* to go and *things* to do," Frost said to him, "but I've got to understand this, you know."

"I object!" Bennett was on his feet again. "Your Honour, there is no reason for Mr. Frost to use voice inflections, sarcasm that doesn't show up on the record."

Another sigh from Mr. Justice Adams. "Continue, Mr. Frost."

Frost continued until almost 12:30 P.M. He had been cross-examining Stewart for five hours. Now he was out of questions. He sat down.

In Bennett's opinion, in the five hours, Frost hadn't laid a glove on Larry Stewart.

The following Tuesday, Judge Adams heard argument from counsel over the two lines in Mike Gurman's notebook. It wasn't much of a contest. Bennett and Bryant had on their side the test results from the two scientists, Greg Boyd of the Ontario Centre of Forensic Sciences and Larry Stewart of the U.S. Secret Service. In their argument, the two defence counsel went through the tests once more; the ink on the two questioned lines from page 62 was different and younger than the ink on the rest of the page, and the lines had been written at least two years after the time Gurman had testified in court that he'd written them. Gurman had lied about the timing, about the writing, about the lines. Damien Frost for the Crown called no scientific witnesses of his own. All he could do in his argument before Judge Adams, as he had done in his cross-examinations of Boyd and Stewart, was dump on their techniques, to insist that they were inadequate or misleading or incomplete. In the end, Frost's contentions weren't persuasive, and Judge Adams ruled that, on a balance of proba- bilities, Gurman had been untruthful in his answers to Bennett and Bryant about the two lines. For that matter, he'd been untruthful to Kofi Barnes. "When did you make your notes?" Barnes had asked Gurman as part of the Crown's examination- in-chief on the first day of Gurman's testimony several weeks earlier. "I made the notes during the course of the investigation," Gurman answered, "and specifically on the evening of the take- down of this drug project." That appeared not to be true, not in the case of the infamous two lines on page 62 of the notebook. And Judge Adams so ruled.

Chalk up a point for Paul Bennett and Tony Bryant.

But Judge Adams wasn't finished with his rulings in the matter of Mike Gurman and the notebook. He went on to hold that, even though he thought Gurman had been untruthful about the two lines on page 62 – two lines that dealt with his reading, or non-reading, of a caution to Ulpiano Aguilera – the statements that Gurman had drawn from Aguilera on the night of June 28 were still admissible as evidence in the trial. Since the statements included apparent admissions by Aguilera that he was in the cocaine trade – "I think was big mistake to get in this business"

— Adams was allowing the Crown to wield some potentially incriminating material.

Chalk up a point for Damien Frost and Kofi Barnes.

The forty-day-long *voir dire* finally ended. Judge Adams made decisions on the various evidentiary challenges that Bennett and Bryant had brought, some in favour of the defence, more in favour of the Crown. With that at last out of the way, a jury was selected, and the trial proceeded for the next thirty-five days. Frost and Barnes called as witnesses most of the twenty-three police officers who took part in the takedown on June 28, 1990. Conspicuously absent from this list was Mike Gurman.

"If Gurman had testified," Paul Bennett said, "Tony and I would've had a field day."

So they would have. Here was a witness who had been branded untruthful by the judge, not untruthful across the board, but dissembling about a key page in his notebook. That would have been enough for two tenacious defence lawyers. They would have kept Gurman on the stand for a week, revealing to the jury the duplicity that the two forensic scientists had suggested, grilling Gurman to see if there were other inconsistencies in his testimony, maybe another clanger of a deception in his notebook. They would have tried to expand on Gurman's one seemingly established falsehood to take in the entire case. It was *all* based on dubious tactics, Bennett and Bryant would have said to the jury, on mendacious testimony, on lies. And that approach might have worked. The jury might have figured there was a reasonable doubt and acquitted Ulpiano and Maria Aguilera.

But Bennett and Bryant didn't get the chance. In one sense, this meant that they came out the winners in the contest over the two lines in Gurman's notebook; they had prevented Gurman from testifying about the incriminating statements that Ulpiano Aguilera had made to him on the night of June 28. On the other hand, with the Crown holding back Gurman, Bennett and Bryant were denied their field day. To compensate, they considered calling Gurman as their own witness. But that would have been dicey. Gurman would have been a hostile witness, and his testimony would have been, at best, grudging. "We thought about it," Bennett said, "but ended up not seeing the point."

The jury convicted Ulpiano and Maria Aguilera of trafficking in cocaine. Judge Adams sentenced Ulpiano to twelve years in prison, Maria to five years. Both appealed their convictions. While they waited for the Ontario Court of Appeal to hear their cases, both applied for bail. The court refused Ulpiano's request and granted Maria's. She went home to look after the four Aguilera kids. In the late spring of 1995, their appeal was still pending.

The Crown – not Damien Frost or Kofi Barnes specifically, but the Crown's office – laid a charge of perjury against Mike Gurman arising out of his testimony about the notebook in the Aguilera case. Metro Police put Gurman on suspension with pay until the courts decided his guilt or innocence, and Gurman hired a lawyer named Peter West to represent him on the perjury charge. West is a chunky, muscular man in his mid-thirties. The son of a clergyman and devoted father of three children, West is serious, thorough, and assiduous, and he realized that success in defending Gurman would lie, if anywhere, in an attack on Larry Stewart and his science.

For assistance in this job, West turned to two Canadian document specialists. One was Joel Harris, a member of the RCMP documents section in Ottawa, and the other was Brian Lindblom, a former officer in the same section, who now did private consulting in cases involving document analysis. Harris and Lindblom had eye-opening opinions for West. Both insisted that the ink-dating system used by Larry Stewart on Mike Gurman's notebook, the system based on the extractability of ink, was definitely suspect, that it was far from infallible, not nearly as reliable as Stewart had led the court to believe at the Aguilera trial.

Harris and Lindblom claimed that only eight or nine document experts in the entire world regularly used the extractability method, and all of them were, like Stewart, American, all people who had been at one time or another, as Stewart had been, associated with the Bureau of Alcohol, Tobacco and Firearms. This group formed a small club of American scientists who practised the technique, and it seemed, according to Harris and Lindblom, that other scientists, outside the club, who attempted to duplicate the methods of the eight or nine Americans had trouble producing the same results. These other scientists couldn't say for a certainty, based on extractability tests, that one ink was older than another.

This was what Harris and Lindblom told Peter West – and there was more. Harris and Lindblom said they were aware of instances where document experts *within* the exclusive American school of eight or nine scientists had differed not only on the age of an ink but on its *type*. There were actual court cases in which two of the experts, using the same extractability method, had come up with opposing answers in pinpointing the name of a specific ink and its age. All of this encouraged Peter West as he prepared to launch his attack on Larry Stewart's methods.

West's first crack at Stewart came in November 1993. That was when the preliminary hearing in Mike Gurman's perjury case began in court. A preliminary hearing is a proceeding in which a judge of the Provincial Court, sitting alone, determines whether there is sufficient evidence against an accused person to send the accused on for a full trial in a higher court in the General Division. The Crown at such a hearing needs only to reveal part of the evidence accumulated in the case, just enough to persuade the judge that a full trial is called for. It's rare that a judge on a preliminary hearing does *not* commit an accused for trial, and the main job for the defence counsel at a preliminary is to get an idea about

some of the Crown's case, to listen to the Crown witnesses, and
to plan strategy for the inevitable trial.

The preliminary hearing in the Gurman case took place at the
Finch Avenue Provincial Courts in northwest Metro Toronto
before Judge Charles Vaillancourt. Fred Braley was the Crown
attorney, a smart, seasoned lawyer, and he called two witnesses.
The first was Greg Boyd, who explained once again how his VSC
had detected two entirely different inks on page 62 of the notebook. Then came Larry Stewart, who was part way through an
outline of his extractability method in calculating the age of inks
when the court day came to an end. Since just a single day had
been set aside for the Gurman preliminary, and since the lawyers
and Judge Vaillancourt had crowded calendars, the second day of
the preliminary was set over to July 1994, eight months away.

The delay worked to Peter West's benefit; he had more time
to get a grip on the fine points of ink analysis – and he found
plenty of material to work with. Among other documents, he
studied Larry Stewart's working notes from the Aguilera case,
which West had obtained from Fred Braley as part of the disclosure of the Crown's case. These were the notes that Stewart made
to himself as he went through the long process of analysing the
inks in Gurman's notebook, the rough notes that Stewart would
use as the basis of his final report.

Right away, West thought he spotted something curious in the
notes. "It just leaped out at me," West says. What leaped out, West
thought, were errors in some of Stewart's ink identifications. In
West's perception, Stewart had misidentified certain I.F.K. inks
as Bic and certain Bic inks as I.F.K. This, West figured, was at least
odd, and, when the preliminary hearing resumed in the summer
of 1994, he brought up the matter of identification, or misidentification, in his cross-examination of Stewart.

"It was the exchange I had with Stewart over this issue that
really got me thinking there was something wrong with his technique," West says. "I brought up the misidentification of the inks,

the I.F.K. for Bic and the Bic for the I.F.K. on various lines in the notebook, and Stewart answered that, no, no, he wasn't mistaken in his designations. But he didn't stop there. Then he added, 'But if it'll make the court feel better, I'll call these I.F.K. inks Bic inks.' I said, 'It isn't a matter of making the court *feel* better. It's a matter of right and wrong, and I say you're *wrong*.'"

At the end of Stewart's testimony, at the conclusion of the second day of the preliminary hearing, Judge Vaillancourt committed Gurman to trial on the perjury charge. But West came away with the feeling that perhaps he had just begun to uncover holes in Larry Stewart's ink-dating analysis, and that he might find more.

For Mike Gurman, the summer of 1994 was a good-news-bad-news season. The bad news was that the perjury charge still hung over him, something that would haunt him at least until the trial. The good news was that Metro Police reinstated him in his job in the Court Services Department at the College Park Courts. The reason for the reinstatement wasn't clear. Maybe it was a show of support for Gurman from the top brass. Or maybe it was a matter of economics. Maybe the cops thought they were wasting money by allowing a detective with seventeen years of service to sit around his house on full salary. Either way, Gurman was out of the house and back on the desk.

In mid-April of 1995, with Gurman's trial still two months away, Peter West travelled to Raleigh, North Carolina, for a meeting with a man named Al Lyter. West took with him the Gurman notebook and Larry Stewart's report on his analysis of the notebook's inks. West asked Lyter to produce a critique of Stewart's work, to look for flaws in it. But, more than that, he asked Lyter to duplicate Stewart's ink-dating tests. West wanted Lyter to run through the whole process a second time and see what results he came up with.

Lyter seemed to be just the man for the task. He had worked

in the documents department of the Bureau of Alcohol, Tobacco and Firearms several years earlier. Indeed, he had once been Larry Stewart's supervisor. He knew his way around ink analysis, and he was still putting his knowledge to use in private practice as a freelance documents expert. Most of his work these days, he told West, was in medical malpractice cases. Patients sued doctors, and the doctors, to cover their tracks, often returned to old notebooks and wrote new entries that might get them off the hook. But, doctors' notebooks, a cop's notebook, it was all the same to Lyter. He would run the tests.

And he did. He put the notebook through the same process as Larry Stewart. He removed tiny plugs of ink from a variety of lines in the notebook. He put the plugs in small vials. He dropped solvent into the vials, first the butanol, then the pyridine. He placed the inks on plates. He allowed the dyes to run on the plates. He studied the plates under the densitometer. And he took readings from the densitometer, readings that eventually led to numbers that measured the age of samples of each ink in the notebook.

All of this was a repetition of the same process Larry Stewart had carried out in June 1993. But, Lyter told West, his own test was more complete than Stewart's, more comprehensive, ultimately more certain. Why? Well, for one thing, Lyter explained, he tested for more samples of the I.F.K. ink than Stewart had. Stewart tested I.F.K. inks from two pages of the notebook, page 7 and page 97, and compared them with the I.F.K. ink in the two questioned lines on page 62. That, Lyter insisted, wasn't good enough. Two I.F.K. inks, one each on either side of the questioned ink, wasn't sufficient, in his opinion, to draw acceptable conclusions. Lyter himself took nine samples of I.F.K. ink from the pages before page 62 and nine more samples from the pages following page 62, eighteen samples altogether. It was only with these eighteen, Lyter said, that he could carry out a valid statistical analysis of the inks. To Lyter, numbers equalled certainty.

Lyter found other areas where, he believed, Stewart's testing came up short, and Lyter reached many conclusions about the inks that differed from Stewart's. Lyter wasn't even sure that Stewart had correctly identified the second ink in Gurman's notebook. Yes, Lyter agreed, there were two inks scattered through the notebook, and, yes, one of them was a Bic. But the other might not be an I.F.K. Lyter thought it showed signs of being something other than I.F.K.

Still, regardless of what the second ink was, the point where Lyter fundamentally departed from Stewart was on the age of both inks. Lyter said the two inks in the notebook, including most crucially the ink in the two questioned lines on page 62, were of the same general age. Lyter had run all the tests Stewart had conducted, notably the ink-extraction test, and he reached the conclusion that Gurman had written all the lines in the notebook in both inks over the three months that the notebook covered. There was, Lyter wrote in his report for Peter West, no "significant difference" in age between the "questioned" ink and the "known" ink. It was Lyter's view that Gurman had not written the two lines on page 62 at a date long after June 28, 1990, not a year later, not two years later. He'd written the two lines, albeit in a different ink from the one he'd used on the rest of page 62, contemporaneous with the rest of the notes on the page. Two inks, same time.

Mike Gurman's perjury trial was scheduled to begin in the Toronto Courthouse on Monday, May 29, 1995, and, given Al Lyter's analysis, the trial shaped up as a battle between the two specialists in ink identification and ageing. Larry Stewart versus Al Lyter. The Crown scientist versus the defence scientist.

Stewart had already testified at length in the Aguilera trial, and to a lesser extent in the Gurman preliminary hearing, explaining in detail his methods in ink analysis and offering reasons for the results he had arrived at. He had been subjected to a searching cross-examination by Damien Frost and, over a shorter period, by Peter West, and his work and conclusions in the matter of Mike Gurman's notebook were on the public record. Al Lyter's analysis of the writing and inks in the notebook hadn't yet been given the same scrutiny. He hadn't testified in court and hadn't come under fire from an opposing counsel. Now his views, seemingly the opposite of Stewart's, would be put on courtroom display. Now Lyter and Stewart, two scientists whose analyses ran counter to one another, would meet for a showdown, and the trial of Mike Gurman on the perjury charge would essentially hinge on the contest between two heavyweights of ink analysis.

That was what seemed to lie ahead, but it was not how events finally unfolded.

Six days before the beginning of the trial, on Tuesday, May 23, Peter West telephoned Fred Braley, the Crown on the Gurman case, and asked for a meeting, and the two men got together two days later in the Crown's offices at the Toronto Courthouse. West went to the meeting equipped with Al Lyter's report on his analysis of the inks in the Gurman notebook and with Lyter's criticisms of Larry Stewart's work on the same notebook. West showed the material to Braley, and went into a lengthy pitch, playing up what he considered the sound and thorough qualities of Lyter's analysis over those of Stewart's investigation.

Then West offered Braley his own explanation – actually two possible explanations – for the presence of two different inks on page 62 of the notebook.

"It's completely straightforward," West said. "Gurman made his notes as he interviewed Ulpiano Aguilera. Then, later on the same night, he read over everything he'd written that day and realized he'd left something out. So he wrote an additional two lines on page 62, but he happened to write with a different pen in a different ink."

Or, if not that, West said, then this:

"Gurman started out at the top of page 62 writing with the

same pen as he'd used in the previous few pages. Then he got distracted for some reason, something else came up, and when he started writing again, he happened to pick up another pen with a different ink. He wrote the two lines, and then another interruption delayed him. That can happen, somebody coming to the door, another officer asking Gurman a question, whatever, and when Gurman got back to work, he resumed writing with the first pen with the first ink."

This second explanation was the same hypothesis that Damien Frost had suggested in his cross-examination of Greg Boyd during the Aguilera case. It was familiar stuff, but West propped it up with Al Lyter's scientific conclusions. Lyter said both inks on page 62 were written at the same time. There was nothing complex about it, nothing dishonest on Gurman's part. Lyter's testimony at the trial would support either hypothesis – the use of two pens or the later additions – and Lyter would make a more-convincing witness than Stewart. Lyter's science, West claimed, was more complete, more persuasive.

And besides, West went on, Stewart's methodology wouldn't hold up under cross-examination. West said he had already picked a hole in Stewart's testimony at the preliminary hearing, the business about Stewart misidentifying the Bic and the I.F.K. inks, and West promised he had more criticisms he could bring home. He'd call into question Stewart's very qualifications as an expert witness in the Gurman case.

That was what Peter West told Fred Braley at the meeting on Thursday, May 25. Next day, with the trial just a weekend away, Braley phoned West at his office.

"I'm not putting Larry Stewart on the witness stand," he told West.

With this decision, the Gurman case rushed towards anticlimax. The trial went on, but the outcome now seemed inevitable. Judge Donald Talliano of the General Division presided over the trial on Monday morning in the Toronto Courthouse, and, for the Crown, Fred Braley opened by calling two witnesses. First, Ed Tymburski, one of the detectives in charge of Project Narrows, described the events of the Aguilera takedown and Mike Gurman's role in them. Then Greg Boyd explained yet again how his VSC detected two inks on page 62 of Gurman's notebook. But neither man could shed any light on the key issue in the case: when did Gurman write the two questioned lines? Among possible witnesses for the Crown, only Larry Stewart was prepared to give an answer to that question, and he wasn't in the courtroom.

Fred Braley told Judge Talliano that the two witnesses, Tymburski and Boyd, completed the Crown's case. Peter West moved immediately for a non-suit. He wanted a dismissal of the charge against Gurman on the ground that the Crown hadn't proved its case. The charge, West pointed out, was perjury, that Gurman had lied in court during the Aguilera trial when he said he wrote the two questioned lines "during the investigation and specifically on the evening of the takedown of this drug project." But, West continued in his argument, the Crown had offered no evidence that Gurman had *not* written his notes, including the two lines on page 62, at any time other than on the night of June 28 when he said he'd written them.

Judge Talliano nodded in agreement. "There's not a tittle of evidence against the accused," Talliano said, and he ordered an acquittal of Mike Gurman on the perjury charge.

Peter West says, "My own personal view is that the technique of determining the age of ink isn't developed to the point where it's reliable."

Looked at from one angle, West isn't being entirely straight-forward in his appraisal. He doesn't think Larry Stewart's age-determination technique is reliable, but he embraced Al Lyter's technique as part of his strategy in winning Gurman's acquittal. And this ambivalence towards the forensic science of judging the age of ink runs as a theme through the case of Mike Gurman's suspect notebook.

One judge, George Adams, held that Gurman had written the two lines at a later date than he claimed. Adams had the benefit of hearing a scientist's evidence, Larry Stewart's, on the subject. Another judge, Donald Talliano, ruled there was no proof that Gurman had written the lines at a later date. Talliano made his decision in the absence of any scientist's testimony. Mike Gurman found himself in trouble when one scientist, Stewart, testified at one trial. And he found himself off the hook when no scientists, neither Stewart nor Al Lyter, testified at another trial.

So science, in this case, seemed to have been short-changed by the law. Scientists and lawyers came into collision in the forum where lawyers are most at home, the courtroom, and it was the scientists whose story became muted. Whose analysis of the inks in the two questioned lines on page 62 was to be believed? Larry Stewart's or Al Lyter's? That contest never took place, not in a courtroom, and in the end, only one of the people caught in this small, intriguing mystery may have come away believing that justice had ultimately been done. That person was the one who had the most to lose, Mike Gurman.

Footprints:

The Case of the Grounded Air Nikes

Ɪɴ ᴀɴᴅ ᴀʀᴏᴜɴᴅ ᴅᴇꜱᴇʀᴏɴᴛᴏ, Ontario, folks knew Ward Maracle as the man to see if they needed a cheque cashed at night, needed a few dollars to get them through the weekend. Maracle kept money on hand at home and ran a cheque-cashing service, discreetly, for the locals, for Indians on the Tyendinaga Mohawk Reserve, for people who didn't operate with bank cards and PINs. And it was this circumstance of Deseronto society that, just after Christmas 1992, brought into Ward Maracle's life, first, violent events, and, second, the services of Jim Eadie, specialist in footprints and all-round ace member of the Forensic Identification Unit working out of the Ontario Provincial Police office in Belleville.

Deseronto is a lazy little town (population 2,000), sitting prettily on the Bay of Quinte about 30 kilometres east of Belleville and about 180 kilometres east of Toronto. The town's situation puts it off the beaten track, four or five kilometres south of the thundering traffic of Highway 401. Anybody who arrives in Deseronto intends to end up there, cottagers, fishermen, inquisitive tourists, and not many of each group.

Still, Ward's Gas Bar turned a nice business. It was Ward

Maracle's establishment, a gas station with restaurant attached. The place was located a few kilometres outside Deseronto, on Tyendinaga land, and, though patronage wasn't spectacular, it was steady, regular, and mostly familiar. Ward worked there. So did his wife, Diana. They spent busy hours on the job, even if both were crowding middle age, and at night, sometimes long after dark, they took the day's receipts home. Diana counted the cash and wrote the totals right on the bills. Ward locked the money in the house safe.

The house was an object of pride for the Maracles. It was on the reserve, too, about ten kilometres from the gas bar, but isolated. The closest neighbour, down the road and on the opposite side, Lorraine Brant, wasn't within hailing distance. The Maracle house had little in the way of architectural distinction, but for size – two stories and sprawling – for orderliness and care in décor, it beat just about everything in the area. The floors were shiny hardwood, and the first thing Ward and Diana did when they stepped inside the front door was take off their shoes and slide their feet into slippers.

As things turned out later, Jim Eadie was awfully glad to see those hardwood floors.

Pete Benedict and Frank Lanoue had heard about Ward Maracle's practice of cashing cheques, of keeping money around the house – and they were the wrong couple of guys to come into that piece of information. Benedict and Lanoue, both in their early twenties, were rounders. They robbed and thieved. They had records. They'd seen the inside of jails. They lived in Cornwall, a larger town an hour's drive east from Deseronto, close to the Quebec border, but they developed designs on Ward Maracle's cache.

"Thieves move around a lot," Jim Eadie explains. "What happens in our area, the thieves might live down south in, say, Picton, and one night they'll drive way up north to Bancroft, do three or four break-ins, then drive home the same night. They expect the police'll go looking for Bancroft bad guys. But we've learned to spread the net a little wider."

Benedict and Lanoue hatched a plan. Masks. A gun. A car. It wasn't an elaborate plan. They'd crash into the Maracle house at night, scare the shit out of the couple, and beat it with the money. That was the plan.

Lanoue's mask was homemade. He got out an old navy-blue toque, pulled it down to cover his face, then cut holes for his eyes and mouth. Benedict's was store-bought, a rubber mask with a face that was either a bad Elvis or just a guy with slick features and a Brylcreemed pompadour.

The gun, picked up third- or fourth-hand from another rounder who bought it across the St. Lawrence in the States, was a mean little thing, a Beretta .22-calibre semi-automatic, small enough to disappear in the palm of a man's hand, not much power but a sneaky weapon and illegal in Canada.

The car was a rental, a red Pontiac, and, in the very early morning hours of December 30, Benedict and Lanoue drove it to the Maracle house. They parked in the driveway in the dark and quiet of the countryside. The time was just past 5 A.M.

Lanoue carried the .22-calibre pistol.

"I need something in my hand," Benedict said. "Like, for threatening these assholes. A weapon."

The two guys walked to the back of the Maracle house. It was bright enough in the moonlight to make out some stuff strewn around the yard. A sawhorse. Benedict picked it up and cracked off one leg. He waved the leg in the air.

"Fuckin' all *right*."

Masks in place, weapons in hand, gloves on, Benedict and Lanoue stormed the house. They went in through the front door. Nothing subtle, just put their shoulders to the door and smashed the frame.

Upstairs in the master bedroom, Ward and Diana Maracle

came awake to the sound of the splintering door and of shouting on the floor below. The voices were muffled at first, the words indistinct, but there was definitely somebody unfriendly down there. The Maracles heard shoes pounding on the hardwood floors. Whoever it was, they were on the stairs.

Two men appeared at the bedroom door.

"Get out here, Ward!" Lanoue shouted. "We want to see you!"

Lanoue, in the navy-blue toque, waved the pistol at Ward Maracle. Benedict, in the Elvis mask, held the sawhorse leg in position to whack somebody.

"Come on, Ward!" Lanoue said. "We know you got money around here!"

Ward Maracle is a powerful man, not tall, about five-foot-eight, but heavy, almost three hundred pounds. He's also a stubborn man, probably a brave man. He wasn't going to give up his money, the money he and Diana worked hard for, not hand it over to these two punks, to a couple of pipsqueaks in ridiculous masks.

"Where's the goddamn money?" Lanoue said.

It also occurred to Maracle that the two bandits hadn't said anything about the safe. Maybe they didn't know about the safe, didn't know that that was where the money was kept, and in this, Maracle was right.

"You gonna give us the money?" Lanoue demanded. "Or do we hafta get fuckin' serious here?"

Ward Maracle charged at Frank Lanoue.

"Shoot him!" Benedict screamed to Lanoue. "Shoot him!"

Lanoue fired.

Diana Maracle ran into the bathroom off the master bedroom. A connecting door led to a second bedroom. Diana intended to escape through it, into the hall, down the stairs, and out the front door.

Pete Benedict caught her at the bottom of the stairs.

"I don't want to hurt you, lady," he said to Diana. "Just give me the money."

Diana led him into the front room and reached under a desk. She pulled out a briefcase. It held bundles of bills, tens, twenties, fifties, hundreds. Ward hadn't locked the money in the safe that night, and there was more of it than he normally carried in the briefcase. That was because the Christmas holidays had disrupted his usual banking routine. He hadn't been to the bank in a few days. The bundles of bills added up to about ten thousand dollars.

Frank Lanoue thumped down the stairs. Ward Maracle came right on his heels. Benedict stood in Maracle's way on the first floor. Maracle bashed Benedict and sent him tumbling through an open door and down the basement stairs.

Lanoue shot at Maracle again.

Diana fled through the living-room and sun-room and out the back door. She headed across the field towards the road and her neighbour's home.

Back in the kitchen of the Maracle house, Lanoue shot at Ward Maracle one more time.

All three of Lanoue's shots had hit Maracle, one in the chest, the second in the head, the third in the leg. If Lanoue had been wielding a higher-calibre pistol, something with more power and bigger bullets, Maracle would have been a dead man. As it was, he was badly hurt. He would need years of recuperation, years to recover from the brain damage that the shot to the head had inflicted. At that moment in the kitchen, after Frank Lanoue had fired the third bullet at him, Maracle was out of fight.

Lanoue and Benedict scooped up the ten thousand from the briefcase, and, leaving behind far more money, the money in the safe they didn't know about, they raced out the front door of the Maracle house. They climbed into their rental Pontiac and drove home to Cornwall.

The Tyendinaga Reserve maintains its own small police force to keep order on the Indian land and to investigate petty crimes. For bigger stuff, for major robberies and major bloodshed, the reserve police summon the Ontario Provincial Police from Belleville.

About three hundred officers work out of the OPP's Belleville office. That seems a lot, but the Belleville cops cover four eastern Ontario counties, hundreds of square miles from Algonquin Park in the north to Picton on Lake Ontario in the south, from Trenton at the west limit to Gananoque in the Thousand Islands to the east. Among the three hundred officers, Belleville's "Ident" group – the Forensic Identification Unit – numbers seven people, including three who have expertise in footprint work. These seven attend approximately 5 percent of the crime scenes in the Belleville OPP region – all homicides, all sexual assaults, and many robberies with or without violence.

On the Maracle case, the forensic man who got the call when the police on the Tyendinaga Reserve rang in the OPP was Jim Eadie.

When Jim Eadie was eight years old, growing up in Belleville, he spotted something in a neighbour's trash that intrigued him. It was an aged, out-of-commission ham-radio set. He knocked on the neighbour's door and asked the lady of the house if he could cart home the radio. If you're so interested, the woman said, I'll pay to have it repaired for you. Young Jim Eadie was now in the ham-radio game. He tuned in to people in the world beyond Belleville, spread his contacts to operators in places with magical names, Vienna and Monte Carlo and Buenos Aires. He got his official radio licence at age sixteen, stayed an enthusiast into adulthood, and today teaches classes in ham radio to people in the Belleville neighbourhood who want to follow the path he figured out for himself when he was a small boy.

"Curiosity," Eadie says. "That's what got me interested in radio in the first place. I think I've always been a curious person."

Eadie, who's married, with two children, is of medium height, fortyish, and gently, insistently talkative. He has dark brown hair,

wears a beard, and exudes a warm, *simpatico* presence. It's the presence
and the engagingly garrulous nature that make him an effective
teacher. Besides the ham-radio group, he teaches classes in forensic
identification to student recruits at the OPP Academy in Brampton,
Ontario. He has a talk and demonstration about footwear that he
takes on the road and performs by invitation for such outfits as The
Bootmakers, a Canadian society devoted to the stories of Sherlock
Holmes, and Sisters in Crime, a club of women crime writers.
(Although Eadie is a keen reader, he never cracks a crime novel; he
says he prefers the real stuff on the job.) He also plays the piano and
guitar, sings in his church's choir, and is secretary to a Belleville organization that helps people with family abuse problems.

Curiosity, he feels, fuels all of his various passions, a kind of
benign drive to understand how things work, how people think,
and it's that same curiosity – in part, wanting to know how criminals or, as Eadie calls them, "bad guys," function – that helps to
qualify him as a superb forensic identification officer.

After high school in Belleville, and after studying electronics
at a community college in Kingston, Ontario, Eadie joined the
OPP. His first assignment took him to regular duty in the Niagara
Peninsula, then to ten more years of the same thing in Madoc, a
town north of Belleville. At that point, in 1986, he'd been attend-
ing crime scenes for a dozen years, been fascinated with them,
with the clue-gathering process, but hadn't been as involved in
that process as he would have liked to be. He decided to get into
forensic work, so he enrolled in the sixteen-week course in forensics at the Ontario Police College in Aylmer, Ontario. That gave
him a smattering of expertise in photography and fingerprinting,
a bit of technique in footprints, something in a few other areas.
It was enough training to get Eadie an appointment to the
Forensic Identification Unit at the Belleville OPP.

Work for an Ident unit, big city or small town, puts someone
like Jim Eadie in a middle position. In some procedures, he carries
on as an independent operator; in others, he's more of a conduit.

For fingerprinting and shoe identification, Eadie's strictly on his own. He handles the operation, from the print-lifting at the crime scene to the consultation with the investigators who follow up on the clues Eadie unearths. But in more complicated scientific matters, in dealing with blood, hair, semen, with other bodily fluids that might yield DNA, Eadie acts as the expert on the scene for the people at the Centre of Forensic Sciences in Toronto. He gathers the raw material. They analyse it. To be sure, the CFS scientists depend on Eadie to get it right, to collect the blood and hair and semen in the sort of intact form that they can work on. That isn't always an easy task in the violence and chaos of a crime scene. But whatever Eadie does in this clue-gathering aspect of his job, it's the scientists who by necessity have the last word.

In another sense, Eadie's work sets him apart from most other OPP officers. He's scientific; they're investigative. There's a difference, and Eadie rather relishes it. "I have to be a person with an open mind in my job," he says. "I have to think like a scientist. That means there's sometimes a clash between officers who are in the investigative end and people like me who are in identification. I have to be absolutely impartial in studying something at a crime scene. That can make the investigators impatient. They want to get on with catching the bad guys. But I have to be scientific about deciding who the bad guys really *are.*"

In addition to the open, scientific mind, there are two or three other qualities that Eadie brings to forensics. That old standby, curiosity, is one. "Even after twenty years of crime scenes," Eadie says, "I never get bored with the work. What do bad guys *do* at crime scenes? I'm fascinated to find out."

And a tough streak of competitiveness is another Eadie attribute, and, in a sense, he's in competition with the "bad guys."

"Suppose," he begins, explaining his competitive nature *vis-à-vis* the bad guys, "somebody, a singer, asks me to accompany them in a song they're going to sing at a wedding in a couple of weeks. I tell the person, okay, give me the sheet music, and I go home and practise it on the piano. I'm very conscientious about that. I practise, practise, practise. I'm not really *that* good at playing the piano. And I know I'm not going to give my best performance on that particular song at the wedding. I'm going to give my best performance during my practice. But in practice I'll overcome most of my mistakes, and at the wedding I'll have an error percentage of about five. A 5-percent error margin, and it'll take a very good musician to pick out the 5 percent.

"Okay, with bad guys, with criminals, they aren't as committed to doing a good job as I am. They may talk about the crime they're going to do, think about it, plan it, decide they've got everything covered. But, no matter what, they aren't going to have a lower margin of error than 5 percent. They're always going to be higher, and that's where I have the edge."

Eadie offers a small example.

"In robberies," he says, "you don't catch the thieves on the obvious things. Take cash boxes. People in stores, in businesses, sometimes in homes, they keep their money in locked cash boxes. Okay, in all the time I've been doing forensic identification work, I've never once found a thief's fingerprints on a cash box. The thief thinks of that. It's obvious: don't touch the cash box. But while he's thinking about not touching the cash box, he's usually leaning on the table or the counter that the cash box is sitting on. Maybe he's just steadying himself for the job, studying the cash box. Whatever the reason, he leaves his prints on the table or the counter, and that's where I find them. Not on the cash box, but on the table. So I'm working on his error margin, which is larger than mine."

In robberies, Eadie thinks the most important part of the crime scene for his work is the point of entry, the specific place where the thieves break into the house or store or business.

"The reason," he says, "is that the point of entry is the most high-intensity part of the whole break-in. The bad guys are nervous, the sweat is running, the heart is pumping. If they're going to make a mistake, it'll be right there, right where they go in. No matter how much planning they've done, they'll slip up at the entry. They'll leave a shoeprint, a fingerprint. Ninety percent of the fingerprints that I identify as belonging to criminals I find at the point of entry."

There's just one thing wrong with this perfect little forensic arrangement: frequently, by the time Eadie arrives at the crime scene, other police officers, the first cops on the scene, have somehow messed up the point of entry. They're in a rush, hurrying to answer a frantic 911, and, in the scramble, they trample over footprints and rub their hands across fingerprints.

"One time," Eadie says, "and this is almost typical, I went to a break-in at a store in town. The thieves had gone in through a large window. Broken it and left glass all over the ground. The thing is you get fantastic footprints off glass, the *best* footprints. They come up two-dimensional. Just a simple shard of glass is going to give you stunning detail. But at this store break-in, it was winter and frigid, and, when I got to the scene, the officers had already removed all the glass and covered over the window because it was getting cold in the store. Where was the glass? In the garbage. But the whole episode ended up okay. I fished the glass out of the garbage can and found a pretty good print."

The point of entry in the break-in at Ward Maracle's house fell into the messed-up category. When Eadie reached the Maracle place later on the morning of the robbery and shooting, the first people on the scene – the Tyendinaga Reserve police, OPP officers, an ambulance crew, and a Maracle employee whom Diana Maracle had phoned – all responding to the crisis, had given the main entrance and the immediate surrounding outside area a thorough treading and crushing. No identifiable footprints, no fingerprints – Eadie couldn't locate anything that might point to the bad guys.

But inside the house, Eadie got lucky two or three times over. First, there was the hunk of wood lying on the kitchen table.

What was it doing in the house? What *was* it, anyway? It looked like a leg broken off something larger. Eadie and the other officers got on the hunt. The trail led out to the backyard, to the broken sawhorse, and there, in the snow beside one of the sawhorse's remaining legs, Eadie beheld an Ident officer's dream – a pure, untrammelled, pristine shoeprint. It was a print from a running shoe, if Eadie read the signs correctly, and it was for the right foot.

Eadie went to work. His aim was to make a cast of the print in the snow, but there were things that had to be attended to before that could be done. Photography came first. If he didn't snap pictures of the print, he might later find mysterious little details in the cast that he couldn't account for, small marks and irregular ridges. The photographs would answer his queries. They'd reveal that the irregular details, the funny little marks, were caused by wedges of mud or pieces of grass stuck to the shoe's sole.

The actual photography was no piece of cake. A print in snow makes a tough subject. The combination of white snow and bright daylight meant Eadie had to manoeuvre with some skill to get the angle that would give him the sharpest definition. It didn't help matters that the temperature was rising, the snow growing softer. Indeed, the next day, rain would fall and wash away the snow and the print. Eadie couldn't afford to dawdle.

The camera he used was a Bronica. For most crime-scene shooting, a Nikon in the 801 series was Eadie's camera of choice, efficient and reliable. But for footprints, for this particular footprint in the snow, the Bronica would give him a much larger negative than the 35-mm Nikon, better closeups in the snow, clearer definition.

Eadie moved around the print, setting the Bronica, adjusting to the light, and, as he found the right angle, he snapped off shots until he was satisfied he'd got the photograph that would hide no secrets.

Now he was ready to make a cast of the print. For footprints on plain, uncovered ground, on earth or mud, the casting material he uses most often is dental plaster; it's exceptionally hard and records very fine detail. But plaster is too heavy for snow. So the material Eadie employed to cast a print in the snow of the Maracle yard was flour sulphur, the stuff that's tossed into farm animals' feed.

For casting, the sulphur had to be reduced to liquid form. That meant it would be runny, and so, before Eadie did anything with the sulphur, he had to shore up snow around the footprint. That would keep the liquid sulphur from leaking away and would preserve the print's integrity during the casting procedure.

Eadie carried from his car all the necessary equipment. This was nothing grand, just a small bag of flour sulphur in solid form, a propane stove from Canadian Tire, and a slightly battered pot that looked like a refugee from a yard sale.

Eadie lit the stove, set the pot on top, and dumped in a small quantity of sulphur. The sulphur began to heat and to melt. It was no swift process. Sulphur's boiling point is somewhere above water's, and for ten, fifteen minutes or more, Eadie heated and stirred the sulphur in the pot. The stuff began to take on the consistency of maple syrup. It approached the colour of maple syrup too, dark brown.

When the sulphur had become totally liquid, Eadie whisked the pot off the stove and waited another minute or two until the sulphur began to crystallize again. At that delicate juncture, Eadie held the pot over the footprint and, in a smooth, sweeping motion, he poured the sulphur into the print.

The sulphur started to harden the instant it hit the snow – without melting the snow. It all happened swiftly, the sulphur hardening from the bottom up, covering the entire print to a thickness of about an inch. In fact, it was sulphur's quick-hardening qualities that made it ideal for this job. Then Eadie waited for the sulphur to cool off. In cooling, its colour grew lighter, from a maple-syrup shade to something closer to yellowy beige.

When the sulphur was cool and hard, Eadie lifted the cast out

of the snow. It made a perfect little specimen, showing the sole
of a running shoe with a fancy, intricate design of swirls and
circles. It looked like the bottom of a shoe an NBA point guard
might wear – or a kid on a playground. But in this instance, it
had probably been worn by a break-and-enter man, by a bad guy,
and it was a crucial piece of evidence in a criminal case.

Eadie put the cast, thin and dangerously brittle, in a cardboard
box and surrounded it for protection with crumpled paper towels.
He'd study the cast later, back at the OPP offices.

Inside the Maracle house, Eadie photographed the crime scene
in detail, trained his Nikon on all the rooms, all the surfaces, every
space the intruders had moved through the night before, everything they might have touched. He shot roll after roll of film.

Shell casings were found in the course of the tour through the
house, casings from the .22 pistol. There were three of them, one
in the bedroom, a second in the hall, the third in the kitchen. By
themselves, the casings weren't conclusive of anything except
that one of the assailants had fired shots and hit Ward Maracle,
but when the cops found a pistol that matched up with the
ejected casings, the evidence might go a long way towards tying
in a specific bad guy to the crime.

Then Eadie went looking for more footprints. It wasn't a
difficult search, not on the Maracles' clean, proud, shiny hardwood
floors. Even if the cops and others had been striding through the
rooms all morning, Eadie had no trouble spotting the prints from
running shoes. There were definitely two pairs, two kinds of
running shoes, worn by the two bad guys. Eadie set up his lights
and camera, and patiently, diligently, he shot each footprint. But
he was most excited by one particular print. It was on the stairs,
it was headed upwards; it was a right foot, and it looked very much
as if it had been produced by the same shoe that made the print
in the snow in the Maracles' backyard. Eadie photographed this
print with much care.

~

Eadie figures that, on balance, it's more a blessing than a curse to people in his business that running shoes enjoy such a terrific vogue, that everybody wears them, that dozens of companies manufacture the shoes and spend millions promoting their brands, that there's a rapid changeover in the style of the shoes, that the patterns on the soles of running shoes are in constant flux, as new designers conceive fresh arrangements of swirls and circles and exotic combinations of figures.

"It'd probably be helpful to me if somebody compiled a book of shoeprints," he says. "Then I'd have something to refer to with the prints I find at crime scenes. But it'd be impossible to put together a book like that, because there are just too many running shoes being produced. A line of a certain kind of shoe doesn't last more than six months or a year on the market. Companies regularly change the style of their shoes, and that includes the patterns on the bottoms."

But this unceasing turnover, Eadie goes on, works to his advantage.

"It means there are a limited number of each pattern out there," he says. "I don't have to worry about a billion shoes with the same pattern on the sole. I just have to worry about a couple of manufacturers' runs of the same pattern. And, another positive thing, I might spot a shoeprint at a crime scene and think, gosh, this guy's wearing an old pair of shoes, I saw that particular pattern two years ago. These things make it easier to catch the bad guys."

On the Maracle case, Eadie developed the photographs he'd taken of the shoeprints on the hardwood floors. He concentrated on the particular print, the one from the running shoe that was headed up the stairs to the second floor. He compared the print in the photograph with the print in the cast he had made in the snow of the Maracles' backyard. Definitely the same shoe, Eadie concluded. Same size – an eight. Same pattern on the sole. Same marks of wear. This was a relatively new shoe, Eadie deduced, without many signs of long and heavy use. Now he had two prints, one on film and the other in sulphur impression, of a right shoe worn by one of the bad guys.

Eadie composed a small circular, incorporating everything he knew about the shoe. He included a clear reproduction of the photo of the print on the stair, filled in a few particulars about the robbery and shooting at the Maracle house, added dates and the case number, and ran off several copies of the circular. He distributed the copies to the OPP investigators who were working on the Maracle case.

"From a scientific point of view," he says, "the circular isn't particularly useful, because the reproduction of the print doesn't show enough detail. But the investigators like it. It gets them excited for the hunt. They go out there, and eventually, in a lot of cases, they find the shoes."

At 4 P.M. on New Year's Day, a message turned up on the Belleville OPP's Crime Stoppers line: "In that break-in out by Deseronto, the one where the gentleman got shot, you oughta be looking at two people in Cornwall by the names of Pete Benedict and Frank Lanoue. Thank you."

"Usually on Crime Stoppers," Eadie says, "it's thieves telling on one another. That's probably what happened in the Maracle case. There isn't a lot of honour in the criminal culture."

The OPP drew an early blank on Frank Lanoue. No address for him right off the bat. But they came up with a street and house number in Cornwall for Pete Benedict. The cops swore out a search warrant, and, on January 2, two officers went calling on Benedict. The two were Det.-Sgt. Rick Myers of the OPP and Const. Dave Lewis of the Tyendinaga First Nations Police, and before they set off on their mission, Eadie reminded them about the shoes. Look for the ones in the circular, Eadie said, shoes with soles that match that particular pattern.

Pete Benedict's closet held no shoes that fit the pattern Eadie was talking about. Filas, yes; Myers and Lewis noticed a pair of nifty-looking new Fila runners. Benedict was wearing them. And the officers found four other pairs of shoes in the place. But not the shoes from Jim Eadie's circular, the ones that would inextricably tie Benedict to the scene of the crime.

Myers and Lewis asked Benedict questions. Benedict mumbled answers of a sort. Frank Lanoue? Not only did Benedict not know where anybody named Frank Lanoue lived, he didn't know who Frank Lanoue *was*. Not a buddy of mine, Benedict insisted, waving his hands in denial and indignation.

Something glinting from Benedict's waving hand caught Rick Myers's attention.

"Nice ring you got, Pete," he said. "On your finger there."

"So?"

"Looks new," Myers said. "Let's see what you got in your pockets."

The ring, a chunky piece of work featuring diamonds and a ruby, *was* new. When Myers rummaged through Benedict's wallet, he found a receipt for the ring. It came from a store at the Rideau Town Centre, a shopping mall in Ottawa, a couple of hours' drive from Cornwall. The receipt showed the ring's price, $1,100, and the date of purchase. Benedict had bought the ring, paying cash, on December 30, later on the very day of the Maracle break-in.

Myers and Lewis turned up some other interesting items in Benedict's place. Bundles of bills in denominations of tens, twenties, fifties, and hundreds. A .22-calibre handgun. And, on the street out front, parked at the curb, there was a red Pontiac, something like the vehicle Diana Maracle thought she saw in her driveway as she fled her own home.

Myers and Lewis arrested Pete Benedict.

Jim Eadie says this about thieves and their footwear: "It's fairly common for thieves to get rid of their shoes. They know they might leave shoeprints at their break-and-enters. Or, if the thief isn't too bright, he might put nicks and marks in the bottom of his shoes, cut out parts of the soles. By doing that, he thinks he's disguising his shoeprints. One time, we had this suspect in some break-ins. An officer went around and interviewed the guy, and, during the interview, the officer checked the guy's shoes. We had shoeprints from the different crime scenes, same prints at each one, but they didn't match the shoes this particular suspect had on at the time. We let him go. But something twigged in the guy's head that shoeprints were a clue. So he got out a knife and went at his burglar shoes. He carved whole chunks out of the sides and made divots in the bottoms. Then he continued doing his break-and-enters. I got prints from the new crime scenes, and I thought, wait a minute, it's the same guy from the other break-ins but he's done something strange to his shoes. Now they're *really* unique. We caught him a few weeks later, and the shoes with all the gouges in them nailed him cold."

Eadie also says this about thieves and their footwear: "One thing about thieves, they always wear expensive shoes."

Eadie was of two or three minds about Pete Benedict and the shoes that weren't in his closet.

If Benedict didn't have shoes whose bottoms matched the prints at the crime scene, then maybe the police were on the wrong track. Maybe Benedict wasn't one of the robbers.

Or maybe Benedict *was* one of the robbers, and he'd simply got rid of the incriminating running shoes.

Or, another thought, maybe Benedict's purchase of the ring a few hours after the break-in was more than a coincidence.

Eadie talked over the various possibilities with the two investigators, Rick Myers and Dave Lewis. Suppose Benedict had bought more than just a ring at the Rideau Town Centre. Just suppose he'd also got himself a new pair of running shoes. The Filas, maybe? And suppose he left his old running shoes at the store. Left them for the clerk to get rid of. Was that a possibility?

Well, it was worth checking.

On January 3, Myers and Lewis drove the two hours to the Rideau Town Centre in Ottawa.

It was the last shoe store in the mall that the two officers canvassed. So far they'd struck out. Nobody in the other stores recognized Pete Benedict from the photograph that the officers showed around. Now they were at the final store, a Foot Locker outlet.

"That guy?" said the clerk, a man named Scott Debellefeuille. "I particularly remember him. He was in here before New Year's. Bought a pair of Filas from me."

"That's why you remember him?"

"No, no, it was for what he didn't take with him that I remember the guy," Debellefeuille said. "Perfectly good shoes, Air Nikes. Hardly had any wear on them. He comes in here with them on his feet, he buys the Filas, which aren't as good a shoe as the Nikes, and he tells me to throw the Nikes in the garbage. This is a hundred-and-forty-dollar shoe, you know?"

"That's what you did?" Myers asked. "You threw the shoes in the garbage?"

"Well, yeah. I put them in the shoebox from the Filas the guy bought. Got them ready for the garbage."

"That's too bad," Myers said.

"But listen," Debellefeuille said. "You know how garbage collection is messed up right now, the holidays and everything, New Year's Day? Ours still hasn't been picked up. You want me to go out back and get those Air Nikes?"

"We'd like that very much," Myers said. "Yes, sir, we would like very much for you to do that."

There's a definite drill, as Jim Eadie explains it, to shoeprint comparison.

For starters, Eadie doesn't compare the actual shoe with a

photograph or an impression of a shoeprint taken from a crime scene. He makes an impression of the shoe, a cast, and compares *it* with the crime-scene prints. The trouble with a real shoe is that it's usually difficult to make out the small identifying marks and abrasions in the sole. But those marks show up nicely in a cast of the shoe bottom.

Obviously, the very first point to check in the comparison process is shoe size. If Eadie isn't working with the same size in the shoe and in the print impression from the crime scene, then it's instantly game over.

Next, Eadie compares the pattern on the bottom of the suspect's shoe with the pattern in the print from the crime scene. For each size of shoe in each make, the manufacturer has probably produced a dozen different patterns. Are the two in the comparison study from the same pattern? If so, Eadie presses on with the rest of the comparison.

Now he's into the fine, detailed, demanding work of comparing, the examinations that require an experienced, active eye. He compares the two shoe bottoms – the impression of the suspect's shoe and the print found at the crime scene – for ordinary wear-and-tear. Are the shoes run down at the heels to an equal degree? Do they show an identical and idiosyncratic rubbing away at the toe? That's the sort of thing Eadie looks for. He's learned from long practice in studying shoe bottoms that it's highly unlikely to find the heels from two different shoes run down in exactly the same way. If the impression of the subject's shoe and crime-scene shoeprint display identical wear in the heel, they are more than likely the same shoe.

But that doesn't yet bring Eadie to the end of the comparison. He takes one more step. He looks for similarities in nicks, cuts, and other "accidents" to the bottoms of the two shoes under comparison. Are the nicks, these "gross accidents," as Eadie refers to them, in the same places on each impression? It takes a while to arrive at the answer, as Eadie swings his eyes back and forth between the impression of the suspect's shoe and the print taken at the crime scene, checking the positions of the nicks and gouges, measuring, verifying. But if all the cuts are in precisely the same location on each impression, then Eadie has the clincher. The two items under comparison belong to the very same shoe. Case closed.

With the pair of charcoal grey high-top Air Nikes that Rick Myers and Dave Lewis retrieved from the garbage at the Foot Locker in the Rideau Town Centre, Eadie followed his usual comparison procedure. He made a plaster impression of the right shoe from the pair of Nikes and compared it in all respects with the two shoeprints he'd lifted from the Maracle crime scene, the print in the snow of the backyard and the print on the stairs.

He began by checking for size. Yes, same size all round, an eight.

Next, pattern. The impression of the Nike bottom displayed the same design of circles and swirls as the bottoms in the cast from the snow and in the photograph from the stair. Again an affirmative.

Ordinary wear-and-tear? Same in all three. The wear was negligible in each case, since the Nikes were fairly new, but the shoes were slightly run down at the heels at the same angle on all the shoe bottoms.

Finally, the nicks and scrapes and gouges. Almost immediately, Eadie spotted three tiny nicks in an orderly row near the centre of each shoe bottom. It was as if the wearer had stepped on a small piece of wire that had forever engraved the three cuts, all in a row, on the shoe's sole. They would identify the shoe for the rest of its life. But Eadie didn't end his study with the three little nicks. He kept going until he had isolated a grand total of sixteen points of comparison between the shoe and the shoeprints from the crime scene. There were sixteen cuts and abrasions and scoops that appeared in the same places, in the same shape and intensity, in the various prints and casts and photographs under study.

Eadie didn't have a doubt. The shoe that had left the print in the snow of Ward Maracle's backyard and that had stamped another print on the Maracle stairs was the right shoe from the pair of Air Nikes that Pete Benedict thought he had ditched at the Foot Locker.

Meanwhile, other elements were falling into place in the case of the robbery and shooting at the Maracle house.

Eadie put together a package that he sent to the Centre of Forensic Sciences in Toronto. The package contained the .22-calibre pistol that Rick Myers and Dave Lewis had found at Pete Benedict's place, plus the three cartridge casings that had been recovered from the floor of Ward Maracle's house. Sam Barbetta, the firearms and toolmark examiner at the CFS, carried out his tests and reported back that, without question, those three Remington cartridge cases had been fired from that .22 short-calibre semi-automatic pistol.

The bundles of bills of various denominations that Myers and Lewis took from Benedict looked familiar to Diana Maracle. The distinctive way the bundles were folded and tied was just how Diana folded and tied bills at the end of a day's business at Ward's Gas Bar. And the writing on some of the bills, the additions and totals – no question, Diana said, that was her very own hand-writing. It was a habit of hers to jot down totals on the bills after she'd added up a stack of money.

Jim Eadie got out his fingerprinting equipment and went at the interior of the red Pontiac that had been parked outside Pete Benedict's house (a car, police learned, that had been rented in the name of Benedict's mother). Eadie found plenty of prints inside the Pontiac from both Benedict and Frank Lanoue (because Lanoue had a record, his prints were on file). Benedict's were mostly on the driver's side, Lanoue's on the passenger side. There was nothing ultimately incriminating about the prints, nothing that necessarily put Benedict and Lanoue at the scene of the crime. But the prints established one key fact: Benedict had been lying when he insisted that he didn't know Frank Lanoue.

And, finally, towards the end of January, the OPP traced and arrested Frank Lanoue himself.

The police figured they had enough evidence to take both Lanoue and Benedict to court, and they charged each man with several offences, topped off by attempted murder.

The trial took place before Mr. Justice Richard Byers in the court-house for Hastings County in Belleville in mid-October 1993. Both men pleaded not guilty to all charges, but, very early in the trial, Benedict switched to a guilty plea on aggravated assault and a couple of other lesser charges, sticking to not guilty on the attempted-murder count. The next day, Jim Eadie was scheduled to give his testimony. The defence lawyers knew what he was going to say, especially about the footprint evidence, because Eadie had testified for several hours during the preliminary hearing a few months earlier. The defence lawyers went into a huddle with their clients. The Crown attorney got into the dis-cussion, and a bargain was struck. The Crown attorney would withdraw the charge of attempted murder against both men, and both would plead guilty to the remaining charges, guilty to robbery with violence, use of a firearm in the commission of a crime, using a face mask in the commission of a crime, and wounding so as to endanger a life, Ward Maracle's. Judge Byers went along with the deal, and two days later, he pronounced sen-tence on Benedict and Lanoue.

"I want the message to get out," Byers told the two men, "that, if you come into Hastings County with a weapon and use it, you'll pay big time."

Byers gave both Benedict and Lanoue six years in the peni-tentiary.

~

Jim Eadie thinks it was principally the footprint evidence that put
Lanoue and Benedict away.

"This was a case where almost everything was circumstantial,"
he says. "Nobody saw the two men, not their faces, because they
wore those masks. The Maracles couldn't positively identify them.
And the other evidence was circumstantial, the money in the
bundles, the .22-calibre pistol, the fingerprints in the rental car.
There were possible explanations for all of those things."

But not the shoeprints.

"The shoeprints were compelling for a couple of reasons.
Number one, the major reason, the prints showed there was no
question that Benedict's Air Nike, the right shoe of his pair of
Air Nikes, was in the house on the night of the shooting and the
robbery. Benedict was there on that night, and the other evidence
tied Lanoue to Benedict. They were together. And the other thing
that was damning about the shoeprint is that it was on the stairs
going upwards, going up to the bedroom where Benedict and
Lanoue went to threaten the Maracles and demand the money.
The shoeprint put them right into the crime."

Jim Eadie smiles.

"It was the shoeprint that caught the bad guys."

Food:

The Case of Death's Time

SHIRLEY HARPER BELIEVED IN serving her family an ample and an early dinner. A couple of meats, two or three vegetables, relishes, choice of desserts, all on the table in the kitchen shortly after 5 P.M. So, on Tuesday, June 9, 1959, when the daughter of the Harper family, twelve-year-old Lynne, got home from her school softball game close to 5:30 P.M., everyone else was just finishing the meal. Shirley and her husband, Les, took cups of tea into the living-room, and the two Harper boys, one older than Lynne, one younger, scattered to play outside. Lynne ate alone. She had white turkey meat on her plate, turkey skin and dressing, boiled potatoes, and canned peas. She could choose from dishes of onion pickles, relish, celery stalks, and cranberry sauce. For dessert, there were two kinds of pie, plus pineapple upside-down cake. In the fridge beside her, if she wanted a different meat, she could help herself to cold ham or bologna.

Lynne got through her food quickly, in somewhere between ten and fifteen minutes. That was partly because she was feeling hungry and partly because she was feeling antsy, keen to leave the house and find out about the swimming classes that were supposed to be starting in a couple of days. She was also feeling slightly hard done by. She wanted to go for a swim that evening at a nearby indoor pool, but twelve-year-olds had to be accompanied by an adult, and Lynne's parents had told her they had other plans for the evening. Lynne, alone in the kitchen, a little sweaty from the softball game, a little excited about the swimming classes, a little put out over her parents' small rejection, shovelled food into her mouth and finished her dinner not later than 5:45 P.M.

These details of Lynne Harper's dinner on June 9, 1959 – what she ate, how quickly, in what frame of mind – were about to become very important. The dinner was Lynne's last meal. Sometime in the following few hours, somebody murdered her. And it was the examination by pathologists and other scientists of the contents of Lynne's stomach that led experts to fix an hour, within a matter of minutes, when the murderer killed the young girl. In turn, the timing led the police to the person who was with Lynne at the hour of death – as determined by the pathologists and scientists. That person was charged with the murder, and, after a trial at which the people who examined and tested Lynne's stomach contents provided perhaps the most damning testimony, the accused murderer was convicted and sentenced to be hanged.

All of this, the murder of an innocent child, two and a half months short of becoming a teenager, was stunning and evil. What made the crime and the medical and legal events that followed it even more cruel and distressing was that the person convicted of the murder, sentenced to die for it, was another child. He was fourteen years and nine months old. He attended the same school as Lynne Harper, sat in the same classroom. The boy insisted that he was innocent of the murder, and so many people believed him, so many people across Canada were so horrified by the very thought of a fourteen-year-old child receiving a death sentence in a country supposedly as civilized as Canada, that the boy got the equivalent of a second trial.

This time, however, the hearing took place before the nine judges of the Supreme Court of Canada. That had never happened before, the highest court in the land, a court intended only to hear lawyers argue appellate matters, now taking the testimony of witnesses in a murder case, listening to lawyers conduct examinations-in-chief and cross-examinations. And it wouldn't happen again until another controversial murder case, that of David Milgaard, came before the Supreme Court in 1993. But in the case of the fourteen-year-old boy, the court set a precedent. It heard evidence. And it paid particular attention to the medical and scientific testimony, to expert witnesses who were brought before the court from England, the United States, and across Canada to speak on the curious – the curiously primitive – subject of determining time of death by an analysis of the victim's stomach contents.

The nine judges listened, asked questions, pondered what they had heard, reviewed the scientists' words, and, after three months, they decided by an eight-to-one margin that there was no reason to interfere with the conviction of the fourteen-year-old boy. The matter was finally settled, at least as far as the courts were concerned. But among lawyers, writers, and much of the general public, the doubt and arguments and outrage never entirely died away in what was undoubtedly the most troubling and divisive murder case in recent Canadian legal history.

This was the case of Steven Truscott.

Ontario Highway Number 8, mostly two lanes, drifts more or less east-west through the middle of the province. If you drive west on Highway 8 from Toronto as far as you can go, past Stratford and its Shakespeare Festival, farther past a pancake-flat stretch of farmland, you reach the really beautiful part of southwestern Ontario, right up against Lake Huron. It is landscape with a gentle roll to it, up and down, roads twisting around the hills, everything green in the summer as far as your eye can see, except for the dashes of colour from the purple milkweed and the black-eyed Susans. This is Huron County.

This is also Alice Munro country. She grew up on a farm on the outskirts of Wingham in the northern part of Huron County, and, since the mid-1970s, she has lived with her second husband in what was once her husband's mother's house in Clinton, a town closer to the middle of the county. Munro's short stories have never been specifically about the people, towns, geography, and attitudes of Huron County. But, written on things Munro grew up with and has lived among, her wonderful stories tell you something close and true of that world. "People's lives in Jubilee were dull and simple, amazing and unfathomable – deep caves paved with kitchen linoleum."

Huron County began to be settled in the early nineteenth century by Scottish Presbyterians, by Congregationalists, and by Methodists from the north of England. The Dutch came later, with their strong, conservative religious streak. Farming was almost everybody's principal enterprise, and, by the late 1960s, the population of the county peaked at 60,000 – and has pretty much stuck there. Goderich on Lake Huron is the county town. A place of 7,500 citizens, its two businesses are the salt mines and the Champion earth-moving equipment company. All of these people, in Goderich and out in the country, form a rooted, permanent kind of society in which "everybody seems to know what is expected of them." Alice Munro wrote that, too.

During the Second War and for about fifteen years afterwards, one group of Huron residents, impermanent and transient, was set apart from the real locals. These were the families at the Royal Canadian Air Force base, a mile and a quarter east of Clinton. The men at the base took training in radar, meteorology, radio, and almost everything else that concerned the air force – except flying. The base had all the amenities of a small village: a grocery store and post office, houses for the married people, an Officers' Mess and a Sergeants' Mess, the Air Vice Marshal Hugh Campbell

Public School for the children of the base. It was a self-contained, separate community, and "separate" seemed to be the way the rest of Huron County liked it. County people didn't much care for the base or for the people who lived there.

The base is gone now, but the houses remain, inhabited by civilians, small and freshly painted, the lawns green and mowed short. The streets have the same designations as in the RCAF days: Quebec Avenue, Victoria Boulevard, Winnipeg Road, and so on through the Canadian geographic litany. But the houses and streets form a real village now, a municipal entity with a name, Vanastra. The Air Vice Marshal Campbell School is called Vanastra Public. There isn't much left to recall the time of the air force presence except a sign outside Clinton that reads "Home of Radar" and a huge radar detector, set up like a slightly eccentric sculpture in the Clinton town centre. And, for people with medium-length memories, the RCAF base also left the legacy of a ghastly murder, because, in the Truscott case, both victim and convicted murderer, Lynne Harper and Steven Truscott, were the children of air-force families.

The weather on the early evening of June 9, 1959, was, as it had been all day, glorious. It was warm and sultry, in the mid-eighties Fahrenheit, maybe a trifle on the humid side, but windless, the kind of weather that drew the kids of the air-force base outside to play games and go swimming in the Bayfield River up by Highway 8.

Lynne Harper ran off after dinner to ask about the swimming classes. Then she returned home, washed the family's dinner dishes, and was gone from the house again by 6:30. She was a perky, pretty little girl, five-foot-three, about one hundred pounds, with short, dark hair, dark eyes, full lips, and heavy eyebrows. Her body was just edging towards adolescence, no breasts yet, but her hormones were starting to rage. On this evening, she wore turquoise shorts, a sleeveless white blouse printed in red and blue, underpants, an undershirt, short white socks, brown loafers, a red plastic hair band, and, around her neck, an air-force locket that her aunt had sent her three weeks earlier.

At 6:35, Lynne arrived at the small woods opposite AVM Campbell School. She was drawn there by the scavenger hunt that the Brownies were about to go on. Lynne wasn't a Brownie. She was older, a Girl Guide, but, always eager, she helped the two women in charge of the Brownie pack to organize the hunt. That kept her busy for fifteen or twenty minutes, until she noticed a boy on a bicycle riding along the path through the woods. She knew the boy. He was from her grade-seven class. She may have had a crush on him. The previous Friday night, she'd danced with him at a party at Lorraine Wood's house. Lorraine was another classmate, and the boy had told Lorraine that Lynne was "following him around." The boy was Steven Truscott.

It was easy to see why Lynne might be attracted to Steven. He was two years older – he had flunked a grade earlier in his educational history – and he was bigger, about five-feet-six and 125 pounds. Steven was handsome in an undeveloped, early-teenage way. He had a long, narrow face, a lot of smiling mouth, and large ears that lay flat to his head like Leonard Nemoy's as Mr. Spock. Steven carried himself well, not like an awkward adolescent, but like an athlete. In fact, he had won AVM Campbell's senior boys' championship in track and field for that year. Steven Truscott was kind of a hero around the school, popular with the boys *and* the girls.

Steven stopped his bike on the path, and Lynne walked over to talk with him. It seemed to the two women in charge of the Brownies, though they weren't really paying much attention to Lynne and Steven, that Lynne was doing most of the talking; she perched herself on the front wheel of Steven's bike and chatted away. This lasted for perhaps three or four minutes, and, when the Brownies women next noticed Lynne and Steven, they were moving away, Steven wheeling his bike, Lynne walking beside him, both of them headed towards the County Road that led north to Highway 8. At the last glimpse of the two – the Brownies women saw this and so did some boys playing in the school football field next to the small woods – Lynne had hopped onto the crossbar of Steven's bike, and Steven was pedalling the two of them up to the County Road. The time was just about 7 P.M.

Lynne Harper didn't come home that night. By 9:15, her father, Flying Officer Les Harper, began knocking on doors. Was Lynne visiting one of her friends? No, Les kept hearing, Lynne wasn't with this friend or that friend. No one whom Harper called on had spent time with Lynne that evening. No one knew where she'd gotten to. At 11:15, Les Harper reported to the RCAF base police that his daughter was missing. The base police passed on word to the Ontario Provincial Police detachment in Goderich, who arranged for a local radio station to broadcast a description of Lynne. The Harper family spent the rest of the night worrying.

First thing in the morning, Les Harper was back outside searching for Lynne. At about 7:30, he passed a warrant officer who was on his way to work, Dan Truscott, Steven's father. Truscott knew that Lynne was in Steven's class at school, and, when Harper told him that Lynne was missing, Dan suggested that Harper might speak to Steven. Les Harper walked to the Truscott house and knocked on the side door.

"Hello, Mrs. Truscott," he said to Doris, Steven's mother. "I'm Leslie Harper. You don't know me, though I know your husband, of course."

Les Harper was an officer. Dan Truscott came from the OR, Other Ranks. There was a sharp social divide between the two classes. They didn't mix in the same circles.

"My daughter, Lynne, didn't come home last night," Les Harper went on, "and I was wondering if your boy saw her yesterday."

"Steven," Doris Truscott called. "Flying Officer Harper would like to talk to you."

"Yes, sir?"

"It's about Lynne. By any chance, did you see her after dinner last night?"

"Yes, sir. I gave her a lift on my bike to Number 8 Highway."

"A lift? Where was this exactly?"

"From the school down to Number 8. I gave her the lift, and after I rode back to the bridge, I saw her getting into a grey car up at the highway."

"Into a car?"

"She hitched a ride."

"Oh my God!"

The County Road, two lanes and paved, ran north from a point opposite the Campbell School to Highway 8. The O'Brien farm lay on the west side of the road, the Lawson farm on the east. The road was more or less level for about 3,400 feet from the woods by the school. Up to that point, the Lawson property was cleared for pasture and crops, but at the 3,400-foot mark, the cleared land was interrupted by a large pocket of trees, shrubbery, and brush. The trees included ash, elm, maple, and basswood, and the brush was thick and dense. A wire fence separated the road and the Lawson property, but it was old and broken, flattened to the ground in many places, and a partly overgrown tractor trail led off the road and along the north side of the brush for about three hundred feet. The trees and shrubs radiated south of the trail and another hundred feet to the east. Everybody on the air-force base knew this clump of trees and brush as "Lawson's Bush."

From Lawson's Bush, the County Road, going north, went into a slight and gradual dip. The road crossed a railroad track about 1,500 feet from the bush. Then, 500 feet on, it came to a bridge over the Bayfield River, which the kids of the base used as their swimming hole. It was another 1,300 feet along the County Road from the river to Highway 8.

Steven Truscott's story was that he spent all of the time between seven and eight on the evening of June 9 at different points on the County Road. It was the story he told Les Harper in précis form, the story he later told the police in more detail, the story he told his lawyers, the story he never deviated from during the entire history of the Steven Truscott case. He said that Lynne Harper asked him for a ride from the woods by the school to Highway 8. Lynne, he said, told him she intended to hitch-hike to a white house farther east on Number 8, a house where a man let kids play with his ponies. Lynne had been there before, a year earlier.

Steven rode her to the highway, no hurry, a leisurely cycle up the County Road, past Lawson's Bush, over the railway tracks, across the bridge, all the way to the highway. He let Lynne off the bike and rode alone back to the bridge. When he glanced behind him, up to the highway, it was in time to see Lynne getting into a car. Steven knew cars. He was a car fanatic. And he recognized the make of the car Lynne got into. It was a 1959 Chev Belair. The car was grey, and it had something yellow on the back bumper, a licence plate probably, but maybe a sticker of some sort. That was the last Steven saw of Lynne. He didn't think much of it at the time. He stayed on his bike, dawdling back along the County Road, no particular purpose in mind. He got to the playground beside the school, the one with the swings, at eight o'clock. His older brother Ken was there, Ken and a bunch of other boys. Steven kidded around with them for a few minutes, then rode home. He was supposed to babysit his younger brother and sister at 8:30. He arrived on time.

That was Steven's story, and there were people, other children, who provided information that backed it up. Steven's brother Ken and the rest of the kids at the playground confirmed that their pal Steven, looking his normal self, joined them at about eight o'clock that night. And two boys remembered seeing him on the County Road. One boy, twelve-year-old Douglas Oats, said he was standing on the bridge over the river some time after seven, when he noticed Steven *and* Lynne ride by on Steven's bike, heading north towards the highway. He didn't see either one, Steven or Lynne, come back the other way. And another boy, thirteen-year-old Gordon Logan, said he spotted Steven and Lynne riding north over the bridge at 7:30 or so, and five minutes later, he saw Steve, alone, cycle back across the bridge going south. Gordie was swimming in the Bayfield River at the time of both sightings. He was about six hundred feet east of the bridge, and the bridge was ten feet above the water. That put Gordie at a considerable distance from the people on the bridge, but he was positive he saw Steven and Lynne.

Other kids were just as positive that they didn't see Steven Truscott on the County Road that evening, at least not at the right times to fit in with Steven's story. The road was busy with people, mostly boys, but one girl in particular and a few parents, all going to or coming from the swimming hole in the Bayfield River. And none of them had memories of Steven that matched up with Gordie Logan's sighting or Douglas Oats's.

Kenneth Geiger, who was eleven, noticed Steven sitting on his bike, alone, on the County Road opposite Lawson's Bush at about 6:25. Kenneth's mother, Beatrice, remembered seeing Steven a little earlier, on his bike, on the County Road closer to the bridge, alone, apparently aimlessly tooling around. Twelve-year-old Robb Harrington noticed Steven a few minutes later, about 6:45, sitting by himself on his bike on the County Road near Lawson's Bush, but, when Robb walked home from the river an hour later, he saw no sign of Steven. Richard Gellatly, also twelve, recalled seeing Steven riding Lynne on his bike on the County Road. Richard was going in the opposite direction, biking home to get his bathing suit, and the point at which he passed Steven and Lynne was about three-quarters of the way between the school and Lawson's Bush; Steven and Lynne hadn't yet reached Lawson's Bush. The time, Richard thought, was around 7:25 or it might have been some minutes earlier. Philip Burns, eleven, Butch George, thirteen, and Bryan Glover, fourteen, were all on the County Road at different times between 7:10 and 7:30. None of them noticed Steven or Lynne. But all of them saw a girl named Jocelyne Goddette. In fact, Butch and Philip talked to her. Jocelyne was standing near the tractor trail into Lawson's Bush. She didn't see Steven either, but – unlike the others – Jocelyne was actually *looking* for Steven Truscott.

Jocelyne Goddette was thirteen and in the same grade-seven class as Steven and Lynne. Jocelyne was a tall, slightly built girl, a bit of a flirt, a tease, and her story was that she had a date of sorts with Steven Truscott for Tuesday evening. Steven, she said, had spoken to her earlier in the day at school and had invited her to come with him and look at two newborn calves. The calves were in Lawson's Bush, and Jocelyne was to meet Steven on the County Road near the tractor trail at six o'clock. "He kept on telling me not to tell anybody," Jocelyne said, "because Bob" – Bob Lawson, the farmer – "didn't like a whole bunch of kids on his property." But Jocelyne's mother was late serving dinner that evening, and Jocelyne was way behind schedule for her date with Steven. She hurried out to the meeting place on the County Road anyway, riding her bike, and she found no Steven. She walked up the tractor trail, about three-quarters of the way in, and shouted Steven's name, but there wasn't any sign of him. Jocelyne didn't have a watch, and she was fuzzy on times. She wasn't sure when all of this happened, but, if she saw and talked to Butch George and Philip Burns on the County Road, it must have been about 7:15 or 7:30. Jocelyne didn't have her date with Steven that evening, and, when she asked him at school the next day why he hadn't shown up at the meeting place, Steven, she said, just shrugged.

On Thursday, June 11, 1959, at ten minutes to two in the afternoon, a leading aircraftsman named Joe Leger, who was part of
a search party of 250 air-force personnel and OPP officers, found
Lynne Harper's body in Lawson's Bush.

The body was lying, face up, in a natural depression in the
ground. The depression was about eighteen inches deep, six feet
long, and four feet wide, and, in relation to the rest of Lawson's
Bush, it was about 280 feet east of the County Road and eighty
feet south of the tractor trail. That put it in a dense section of
trees and brush, so thick that anyone standing at the spot where
the body was found couldn't be seen from the road or the trail.

Lynne's body was almost naked. Her undershirt was bunched
up high on her chest, and her sleeveless blouse was still in place
in the right armhole. But the blouse had been pulled free of her
left arm and shoulder and had been knotted around her neck.
Those were the only clothes on her body. Her shorts, shoes,
socks, and red plastic hairband lay, fairly neatly, not in any violent
disorder, at her right side. The panties were farther away, about
thirty feet from the body, towards the tractor trail. Lynne's air-
force locket, the one her aunt had given her, was nowhere in
sight. It didn't turn up until eight days later, when a little girl
who was picking berries found it. The locket was hanging on
the bottom strand of the wire fence between the County Road
and Lawson's Bush.

Dr. John Llywellyn Penistan reached the body site at 4:45 P.M.
He was English, trained at the University of London, with a
medical degree in pathology. But for the previous ten years he
had been both pathologist in charge of the laboratories at Stratford
General Hospital in Perth County and a pathologist in the
Ontario Attorney-General's office. He did all the autopsies for
Perth County and for the next county over, Huron, which didn't
have a pathologist of its own or, given its few violent deaths, much
need for one.

There was another doctor at the body site, another Englishman. He was Flight Lieutenant David Brooks, a graduate of Oxford and the senior medical officer at the air-force base, and he became a bit of a busybody in the Steven Truscott case. Though he had no official status in the case, he offered advice, suggested procedures, performed examinations, took notes, and pushed opinions. Dr. Brooks was always free with his views, and none of them, as it happened, favoured Steven.

But Dr. Penistan was in charge, and, at the site in Lawson's Bush, he made observations and arrived at conclusions. Lynne's body, he noted, had many scratches and one fairly significant wound. That was a deep, stab-like cut in the left shoulder. Blood from the wound had soaked part of Lynne's undershirt and leaked into a pool on the ground beneath the shoulder. Lynne's vagina looked damaged to Dr. Penistan, and he noticed two indentations in the ground between her feet, the kind of marks that might have been left by the shoes of a man having sex with the girl. Dr. Penistan was certain Lynne had been raped, and, from all signs, he was sure she had died on the piece of ground where she was found and still lay.

Dr. Penistan performed the autopsy on Lynne that evening in a room at the Ball and Mutch Funeral Home in Clinton. The room was small and cramped, and its lighting was so dim that the doctor had to ask for an extra lamp. As at the crime scene, John Penistan wasn't the only medical man in the small room. David Brooks was there, too. He made the autopsy notes and volunteered opinions.

Dr. Penistan arrived quickly at the cause of death. Lynne died of asphyxia. She had been strangled. The sleeveless blouse was the weapon, the ligature. The killer had tied part of it, the part that wasn't still fitted on her right upper arm, in a reef knot and had tightened it around her neck until she stopped breathing. The wound on Lynne's shoulder had no direct link to her death. This wound, Dr. Penistan surmised, was probably caused when Lynne was pressed heavily against a branch lying on the ground underneath her. It was bloody and painful, but not fatal.

Penistan also confirmed that Lynne had been raped. Her vagina, he found, was torn and bruised at the entrance and was "tremendously swollen, very discoloured, boggy and seething with maggots." He couldn't say for sure if there was sperm in there, but he discovered plenty of acid phosphatase, the ferment that indicates the presence of semen. All of this, said the doctor, who had a vivid turn of phrase, "was brought about by the blind, violent thrust of the male organ in the direction of the entry to the vagina." Furthermore, Penistan concluded, "I think intercourse took place while the child was dying, when the heart had almost stopped beating."

And when exactly was that? What was the time of Lynne's death? This was where Penistan's examination of the contents of Lynne's stomach came into the picture. First, the doctor checked the stomach, the duodenum, and the small intestine. Food progresses in that order through the digestive tract. According to Penistan's reading of the medical literature on digestion, it normally took two hours for a meal to empty into the small intestine. In Lynne's case, very little of her last meal had left the stomach. Digestion would have stopped with her death, and, when it stopped, most of her dinner remained in her stomach.

Now Penistan opened the stomach and poured its contents into a small jar. He held the jar up to the light in the room at the Ball and Mutch Funeral Home, and he and Dr. Brooks looked at what was in the jar. Their examination was no more scientific than that, a naked-eye check by not-particularly-strong electric light. They figured the jar held about a pint of food, and in the mix they identified onions, pieces of potato, one or two kinds of meat, peas, and something that looked like pineapple. There were a lot of peas; they had a cellulose covering that hadn't digested because the peas hadn't been well chewed, and the cellulose therefore hadn't been broken. None of the food seemed to the doctors to be thoroughly chewed. As Penistan said, "The food looked like it had been bolted, not chewed."

In the doctor's calculation of the time of Lynne's death, he relied mainly on one factor: the presence of most of Lynne's last meal in her stomach. The kind of food, its unchewed state – those didn't figure much in his thinking. He reasoned that, if food normally took two hours to move from the stomach to the small intestine, and if most of Lynne's dinner was still in her stomach, then it would have been there for one to two hours at the time of her death. Penistan knew from information supplied by Lynne's mother that the girl had finished eating her dinner at about 5:45 P.M. on June 9. His conclusion then was that she had died sometime between seven o'clock and a quarter to eight that evening.

Dr. Penistan had arrived at a time of death, a window of forty-five minutes, when one person was known to have been in Lynne Harper's company. The person was Steven Truscott.

That wasn't the end of the story for the humble jar holding the contents of Lynne's stomach.

From Dr. Penistan, the jar went to John Funk, a biological analyst in the office of the Ontario Attorney-General. This was in the days before the Centre of Forensic Sciences became an organized, autonomous unit for forensic study and research. The biologists and other scientists in criminal investigatory work operated out of the Attorney-General's office, and John Funk was one of the people who handled anything that came up in the biological field.

He examined the food in the jar. This was no quick eyeball examination, no simple holding of the jar up to the light. Funk spent hours, parts of every day from June 12 to August 31, separating out the various foods in the jar and determining exactly what they were. In the end, he decided that the jar held celery, peas, pineapple, cucumber, cauliflower, onions (the latter three coming from the onion pickles and relish that Shirley Harper had served), potatoes, and two kinds of meat, one being ham and the other being some type of fowl.

Coincident with John Funk's work, another scientist in the Attorney-General's office, a senior person who held the title of medical director of the Forensic Section, Dr. Noble Sharpe, made a different sort of study of the jar's contents. He wasn't so much concerned with the kinds of food in the jar as with other such elements as gastric juices, acid, and the various fluids associated with the digestive process. Actually, Sharpe found, there was next to no fluid in there, but plenty of acid, and that combination of facts led him to believe that the food hadn't been in Lynne's stomach for much time, probably one to two hours. But Sharpe mentioned a couple of general words of caution in arriving at conclusions from the stomach contents. For one thing, the whole digestive process could have been slowed down by a variety of factors – by how much Lynne liked the food she was eating, by how thoroughly her mother had cooked it, by how hungry Lynne was, and by how much fat was in the meal, since fatty foods take longer to digest. And for another thing, Sharpe warned, this notion of basing time of death on the stomach contents was hardly an exact science. Such a judgement, he stated, ranged from "an inspired or educated guess" to "only a probability or a hunch."

But John Funk wasn't through with his analysis. He organized further tests of the jar's contents, and, in these tests, he needed the assistance of other people in the department. One of the people was Doug Lucas, a man who would have a long, distinguished career in forensics, serving as director of the Centre of Forensic Sciences for twenty-seven years. Lucas remembers well his small role in the study of the jar's contents for the Steven Truscott case.

"I guess it wouldn't be too strong to use the word 'gross,'" he says, "because a number of us went out and ate duplicate meals, duplicate of what the little girl had eaten, and then came back and stuck our fingers down our throats to regurgitate the material we'd eaten."

What was the point of this bizarre and unpleasant exercise?

Two points, Lucas says. "One was to help in identifying the food the girl had allegedly eaten at her last meal. And the other was to determine if it really was her last meal or if she had subsequently eaten something else."

The latter purpose was connected to Steven Truscott's claim that he had seen Lynne climb into a car at Highway 8. If Lynne had gone off with another person in a Chev Belair, had the person given her something to eat at some later time in the evening? According to the vomiting tests and comparisons that Doug Lucas and the others took part in, there was nothing else, no other foods, in Lynne's stomach.

And the throwing-up tests, as well as John Funk's analysis of the contents of the jar, also supported, in an indirect way, Dr. Penistan's conclusion about the time of death, since the tests and analysis confirmed Penistan's reading of the stomach contents. Still, the doctor's determination of time of death didn't take into account Dr. Noble Sharpe's words of caution about stomach contents *vis-à-vis* time of death. Later, this issue became the subject of much contention among other doctors and scientists.

Insp. Harold Graham of the Ontario Provincial Police's Criminal Investigation Division was the acknowledged hotshot among OPP sleuths. Graham was so astute and tough that his career eventually took him to the top, to the commissioner's office. And it was Graham who was despatched from OPP headquarters outside of Toronto to Huron County to get to the bottom of Lynne Harper's murder. It didn't take him long to make up his mind about a suspect. Graham arrived in Goderich at 7:45 on Thursday evening, June 11, a few hours after the discovery of Lynne's body, and by the next morning, following talks with the local OPP people who had been handling interviews in the case, Graham fingered Steven Truscott as the probable killer.

As far as Graham was concerned, three pieces of evidence pointed to Steven.

One was Steven's claim that, from the bridge on the County Road, he could identify the car that Lynne had climbed into as a grey 1959 Chevrolet Belair with a yellow licence plate or a yellow sticker on the bumper. Officers of the OPP carried out tests with grey cars and yellow stickers, and, standing on the bridge, 1,300 feet (or close to a quarter of a mile) from Highway 8, they couldn't be nearly as specific about what they saw as Steven had been. (For what it's worth, this writer tried a similar test, watching from the bridge over the Bayfield River as cars turned on and off the County Road going to and from the highway, and concluded that, without the long-range vision of Superman, it was impossible to identify a make of car, to judge its colour, to tell whether it had a licence plate, never mind to determine the plate's colour.)

The second piece of evidence that Inspector Graham fastened on was Jocelyne Goddette's story about her date with Steven, the date that never happened. Jocelyne's account provided a link between Steven and Lawson's Bush, and, looked at in one way, it might be interpreted as indicating that Steven had plans to do something with some girl, *any* girl, in Lawson's Bush on that Tuesday evening.

Finally, and most persuasively, Graham thought Dr. Penistan's estimation of time of death made Steven a near cinch for the murder. Who was with Lynne Harper between 7:00 and 7:45 P.M. on June 9? By Steven's own admission, and by the eye-witness statements of several other youngsters, it was Steven Truscott.

Those three struck Graham as awfully convincing reasons to charge Steven with Lynne's killing, and, on Friday night, he got one more powerful piece of evidence. This came after a day when Graham spent many hours personally interviewing Steven, pushing the boy to exhaustion, insisting that some features of Steven's story were sure proof that he was lying. In the evening, in the presence of Steven's father, Dan, Graham asked Steven and Dan to allow a doctor to examine the boy. Graham used bullying tactics on the two, holding unspecific threats over the son and father, and Dan gave in. Go ahead, he said, examine Steven.

But Dan managed to wring one concession out of Graham. Dan got permission to have a Truscott doctor handle the physical examination. He was Dr. Joe Addison, a general practitioner in Clinton. Okay, Graham said, but one other doctor would also sit in on the examination of Steven. He was the ubiquitous Flight Lieutenant David Brooks of the RCAF base.

The examination took place in the RCAF guardhouse on the base and didn't start until 10:45 Friday night. The doctors, with Dan present, asked Steven to remove his clothes. He stripped to his underpants, and the doctors took note of scratches on Steven's left arm and on his knees. The scratches seemed to be three or four days old. Steven took off his underpants. To the doctors, his penis appeared red and swollen on the distal end, the very tip. Dr. Addison took Steven's penis in his hands and pushed back the skin next to the distal. Underneath, just behind the groove on each side of the penis, there were two oozing sores. Both were about the size of a twenty-five-cent coin. They were red, raw, and ugly, and were so recent that scabs hadn't yet formed over the sores.

Addison and Brooks left the room.

"I haven't seen a penis as bad as that," Addison said, "except one that had a cancer and another that a cow stepped on."

"It's the worst lesion of this nature I've *ever* seen," Brooks said.

The doctors agreed on how the sores might have developed.

"My opinion," Brooks said, always correct in his language, "is that those lesions were caused by the insertion of the erect organ into a narrow orifice."

"Looks that way," Addison said.

"The situation," Brooks said, "is that we have the deceased, who's a girl of tender years, who hadn't reached maturity in her sexual organs, and the injuries she suffered to her labium and so on are consistent with a very inexpert attempt at penetration, if you follow my thinking."

Addison went alone back to the room where Steven and Dan waited.

"How on earth did you get such a sore penis, Steven?" Addison asked. "Have you been masturbating?"

"Well, it's been like this for four or five weeks," Steven said.

"Did you masturbate?" Addison asked again. "Or cut it in a knothole or something?"

"It isn't sore," Steven said. "It doesn't hurt or anything. I masturbated a week or so ago and took some skin off, but it isn't sore."

Addison wasn't satisfied. "Did you have intercourse with another girl?" he asked. "Are you trying to protect someone? If you are, you'd better forget that, because there is no other girl that we know of who came to the same end as Lynne Harper."

At 2:30 in the morning on Saturday, June 13, Inspector Graham took Steven into Goderich, woke up a justice of the peace named Mabel Gray, and had Steven charged under the Juvenile Delinquents Act as a delinquent boy. This was to keep Steven in custody. He was locked in a Goderich detention home. Later the charge was changed to the murder of Lynne Harper, and Huron County's Juvenile Court judge granted a Crown motion to move the trial of the juvenile, Steven, to adult court, in the trial division of the Supreme Court of Ontario. Steven spent the summer of his fourteenth year, waiting for his trial, in the Goderich Jail.

Dan Murphy is a tall, loose, wry man in his mid-sixties. He lives in a comfortable old stone house that looks over the Maitland River at the edge of Goderich, where he practises law. He arrived in town in September 1959 to join the small firm presided over by Frank Donnelly. Donnelly was Steven Truscott's defence counsel, and, for each day of Dan Murphy's first couple of weeks in Goderich, from September 16 to September 30, he strolled across the street from his new office to the courthouse to watch the Truscott trial. Among other things, Murphy developed a feel for the principals in the case.

"What made it interesting was that I had no place to live when I got here," he says, "so, during the trial, I stayed with Frank in his summer cottage out at Sunset Beach not far from town. It was so damned cold out there in this unheated cottage that I thought I'd die. But Frank, he was a tough old son of a bitch. He used to sleep with his hat on and shave in cold water and never mention the conditions. He was a bulky man, about five-ten and heavily built. His family had been in the lumber business, and he grew up tough as nails. He made himself the big lawyer in Huron County, smart, and never missed a trick. Just before he took the Truscott trial, he'd already been told he had an appointment to the Supreme Court of Ontario. He delayed it until he finished the case, then he went straight to the bench."

Glenn Hays was Donnelly's opponent, the Crown prosecutor in the Truscott case.

"Glenn came from a family that goes back in Goderich forever," Murphy says. "He was in the navy, then he practised law over in Seaforth, then he became the Crown. Glenn wasn't a smart lawyer, not smart at all, but he was trudging."

And the judge in the case was Mr. Justice R. I. Ferguson.

"Ferguson was from Ripley, which is fairly close to Goderich," Murphy says. "The thing about judges back then was that, no matter where they came from in the province, they all worked out of Toronto, and they'd be assigned to different county towns for sittings of a couple of weeks at a time, then they'd get moved to another county town. But senior judges could pick their own places, and all the judges who came from this area of the province, Huron County, southwestern Ontario, they liked to come back here and sit. Well, as a matter of fact, that led to us getting an odd collection of judges. Ferguson was one of them. He was professional enough, but he was hard of hearing, and he was mean and grumpy, which was the way he acted through most of the Truscott trial."

The jury for the trial was all male. It included a barber and a grocer from Seaforth, a dairyman from Exeter, a Blyth hardware merchant, the proprietor of Wingham's bowling alley, a worker from the factory in Wingham that made doors, and six Huron County farmers.

To these men, Glenn Hays, in his trudging way, presented a carefully constructed scenario. Hays had worked out a theory that encompassed every aspect of Lynne Harper's murder. It explained Steven Truscott's motivation in killing Lynne, took into account the stories of all the witnesses, and built on the medical evidence. Hays ran into a few difficulties in presenting all of this to the jury; he got the status and number of his expert witnesses mixed up and was therefore disqualified by Judge Ferguson from putting one of them, John Funk, on the witness stand. He regularly set off Ferguson's temper with his failures in courtroom technique, especially in the matter of asking leading questions of his witnesses, questions that improperly suggested the answers. But Hays persisted, and he thought his murder theory was air-tight.

The subtext to Hays's version was that Steven was a sex-crazed teenage maniac. On the evening of June 9, Hays theorized, Steven was obsessed with having his way with a girl in Lawson's Bush. Jocelyne Goddette was his first choice. But when Jocelyne didn't show up on time for the date to look at the newborn calves – that was Steven's cover story to lure a girl into the bush – he switched his sights to Lynne Harper. "What more likely prospect," Hays said, "than a girl Truscott knows is fond of him, soft on him." Steven, with sex in mind, invited Lynne into Lawson's Bush.

Hays thought his theory was supported entirely by the young

witnesses who saw, or didn't see, Steven on the County Road that night, even though the children weren't always certain about the times they saw — or failed to see — Steven. Two of the boys, Kenneth Geiger and Robb Harrington, as well as Kenneth's mother, Beatrice, had noticed Steven cycling aimlessly in the neighbourhood of Lawson's Bush in the forty-five minutes or so before seven o'clock. It was obvious what Steven was doing, Hays said — Steven was waiting for Jocelyne Goddette to show up for their date in the bush. Then Richard Gellatly passed Steven and Lynne riding Steven's bike on the road, but, at that point, Steven and Lynne hadn't yet reached the tractor trail into Lawson's Bush. Richard's sighting happened not too long after seven. Philip Burns came up the County Road a few minutes later, going in the same direction as Richard, but Philip didn't see Steven and Lynne. That, Hays said, was because Steven had by then turned off the road and taken Lynne into the bush. He was still in there, doing his unspeakable deeds to the girl, when three more children passed or stopped in the neighbourhood of the tractor trail, Jocelyne Goddette, Butch George, and Bryan Glover. They didn't see Steven either. Jocelyne shouted his name. But Steven couldn't answer, Hays said, because, though he was nearby, he was occupied with the rape and murder of Lynne Harper.

But what of the two boys, Gordon Logan and Douglas Oats, who swore they saw Steven riding Lynne across the bridge over the Bayfield River sometime between seven and seven-thirty? If Gordon and Douglas were to be believed, then Steven had not turned in to Lawson's Bush as Hays insisted, and Hays's entire theory fell apart. But the prosecutor dismissed the stories of the two boys as "part and parcel of the Truscott conspiracy." Steven had "rigged" the alibis with the boys. Logan and Oats had lied. Their stories, Hays said, must be ignored.

Hays built other pieces of evidence into his theory. He mentioned the flimsiness of Steven's claim that, from the bridge 1,300 feet away, he saw Lynne climb into the 1959 grey Chevy. Hays also mentioned, just in passing, that the owner of the white house where – according to Steven – Lynne had been headed to see the ponies had received no visitors that evening. And anyway, Hays went on, the white house was a mere four hundred yards down Highway 8 from the County Road, more walking distance for a twelve-year-old girl than hitchhiking distance.

Hays worked the locket into his scenario too, the air-force locket that Lynne had worn around her neck that night, the locket that was found eight days after the discovery of her body, hanging off the bottom strand of the wire fence between the County Road and Lawson's Bush. According to Hays, Steven had "planted" the locket on the fence, hoping it would mislead the police into supposing that the locket had caught on the strand when some mysterious third party was carrying Lynne's dead body into Lawson's Bush under cover of darkness.

The most conclusive evidence of all, to Hays's way of thinking, came from the three doctors. Their findings, he contended, beautifully supported his theory of the crime.

Dr. John Penistan, the pathologist, pegged the time of death at precisely the three-quarters of an hour, between 7:00 and 7:45, when Hays theorized that Steven was carrying out his terrible acts.

Dr. Joe Addison left no doubt about what he thought one of those acts had been.

"Is there anything inconsistent," Hays asked Addison at the trial, "with the sores on the accused's penis having been caused by the entry of the male organ into the private parts of a young, small virgin?"

"Nothing," Addison answered. "Steven is sexually developed, the same as any man, and trying to make entry could cause those sores on his penis. Masturbation couldn't have caused them."

And Dr. David Brooks, the RCAF man who had been present at the murder site in Lawson's Bush, at the autopsy in the funeral home, and at the examination of Steven's penis in the air-force guardhouse, backed up every finding that the other two doctors had reached.

"I suggest," Glenn Hays summed up for the jury, "that a review of the facts narrows those facts like a vise on Steven Truscott and no one else."

In defence of Steven, Frank Donnelly relied on the evidence of the two boys, Douglas Oats and Gordon Logan, who stuck to their stories that they'd seen Steven at the bridge, and he called witnesses, including Steven's mother, who said that, later in the evening of June 9, Steven didn't *look* like a boy who had just finished raping and murdering a classmate. Donnelly decided not to put Steven on the witness stand, probably because he saw no advantage in exposing a fourteen-year-old boy to Glenn Hays's cross-examination. But Donnelly's strongest witness was Dr. Berkeley Brown, a medical expert whose expertise placed him distinctly at odds with the three Crown doctors.

Brown practised medicine in London, Ontario. He lectured at the University of Western Ontario, and specialized in internal medicine with an emphasis on diseases of the digestive system.

"In your study and work," Donnelly asked Brown at the trial, "do you have any experience as to the length of time it takes the stomach to empty after an ordinary meal?"

"Yes," Brown answered. "It would take three and a half to four hours to empty from the stomach if it were well masticated. If it were poorly masticated, that would add on another hour for emptying. If there were ham in the stomach, that would also slow the emptying time, because food with protein and fat evacuates more slowly than starchy foods. The skin from turkey would have the same slowing effect."

In a couple of aspects, Brown's testimony somewhat echoed the views on stomach contents of Dr. Noble Sharpe, the medical scientist from the Attorney-General's office. Perhaps significantly, the Crown did not call Dr. Sharpe as a witness.

Next, Donnelly showed Brown the jar containing the contents of Lynne's stomach after her death, and asked him to comment on what he saw.

"Well," Brown said, "I would anticipate that we are seeing the material nearer to the time when it is getting ready to leave the stomach. I would say this food had been in the stomach for three or four hours."

Then Brown added a general comment.

"Judging the time of death by the contents of the stomach," he said, "must be done with great caution, because there are such wide variations, and so many factors can enter into the situation."

That, too, echoed one of Dr. Noble Sharpe's views.

Berkeley Brown performed double duty as an expert witness for the defence. That was because Frank Donnelly, financed from the humble salary of RCAF Warrant Officer Dan Truscott, couldn't afford to bring in a range of experts. Fortunately, Berkeley Brown's experience equipped him to be as learned about penises as he was about stomachs.

"Dr. Brown," Donnelly asked, "you spent five years during the war as a medical doctor in the army?"

"Yes, with a regiment."

"And in this time would you have had occasion to do medical examinations of many penises?"

"Thousands, I would say."

"Pardon?"

"Many thousands of penises."

"Many thousands, yes," Donnelly repeated. And then he described the sores that Drs. Addison and Brooks had found on the shaft of Steven's penis. "What is your opinion, Dr. Brown, as to whether or not such lesions could be caused by the insertion of the organ into the private parts of a young small girl?"

"I would think it would be highly unlikely that penetrating would produce a lesion of this sort. It is interesting that the penis is rarely injured in rape. When it *is* injured, it is usually a tearing injury confined to the head of the penis. The shaft doesn't bear the same traumatic brunt, and the skin of the shaft is fairly durable."

"Doctor," Donnelly asked, "what is your opinion as to whether these lesions were caused by masturbation?"

"The lesions are consistent with masturbation."

Dan Murphy, watching the Truscott trial wind to its end on the night of the last Thursday in September, thought the jury would acquit Steven.

"That's what everybody around the courthouse expected," he says. "As a lawyer, I'd chat with people, and the feeling was pretty consistent. Donnelly had medical testimony that raised a reasonable doubt. And the timing of the whole thing, the story Glenn Hays presented, didn't feel right. Truscott hardly had the time to go into the bush and kill the girl and get out during the few minutes that the kids on the County Road didn't see him. That was the attitude among the people I spoke to. It was my attitude. Nine juries out of ten would have acquitted Truscott. There was just one problem – he got the tenth jury."

The jury in the Goderich courthouse retired to make its decision at 8:38 on the night of September 30 and came back to the courtroom at 10:55 with a verdict of guilty as charged with a plea of mercy. Judge Ferguson sentenced Steven to be hanged on Tuesday, December 8. The hanging was postponed while Truscott's new lawyer, an excellent young criminal counsel named John O'Driscoll, who replaced the newly appointed Judge Donnelly, launched appeals.

On January 21, 1960, the Ontario Court of Appeal turned down O'Driscoll's arguments for a new trial, and, within the month, the Supreme Court of Canada declined to hear an appeal from the Ontario court's decision. John Diefenbaker's federal cabinet immediately commuted Steven's sentence to life in prison, and he served the first four years of the sentence in the Ontario Reformatory near Guelph. After he turned eighteen, he was moved to Kingston Penitentiary to do the rest of his time. He remained there, mostly forgotten, until 1966, when a woman named Isabel LeBourdais wrote a book called *The Trial of Steven Truscott.*

Isabel LeBourdais was an old-fashioned do-gooder. In the early 1930s, she had joined the crusading new CCF party, and later she worked for such causes as Negro rights in Canada. She came from a literary family. Her sister, Gwethalyn Graham, won two Governor-General's Awards in fiction for her novels, and LeBourdais's husband, Don, wrote books about mining and exploration. LeBourdais herself dabbled at short fiction and journalism, but she needed a cause to get her fired up about writing, and she found it in the Steven Truscott case. She had a son Steven's age. That helped her to identify with the case. But mostly she felt that the boy had received a raw deal from the justice system, and she intended to rally the country in Steven's support.

She read the trial transcript, picking out what she considered to be flaws in Glenn Hays's case against Steven, errors in Judge Ferguson's rulings, and failures in Frank Donnelly's defence. She spent weeks in Huron County, where she interviewed many of the locals, including eleven of the twelve jurymen, and where she sussed out the general feeling towards Steven. And she put everything she learned and everything she thought, some of it self-serving speculation, some of it solid detective work, into one long, complaining rant of a book.

To LeBourdais, there were many villains in the case: Judge Ferguson, because his charge to the jury was slanted against Steven; the police, because their investigation was directed single-mindedly to convicting Steven, ignoring other possible suspects; Donnelly, because his defence was too tentative in Steven's interest. But most of her disdain was saved for the people of Huron

County. From the start, LeBourdais argued, they were biased against Steven, the brat from the RCAF base, and that bias was reflected in the mindset of the jury. "I knew by the third day no one was going to prove that young monster innocent," LeBourdais quoted one anonymous juryman as saying. With a jury like that, LeBourdais concluded, Steven didn't stand a chance.

Not surprisingly, Steven agreed with her assessment of the jurors. In a 1971 book that freelance writer Bill Trent ghost-wrote for him, Steven said, "I could feel the antipathy of that small-town jury, moved not by sympathy for Lynne but hatred for me." Also not surprisingly, Dan Murphy disagrees with both assessments. "The jurors seemed a fairly typical, decent sort," he says. "I sat on the Huron School Board with one of them later on, and he was no dummy. One thing, though, the Truscott jurors used to have an annual reunion, a picnic, every summer. Then somebody found out about it. It just looked bad, and there was a terrible stink, so they discontinued the picnic."

Isabel LeBourdais approached several Canadian publishers with her manuscript. All turned her down. Jack McClelland of McClelland & Stewart came closest to publishing the book. He signed LeBourdais to a contract in 1962, but, when McClelland & Stewart's lawyers warned that the book had crossed the line from indignation to libel, McClelland backed off. LeBourdais then took the manuscript to her old CCF friend Ted Joliffe, the former party leader in Ontario. Joliffe, a lawyer, tinkered with LeBourdais's writing, slicking up the possibly libellous passages, and, in its more-sanitized form, the manuscript was snapped up by Gollancz, the English publisher, who offered the book's Canadian rights to McClelland & Stewart.

Jack McClelland did a canny job of promoting *The Trial of Steven Truscott*. In advance of its publication in March 1966, McClelland had a copy delivered to each member of Parliament. One of them, a man named Byrne of Kootenay East in British Columbia, made a speech in the House, in which he staked his

seat on a royal commission finding Steven innocent of Lynne
Harper's murder. The book both became a remarkable bestseller
– fifty thousand copies sold in two weeks – and raised a hot political issue. The federal cabinet, besieged by demands like the one
from the Honourable Member for Kootenay East, passed the
buck to the Supreme Court of Canada in the form of an unprecedented Reference:

"From His Excellency the Governor General to the Supreme
Court of Canada the following question is referred for their
Hearing and Consideration: 'Had an appeal by Steven Murray
Truscott been made to the Supreme Court of Canada what dis-
position would the court have made of such an appeal on a consideration of the existing record and such further evidence as the
court in its discretion may receive and consider?'"

The Reference, which began on October 5, 1966, and lasted for
two weeks, with oral argument later in January of 1967, turned
into a contest of duelling doctors, and, in at least two significant
instances, the medical and scientific experts, who were made to
look like fools by cross-examining counsel, may have left the nine
Supreme Court justices more confused than enlightened on the
case's key issues.

Steven's lawyer on the Reference was Arthur Martin (assisted
by Isabel LeBourdais's old friend Ted Joliffe). An even-spoken,
exceedingly polite man, an authentic scholar of the law, Martin,
whose legal career ended on the Ontario Court of Appeal, was
a giant of the criminal courts, the Canadian equivalent of
Clarence Darrow – but with more principles. Bill Bowman and
Don Scott took the case for the Crown. Bowman, the old hand
of the pair, was in charge of the arguments to the judges, while
Scott, a whiz at cross-examination, handled the questioning of
witnesses.

The witnesses, thirty-one of them, didn't appear in the rigid
order they would at a trial – first the witnesses for the Crown,

then the witnesses for the defence. Instead, both sides called witnesses in a sequence that was close to random. This gave the Reference a loose structure, but it also made for exciting courtroom drama, especially when the Crown and the defence began to parade to the stand medical experts who testified on perhaps the most critical issue of the case: the time of Lynne Harper's death, as arrived at by Dr. John Penistan, and the efficacy of assessing stomach contents to determine that time.

Arthur Martin led off for the defence with an eminent pathologist from Baltimore, Maryland, named Charles Petty. "The question I want to ask you, Doctor," Martin said, "is, can in your opinion the time of death be put within narrow limits based on the stomach contents?"

"Based on the appearance of the stomach contents," Petty answered, "I would find myself completely unable to pinpoint any time, a figure such as seven o'clock to 7:45."

Nothing could be plainer. Or it was until the Crown countered with Dr. Milton Helpern, chief medical examiner for New York City, a veteran of twenty thousand autopsies.

"In my opinion," Helpern said, in answer to Don Scott's questions, "from the amount of food in the stomach I would conclude that death had occurred no more than two hours after the food was ingested."

Which expert was to be believed?

The defence called Dr. Frederick Jaffe of Toronto, the most famous Canadian pathologist of the day, who testified that he certainly couldn't place Lynne Harper's time of death between 7:00 and 7:45, not based on her stomach contents. Dr. Samuel Gerber of Cleveland, Ohio, begged to differ. He was both a doctor and a lawyer, and, testifying for the Crown, he said that, judging from what he'd heard about the volume, nature, and consistency of Lynne's stomach contents, the food had definitely been in her stomach for less than two hours at the time of her death. Dr. Noble Sharpe from the Ontario Attorney-General's office, also testifying for the Crown, agreed with the two-hour time frame, though he again mentioned that other factors – Lynne's appetite, her mother's cooking, the presence of fatty foods – might affect the rate of digestion and that, anyway, stomach contents weren't always an entirely reliable indicator of time of death.

This seemed to be getting out of hand, men with equally impeccable credentials in medicine and pathology disagreeing diametrically on a fundamental matter that ought, one would have thought, to have been straightforward stuff. And the disagreement hadn't yet reached its peak. That, plus two masterly demonstrations of the art of cross-examination, came when the experts from England were heard from.

First up, for the defence, was Dr. Francis Camps. His curriculum vitae was formidable: professor at the University of London, the forensic-medicine consultant to the British Army and to the Ministry of Defence, editor of one of the most widely quoted textbooks on legal medicine.

"First of all, Dr. Camps," Arthur Martin began, "what is your opinion as to whether the contents of the stomach is a reliable guide to the time of death?"

"It is so variable that this generally has been described as being of no value in assessing the time of death."

"Assuming the correctness of Dr. Penistan's observations of the stomach contents," Martin continued smoothly, "what is your opinion as to whether you could, on the basis of those observations, state with any reasonable degree of certainty that the time of death of the deceased was between the hours of 7:00 and 7:45 P.M., having regard to the fact that the victim finished her last known meal at 5:45 P.M.?"

"I would say it's quite impossible," Camps answered, utterly confident, "and in fact I would say it could be dangerously misleading to the investigating officers. Had I been there, having found the stomach contents in that condition – which would indicate death at the end of one hour or up to nine or ten hours

– and with other observed post-mortem changes, I would put my time of death closer to ten hours than one."

Don Scott rose to cross-examine the witness.

"Dr. Camps," he said, "it appears that you have considerable experience in these matters. I would suggest to you that you yourself might have given the police a similar time of two hours."

"I should not have, actually."

"Well, do you agree that this girl could have died within that period of Dr. Penistan's?"

"She could have died within two hours. Could have been nine, ten, eleven hours. But I do not think you can say when she died, fixing a time within half an hour."

"Very well," Scott said. "Now please, sir, I am trying to be very cautious here. I do not wish to reflect on your integrity at all, Doctor, please accept that, but I do feel bound to ask you if you really made up your mind about this matter long before you heard any of the evidence or had anything to go on except a book for which you wrote a review in England saying the medical evidence couldn't possibly stand up?"

Camps was caught badly off guard.

"Well, it is partly . . . but almost completely untrue," he said, his utter confidence now dissipating. "I wrote to a very . . . to a gentleman who had asked my advice . . . and all I said, I wanted to make it clear . . . subject to my reading the evidence –"

Scott interrupted Camps. "Yes," he said. "I have a copy here of the letter you're referring to. I quote: 'I have read *The Trial of Steven Truscott* with considerable interest. As you appreciate more than anybody else, books of this type have a certain emotional involvement of the author with the subject and hence require considerable objective detachment. This I have attempted to achieve and on such basis I do not think the medical evidence for the prosecution can possibly stand up to scrutiny. I should be prepared to support this in writing or in evidence. I have no objection to any communication of my views on the Truscott case.'"

"This is written to whom?" Chief Justice Robert Taschereau asked.

"The Lord Chancellor of England as a result of a personal letter from him," Camps answered. "I had no idea it was ever to be divulged."

Scott pointed out to Camps that, on the contrary, he had said in his letter he had "no objection to any communication of my views on the Truscott case."

"I'm sorry," Camps mumbled. "I must have misunderstood."

"When *did* you read the evidence, Doctor?" Taschereau asked.

"I read the book, and it must have been somewhere around that date. I read the evidence as soon as it was sent over to me."

Scott said to Camps, "I don't wish to pursue this, but frankly it seems that your statement that the medical evidence cannot possibly stand up was made long before you read the evidence. That's my simple question."

Camps answered, "I'm afraid your simple question is very misleading. Your simple –"

Justice Gérald Fauteux interrupted. "I would like an answer to that. As far as I'm concerned –"

Camps interrupted right back. "I don't like him suggesting that my integrity is –"

"No, sir," Scott said. "I am not."

"My Lord," Camps tried again, "the answer was that . . . this was a personal letter but what I had read led me to believe that – and I wasn't saying the evidence was wrong. I simply said it didn't stand up to close scrutiny. In other words, it . . . required more . . . scrutiny. That was the object of . . . since . . . since then I have . . . I . . ."

"All right, sir," Scott said gently, as if to the victim of a traffic accident. "All right."

Scott was riding high. He had just demolished the defence's star witness, and now he was calling to the stand his own prize expert, the only English pathologist who boasted a more impressive c.v.

than Francis Camps. This was Dr. Cedrick Keith Simpson, a man who had performed some 100,000 autopsies, the author and editor of several definitive medical textbooks, the most famous forensic pathologist in the entire world.

"Now, very generally," Scott asked Simpson, "what is your view as to the medical evidence as presented in the original trial of this matter?"

"I think, My Lords," Simpson said, prepared to be generous with his superior wisdom, "I would say that with my experience in these matters, extending over thirty years, I would say that Dr. Penistan and the officers responsible appear to have performed a very competent and conscientious investigation pertaining to the timing and cause of death."

"And what do you say," Scott asked, "as to the conclusion Dr. Penistan arrived at that the stomach contents he examined had been in the stomach between one and two hours?"

"I would say, My Lords, it appears to me in this case most cred-itable that Dr. Penistan paid particular attention to this matter. In my own experience this is not always so. I would say that he was right to conclude that it was likely that death had taken place up to two hours after eating that last meal."

Don Scott turned to Arthur Martin. "Your witness," Scott said.

Martin got right into the destruct part of his cross-examination.

"Dr. Simpson," he said, "I believe you wrote a review of the book *The Trial of Steven Truscott*?"

"Yes, sir."

"And had you read the evidence when you –"

Simpson jumped into the middle of the question. "No, sir. This was a review of a book."

"Yes," Martin said. "I didn't intend to put this to you, but in view of the fact that my friend put the questions he did to Dr. Camps, did you not form opinions from the book which you expressed?"

"I formed an opinion *about* the book, sir."

"Yes," Martin said. "I quote, 'This critical review of a Canadian case is so biased by the outraged feeling of the authoress that it is difficult to weigh the facts. Medical and scientific evidence given seemed to us surprisingly sound, coming as it did from quite moderate experts, and we do not subscribe to the feelings of outrage that are repeatedly called for in this account of the Truscott case.' Now, sir, did you not form an opinion that the medical evidence was quite surprisingly sound?"

"It seemed to me from what I read," Simpson answered, "to be surprisingly sound."

"You formed that opinion?"

"I formed the opinion from the book."

"From the book, yes. Before you read the evidence, that is the opinion you formed from the book?"

"Yes, sir," Simpson conceded.

"Now, Dr. Simpson," Martin went on, "I've read a good many of your books, and one of them is entitled *Forensic Medicine*. It has gone through five editions now?"

"Yes."

"Do you anywhere in this book suggest that the stomach contents and the state to which digestion has proceeded is a reliable guide to the time of death?"

"No, sir. I think that it is, as may be evident to you, a short book for the student."

"It wouldn't have made it much bigger to put in a sentence indicating the stomach contents were a reliable guide."

"No, sir," Simpson said, "I appreciate that. It is not intended to be a comprehensive work, of course."

"Well, it should contain those things upon which there is some consensus and –"

Simpson spoke quickly. "I think you may expect the next edition, sir, to contain some reference."

"Ah, you are going to change the next edition?"

"Why, I think that is how one improves one's textbooks – by experience."

"And when did you decide to change the next edition?"

"Each time I am writing, I am learning."

"Oh, then I will throw this away and buy the next edition."

With that dry aside, Martin turned to another of Simpson's textbooks. "You also deal with stomach contents in the twelfth edition of Taylor, which you have edited?"

"There is a reference to the stomach contents there," Simpson answered. "It is a more comprehensive book."

"Very well," Martin said. "On page 210 under the heading 'Inferences As To the Time of Death,' you write, 'Examination of the body of a woman strangled at about 11:00 P.M. one February night showed meat, peas, mint leaf, and potato still present in the stomach, together with some apple pips. Very little had passed into the duodenum. She had had her last meal of roast lamb, peas, potatoes, mint sauce, apple tart and custard at 2–2:30 P.M., no less than nine hours previously.'"

"Yes," Simpson said, "I remember the case."

"The description is remarkable," Martin said. "First of all, the cause of death was strangulation?"

"Yes."

"The cause of death in the Truscott case was strangling. And the description of the stomach contents, is it not very much like Dr. Penistan's?"

"Yes."

"Very little had passed into the duodenum, you write. Again, that is very like Dr. Penistan's?"

"Yes."

"In fact, the whole process seems to have gone further in the case of Lynne Harper because he used the phrase 'very little had passed *through* the duodenum.' Is that correct?"

"Yes."

"So," Martin said, narrowing in on Simpson, "you have all these analogies in these two cases and yet in yours, you write that death occurred *nine hours* after the last meal?"

"Yes."

"So you get very healthy variations, don't you, in the emptying process of the stomach?"

"Yes, I must comment," Simpson said. "We don't know what the facts were in my case. There must have been some explanation but we did not find out —"

Martin cut him off. "You do not know what the facts were with respect to Lynne Harper either, do you?"

"No, sir, I am saying this is —"

"So, we have *another* parallel."

"Sir, not a parallel."

"Because you have no more evidence as to what duress or fear or things of that nature were working on this girl prior to her death than in your other case?"

Simpson's voice could hardly be heard in the courtroom. "No."

"Thank you."

Simpson made one last vain attempt to rescue his position. "All I am saying," he said, "is that when Dr. Penistan gave his views, they, ah, seemed to be an ordinary, usual, and . . . ah . . . ah . . . reasonable view . . ."

Dr. Simpson's voice trailed off.

There was something more like unanimity among the medical and scientific experts on the second significant medical issue in the case: the cause of the two oozing lesions on Steven's penis. Drs. Addison and Brooks had made the snap decision on the night they examined Steven in June 1959 that he'd probably injured his penis in the act of raping Lynne Harper. That view had been accepted by the jury at the trial — at least it had by implication — over the opinion of the defence's medical expert, Dr. Berkeley Brown, who insisted that violent sex, though it might cause damage to the head of the penis, would never bring about injuries to the penis's shaft such as the ones Steven incurred. The majority of the experts who testified on the Reference tended to side with Brown's interpretation rather than with Addison and Brooks, though there were doubters among the group.

One was Dr. Cedrick Simpson. Testifying for the Crown, before Arthur Martin had left him in tatters over the issue of the stomach contents, Simpson allowed that, if Steven had some pre-existing sores on his penis – "patches," Simpson called them – then if "these patches were rubbed in some way [it would cause] them to become more sore or to weep or crust, and I would regard that as being consistent with the penis being thrust into or being held in some way in a sexual gesture as a part of a sexual assault."

Altogether, six doctors addressed the matter of the penis lesions at the Reference. Some were the same men who testified about Lynne Harper's stomach contents; others were dermatologists who confined their testimony to Steven's sore penis. The majority view of both groups rejected the sexual-intercourse theory as the cause of the sores. Some doctors thought such a cause was "unlikely." Others were more emphatic. Dr. Francis Camps fell into the latter category.

"From a mechanical point of view and from my experience," Camps said, before Don Scott had shot *him* down in flames on cross-examination over his stomach-contents testimony, "I don't think this is the sort of injury which could occur from sexual intercourse. It is the wrong part of the organ for one thing. The commonest injury occurring in this type of forced intercourse is a tear of the prepuce [the foreskin], which mechanically is one place that is vulnerable and which can be pulled on, or when push and force is exerted it is pulled in that way."

So, once again, even though the majority of the medical people lined up on the same side of the penis issue, the two scientists touted as the most expert of the experts, Simpson and Camps, came down with opposing positions.

~

Steven Truscott, who was now twenty-one, testified at the
Reference. It was the first time that his voice had been heard in
a courtroom, and under Arthur Martin's careful examination-in-
chief, he told his story in his own words.

"I stopped by the school," he explained to the court, "and I
was watching the Brownies who were having a meeting there,
and Lynne Harper came over to the bicycle and asked me if I was
going down to the river, and I replied that I was, and she asked
me if she could have a lift down to the highway. And several
minutes later we proceeded to the County Road, and I gave her
a ride to Number 8 Highway."

Steven talked about cycling back to the bridge, about notic-
ing Lynne getting into the 1959 Chev, about seeing Douglas
Oats and Gordon Logan at the bridge, about riding back up the
County Road to the schoolyard and home.

Steven's story registered as both logical and innocent. But
when Don Scott cross-examined him, things started to come
loose from the story. In answer to a question from Scott, Steven
said he had left the Brownie meeting with Lynne at about 7:30.
That didn't square with the memories of the ladies in charge of
the Brownies, who put the time at seven o'clock. Steven said
he didn't see Richard Gellatly on the County Road. But
Richard testified that he'd certainly seen Steven and Lynne. And
as for Jocelyne Goddette's story about the date to look at the
calves in Lawson's Bush, Steven said it never happened. There
was no date with Jocelyne, no conversation with her about
calves in Lawson's Bush.

In answer to other questions from Don Scott, Steven fell back
on a failure of memory, particularly when the questions dealt with
people whose stories contradicted his.

"Sir," Scott asked, "do you recall a Mrs. Geiger giving evidence
[at the trial]?"

"No, sir," Steven answered.

"Well, do you recall Kenneth Geiger giving evidence?"

"No, sir."

"Do you recall Richard Gellatly giving evidence?"

"No, sir."

"Now, you will agree with me, I'm sure, that this was a most serious charge you were facing in 1959?"

"Yes, sir."

"Yes, I am wondering frankly, Mr. Truscott, bearing in mind the nature of their evidence and bearing in mind the nature of the charge against you, why you cannot even recall these people giving evidence."

"I don't recall them giving evidence."

"I know that, sir. My question was, Mr. Truscott, *why* don't you recall?"

"Because I have forgotten."

Of the nine Supreme Court justices who sat on the Truscott Reference – Chief Justice Taschereau and Associate Justices Cartwright, Fauteux, Abbott, Martland, Judson, Ritchie, Hall, and Spence – Wishart Spence of Ontario was the most junior. Twenty-eight years after the Reference, in the summer of 1994, Spence was the only one of the nine who was both alive and in good health, and his recollection of the Reference remained clear and sharp. Asked to assess the testimony of the doctors and scientists, of the experts who came to the courtroom from all over the world, Spence paused. It wasn't because he had forgotten what the experts had said. It was because he was trying to be fair to their memory.

"Well," he said after a few seconds, "the medical evidence was not too helpful."

Still, the medical evidence was what the court had to work with. The trial had turned largely on the testimony of doctors, and the decision of the Supreme Court would depend principally on the testimony of even more doctors and scientists. The written judgment of the eight justices in the majority – Emmett Hall of Saskatchewan was the dissenter – ran to sixty-eight pages, and more than half of them, thirty-eight pages, were devoted to the medical evidence.

The trouble was that the experts insisted on disagreeing with one another. That's what made their evidence, as Mr. Justice Spence expressed it, "not too helpful," and to finesse their way around this problem, the majority judges hit on a couple of ground rules.

For one thing, they would, at least for the record, ignore the two cross-examinations that seemed to put into question the views of the two prominent English pathologists, Don Scott's cross-examination of Dr. Francis Camps and Arthur Martin's of Dr. Cedrick Simpson.

"With each medical expert," the majority wrote, "we chose the opinion which he expressed in his own words in examination-in-chief. We think it is better done this way because we could not see that on cross-examination any expert retracted or seriously modified what he said in chief."

That simplified matters. And to make their decision even more straightforward, on the issue of stomach contents as an indicator of the time of Lynne's death, the judges decided to count heads rather than attempt to break down and analyse the experts' varying opinions. Three doctors – Petty, Jaffe, and Camps – had rejected the idea that the food in Lynne's stomach demonstrated she must have died between 7:00 and 7:45 P.M. But four doctors – Simpson, Helpern, Gerber, and Sharpe, though the latter had reservations – testified that a one- or two-hour time frame for the time of death seemed about right, based on the stomach contents. Ergo, the yeas prevailed.

"The weight of the new evidence," the majority held, "supports Dr. Penistan's position. . . . The effect of the sum total of the testimony of the expert witnesses is, in our opinion, to add strength to the opinion expressed by Dr. Penistan at the trial that the murdered girl was dead by 7:45 P.M."

On the case's other major medical issue, the condition of Steven's penis and the reason for that condition, the justices decided against counting heads. Instead, they were persuaded by the reasoning of one particular expert, Dr. Cedrick Simpson. It had been Simpson's view that Steven had sores of some sort on his penis before June 9, and that the patches had been exacerbated by some later activity, a sexual assault perhaps. The justices thought that made sense. After all, Steven had told Dr. Addison, at the time of Addison's physical exam, that his penis had been sore for four or five weeks. And Steven repeated that observation during his testimony on the Reference. The justices took this admission, together with Dr. Simpson's opinion, and ran with it.

"The serious condition [of the penis] found and described by Dr. Addison and Dr. Brooks," the majority wrote, "was consistent with the aggravation of a pre-existing condition resulting from a sexual assault upon Lynne Harper."

This meant that the eight justices held against Steven on both of the critical medical issues. The time of death, as determined by Lynne's stomach contents, occurred during a period when Steven was known to have been with Lynne, and the sores on Steven's penis probably owed at least some of their cause to a sexual assault on Lynne. Those were the conclusions of the majority of justices, and they were enough to nail Steven. But to cinch the case against him, the justices branded Steven a liar in their court. In all the places where his testimony on the Reference conflicted with testimony given before Mr. Justice Ferguson and the jury at the trial, testimony from Jocelyne Goddette, Richard Gellatly, and the others, the justices chose to reject Steven's version of the events and their timing.

"There were many incredibilities inherent in the evidence given by Truscott before us," the majority wrote, "and we do not believe his testimony."

For the majority, the question asked on the Reference was decided.

"Our conclusion," they wrote, "[is] that the verdict of the jury reached on the record at the trial ought not to be disturbed. The effect of the fresh evidence which we heard on the Reference, considered in its entirety, is to strengthen that view."

As Supreme Court justices go, Emmett Hall was a populist and a maverick. The subtitle of his biography described him as an "Establishment Radical." Still, none of his fellow justices on the Supreme Court of Canada expected him to dissent from the majority in the Truscott case. Some years later, Mr. Justice Ronald Martland said that all the judges had agreed on a unanimous decision until Hall changed his mind at the last minute. Hall, Martland said, was "grandstanding." Hall denied both charges, that his dissent was a last-minute conversion or that he was showing off. But Wishart Spence, speaking in the summer of 1994, supported the Martland view.

"Hall's dissent came out of the blue," Spence said. "I wouldn't say it was slick, but it was awfully coincidental."

Whatever the background and motivation, Emmett Hall's dissenting judgment in Truscott became his most famous decision. It made no law – it was a minority decision – but nothing Hall wrote, before or after Truscott, on behalf of a majority of the court, in cases that did make law, is so often remembered or quoted. Civil libertarians frequently haul out his words in Truscott as an example of what the highest court should say in cases where a citizen's rights to a fair trial may be in question. Edward Greenspan, the eminent Toronto criminal lawyer, once described Hall's decision as "one of the most passionate, blistering dissents ever registered in the Supreme Court," and that's the opinion of most other champions of civil rights.

The thrust of Hall's judgment was that Steven Truscott had not been given a proper trial. Interestingly, Hall had next to nothing to say about the medical evidence at the trial or at the Reference. His objections took him in other directions, and to him, those at fault were the Crown attorney, Glenn Hays, and the judge, R. I. Ferguson. Hays was too fanatical in pursuing Truscott, and Ferguson was too careless in letting Hays get away with his wild theorizing.

"I find," Hall wrote in his judgment, "that there were grave errors in the trial brought about principally by Crown Counsel's method in trying to establish guilt and by the learned Trial Judge's failure to appreciate that the course being followed by the Crown would necessarily involve the jury being led away from an objective appraisal of the evidence for and against the prisoner."

Hall listed chapter and verse of the errors committed by Hays and compounded by Ferguson. These included Hays's speculation that Steven had first planned to have his way with Jocelyne Goddette, that he had "planted" the locket on the bottom strand of the fence, that he had "rigged" alibis with Gordon Logan and Douglas Oats. There was no evidence, Hall pointed out, for any of these or for other fanciful theories that Ferguson allowed Hays to present to the jury. Hall ticked off the sins and errors of the Hays–Ferguson team, and then he let loose his peroration to justice:

> It was inevitable that this horrible crime would arouse the indignation of the whole community. It was inevitable too that suspicion should fall on Truscott, the last person known to have been seen with Lynne in the general vicinity of the place where her body was found. The law has formulated certain principles and safeguards to be applied in the trial of a person accused of a crime and has throughout the centuries insisted on these principles and safeguards being observed. In the great majority of cases adherence to these fundamentals is not difficult but in a case like the present one, when passions are aroused and the Court is dealing with a crime which cries out for vengeance, then comes the time of testing. It is especially

at such a time that the judicial machinery must function objectively, devoid of inflammatory appeals, with the scales of justice held in balance. This standard was not lived up to in the trial under review in a number of instances which one by one were damaging to Truscott and taken collectively vitiated the trial. Nothing that transpired in this Court or any evidence tendered here can be used to give validity to what was an invalid trial. A bad trial remains a bad trial. The only remedy for a bad trial is a new trial. ([1967] S.C.R.)

Steven Truscott remained in Kingston Penitentiary until October 21, 1969, when, having served almost ten years of his life sentence, he was paroled. Under a new name, he settled somewhere in Ontario, married, had two children, and continues to live in an anonymity that must be comforting.

If the events in Lawson's Bush of June 1959 occurred in the present, in the mid-1990s, if Lynne Harper's body was found among the shrubs and trees two days after she had been assaulted and strangled, would the coroner examining the body, a contemporary Dr. John Penistan, employ a new technology to determine the time of the girl's death, something modern and marvellous and foolproof?

"Oh, no," Doug Lucas says. "The examination of stomach contents has the same importance in calculating time of death today as it did back then. There's nothing new."

This is Dr. Douglas Lucas offering his opinion, the eminent scientist who was the head of the Centre of Forensic Sciences, its director for twenty-seven years until his retirement in 1993. He was also the man who played a small and curious role in the Truscott case when he took part in the experiment that tested Lynne Harper's stomach contents by eating a meal similar to her last dinner, then throwing it up. And it's Lucas's view, speaking from his varied experiences, that "there *is* no great way of establishing the time of death in a murder. Examination of stomach contents helps in arriving at a time. But it hasn't got the accuracy of a ticking clock. It doesn't pin the time down to something within forty-five minutes."

Lucas gives a small laugh.

"In fact, he says, "the only reliable way of telling the time of death is to have someone witness the murder, someone who's wearing a watch that keeps very accurate time."

C H A P T E R   F O U R

Numbers:

The Case of the Man Who Took Ten Percent

IT DOESN'T SOUND LIKE MUCH to be Mr. Ten Percent of Trinidad. What's Trinidad? About the size of Prince Edward Island, not many more than a million people, a lot of palm trees, sunsets, and piña coladas. But Trinidad has oil. Its oil industry goes back to 1857, and, by 1946, it was supplying 65 percent of the British Empire's oil production. That still wasn't much, not until the Arab boycott of the mid-1970s drove world oil prices to crazy highs. The Trinidad government owned half of the country's oil resource, splitting it fifty-fifty with a private company, and the government share of revenues zoomed from $206 million (U.S.) in 1973 to $3 billion (U.S.) in 1982. Ten percent of even a little of that added up to plenty, and it was in these years that Trinidad's Mr. Ten Percent, a man named John H. O'Halloran, made himself an extraordinarily wealthy man.

O'Halloran – Johnny O, as he was called on the island, when he wasn't called Mr. Ten Percent – hadn't come as a stranger to Trinidad; he grew up there and managed his family's lime-juice business. But, in Trinidad, he stood out. There was, most conspicuously, his colour; as a cabinet minister, political adviser, and chairman of various boards, he was pasty Irish white in a government

132

that was wall-to-wall black. In other ways, too, O'Halloran styled himself to stand out. He wore white suits, drove big American cars, and even lived on a street called Flambouyant Avenue in the capital city, Port-of-Spain. He owned racehorses (legal) and fighting cocks (illegal). He was charming, roguish, and kept a mistress on the other side of town. She was Pearl Cameron, a nightclub singer, and she once said of Johnny O that "he had a beautiful voice and beautiful large brown eyes."

O'Halloran's clout in Trinidad, his status as Mr. Ten Percent, lay in the sway he seemed to hold over a man named Eric Williams. Williams, charismatic and intellectual but possibly a little simple in the ways of the business world, was Trinidad's father of independence. He headed the People's National Movement, a political party that came to power in 1956, stayed there for thirty years, and won Trinidad's freedom from Britain in 1962. As the new prime minister, Williams named O'Halloran to his cabinet in the best of all portfolios for a man who had his eye on the main chance, minister of petroleum. No one in Trinidad was quite sure why Williams favoured O'Halloran so outrageously – maybe the beautiful voice, the Irish blarney – but O'Halloran's influence on the prime minister appeared absolute.

"In cabinet, O'Halloran was the bridge between all of us and Williams," another minister, Dr. Winston Mahabir, wrote in his memoirs. "Emotionally, he was closer to Williams than any of us. If he appeared swell-headed, it was because of a brain bursting with secrets."

In 1970, a wave of black power on the island compelled O'Halloran to retreat from the cabinet to a less-visible role. But Williams appointed his man to a series of powerful patronage positions – such as chairmanship of the Trinidad and Tobago Racing Authority at a time when the government was planning the lavish Caroni Racing Complex on the outskirts of Port-of-Spain – and O'Halloran continued to have the prime minister's ear. From his insider vantage point, Johnny O took his slice, his

10 percent, his skim off the top, in oil, in construction, in horse racing. And almost everybody in Trinidad knew it.

But nobody could do anything about it. Selwyn Richardson, the attorney-general in the Williams government, launched an investigation into O'Halloran's looting of various tills. The investigation was genuine, but so were the concealments and obfuscations Richardson encountered. These were roadblocks set in place by higher-ups within Richardson's own party, by people who shared O'Halloran's corrupt practices. Richardson gave up. He gave up everything, his investigation, his attorney-general's post, his membership in the People's National Movement. But he continued, in private, to keep files on Mr. Ten Percent, hoping they would one day have a purpose.

In March 1981, Eric Williams died. His death came under what are usually called mysterious circumstances, which usually means – and, in Williams's case, probably was – suicide. His successor in the prime minister's office, George Chambers, called off the Caroni Racing Complex project, even though it was half-finished. Too expensive, Chambers said. O'Halloran began to hear footsteps behind him. He resigned his post as head of the Racing Authority and took stock of his position. He was sixty-five years old, he'd stashed millions in Swiss and other foreign accounts, and he was feeling vulnerable without the shield of the late prime minister. Time to hit the road.

Years earlier, in 1969, Johnny O had sent his young son, John E. O'Halloran, to a private boys' school in Ontario. John E. had stayed in Canada, attended Trent University, and gone into business. Much of John E.'s business put him at the destination end of his dad's transactions in Trinidad. With his son in Toronto, O'Halloran senior headed there, too. But his health was failing, and, in March 1985, he died in Scarborough General Hospital of pancreatic cancer.

Back in Trinidad, a new political party came to power in December 1986, finally toppling the People's National Movement.

The new party was called the National Alliance for Reconstruction. It campaigned on a platform of anti-corruption, and one of its members, a man appointed attorney-general in the new government, was Johnny O's old adversary Selwyn Richardson, who had changed parties.

Suddenly there was new interest in the O'Halloran saga. Surely, the government thought, there must be a way of recovering at least some of the money O'Halloran had spirited away during his long tenure as Mr. Ten Percent.

Or maybe there wasn't a way.

It turned out that the wily Johnny O had died without a will, leaving nothing in his name except ten thousand dollars in traveller's cheques.

What was Trinidad to do? Where should Richardson and the rest of the government search for Johnny O's loot? Who could they turn to for help?

Bob Lindquist has an understated, soft, almost lazy way of speaking. He's in his late forties, about six feet tall, with a round face, dark hair, and a shy, disarming smile. But after talking to him for a while, you realize that there's something else behind the lazy voice and the disarming manner, something tough and competitive. And it's hardly surprising to learn that, years ago, Lindquist drove cars in rally races. He raced a Porsche in Britain and steered a Mercury through cross-country rallies in Canada. His racing partner in England was former rally champ Harold Morley, and the Lindquist–Morley team racked up some great finishes, fifth in the Welsh International, twelfth in the Scottish International, twenty-second out of 240 entries in the biggest race in the world, the Royal Automotive Club Rally in England. Lindquist didn't care merely to compete. He expected to win.

At about the same time, during his racing years in the early 1970s, Lindquist was an accounting student at the Touche Ross firm in Toronto. He performed the usual bean-counter chores

– annual audits, income-tax returns for elderly widows. But he also had a hand in something entirely different: the Harold Ballard case.

Ballard was one of the owners of Maple Leaf Gardens at the time, and had been charged with fraud and theft by an aggressive young lawyer named Clay Powell from the Ontario Attorney-General's office. Powell assigned Touche Ross to document the crimes, and, as the accountants, who included Bob Lindquist, got into the case, they discovered that what Ballard had been up to was a classic instance of back-end fraud. For years, he had ordered tens of thousands of dollars' worth of renovations to his home, equipment for his summer cottage, and personal services for him and for his family, and invoiced everything to the Gardens, which paid the bills. Lindquist and the rest of the Touche Ross team spent weeks documenting each separate fraudulent transaction. ("I learned," Lindquist recalls, "that if you pick up the two-bit frauds, like with Ballard the forty-dollar limo for his daughter's wedding that he charged to Gardens airport transportation, then the guy you're after thinks, my god, if they caught *that*, they must know *everything*.") And in the end, they presented Clay Powell with such an unshakeable case against Ballard, more than $200,000 of fraud and theft, that Powell went to court and got Ballard sent away for three years of prison time.

Now this, Lindquist thought, was accounting with excitement. This was real action. This was worth giving up rally racing for. So, in 1975, along with a couple of similarly minded accountants, Don Holmes and Tedd Avey, Lindquist set up in business. He coined a descriptive for the sort of work he had in mind, "forensic accounting," a term that has stuck to this day. It was accounting with an investigative element built in, tracing people who had pulled scams and frauds, and preparing cases that were strong enough for the cops and Crown attorneys to take to court.

"Eighty percent of the work in forensic accounting is the same drudgery as in any other accounting, just digging for numbers,"

Lindquist says. "But the other 20 percent is a total turn-on. It gives us a chance to do something other accountants never experience. It gives us a chance to play detective."

It was slow at first for Lindquist Holmes, as the firm was named, a hard sell for the new accounting service. They all worked out of their houses and cars. But soon the Metro Police's fraud squad, the Ontario Provincial Police, and others on the prosecution side came to recognize that Lindquist and friends could produce the numbers that put the bad guys away. The three accountants moved out of their cars and into an office, and business picked up.

Don Holmes cites one case that was pivotal to the firm's early years. It involved a man named Tony Foster, and though the case wasn't typical in the style of its villain, it was gaudy and difficult and a winner. Holmes – greying, muscular, handsome in the sturdy fashion of a hero from a Hemingway novel – devoted about fifteen hundred of his own hours to the Foster investigation, supervised associates for another fifteen hundred hours, reviewed 150 boxes of documents, testified at one preliminary hearing and two trials, and, in the end, saw Foster despatched to Kingston Penitentiary. It was this job, "one whole year out of my life," as Holmes says, that contributed substantially to putting Lindquist Holmes and forensic accounting on the law-enforcement map.

"Tony was different from any other fraud artist I've come across," Holmes says, a hint of admiration in his voice. "He was articulate, and he had a lot of smarts. But what really bowled me over was the man's nerve. With most con men, they take the money and run, but Tony always stayed in touch with his victims. He kept them on a string. He'd talk a guy out of twenty thousand dollars for one of his schemes, and then, after he'd broken the news that the scheme had fallen through, he'd convince the investor that, if he just put up another twenty thousand for the next plan, he could recoup the loss for sure. And the victim would go for it every time."

Foster, who cut a dark and dashing figure, was in his early forties when he showed up in southwestern Ontario in 1971. He had been a bush pilot in the Canadian north, a gun smuggler in South America, and an entrepreneur in the crop-dusting business. It was his unique crop-dusting enterprise, using a fleet of four-engine DC-7s to spray agricultural fields around the world on a huge scale, that got him in the front doors of offices in London, Ontario. Once inside, once he had talked up the crop-dusting operation, Foster dangled more-lucrative possibilities before the businessmen. He had plans, he assured them, that could net millions on an investment of just a few grand.

Take, for example, the gold bullion in Brazil. Foster knew this guy, the son of a Paraguayan dictator, who had smuggled sixty thousand pounds of gold bullion out of his old man's country. It was sitting in a warehouse in the Brazilian coastal town of Recife, and Foster was cut in on the deal if he could arrange to haul the bullion out of South America. He proposed to fly down in one of his DC-7s and sneak the gold away to Switzerland in the plane's spraying rig. All he needed was up-front money to finance the flight and pay a few bribes.

And there were other enterprises. Industrial diamonds to be bought cheap in Brazil and peddled dear in Europe. A fleet of F-86 Sabre Jets, originally sold by Canada to Venezuela, now being retired from the Venezuelan air force and ready for purchase by Foster for resale at a whopping profit to the Pakistanis, who needed them in their war with India. And the municipal bonds that the Buffalo Mafia had accepted in return for gambling debts and were now anxious to sell for forty-five cents on the dollar, a steal, Foster said, because the Arabs would buy the bonds for ninety cents on the same dollar.

"Those schemes were perfect," Holmes says, "because they played on the greed of the investors. Men who run their own companies on conservative business principles seem to turn into suckers when they're presented with investments like those Tony put to them, a combination of high risk and phenomenal return."

How much did Foster separate from Ontario investors with his scams? Jim Riley, the OPP anti-rackets-squad officer who eventually took charge of the case, once estimated the sum at $4 million. Holmes doesn't think it was that much, but says it's difficult to be exact, because most of the money was advanced, on Foster's instructions, in untraceable cash. One fact is certain: none of the businessmen saw a return on his money. Indeed, none of them ever again laid eyes on the original investment.

Invariably, Foster offered explanations – either plausible or hilarious, depending on your point of view – for the collapse of his schemes and the loss of the funds. The gold-bullion venture went down the tubes, Foster claimed, when Recife suffered a devastating flood and Brazilian troops, moving in to shore up the town, closed off the route to the bullion. The F-86 jets from Venezuela were on board a vessel bound for Pakistan when an unfriendly coast-guard ship menaced it off the African coast. The vessel had to be scuttled, and the F-86s sank to the bottom of the ocean. As for the Mafia bonds, they were lost when a Lear jet, carrying the bonds from Sicily to Egypt, ran out of fuel and ditched in the Mediterranean.

Foster's stories, growing more fanciful, at last persuaded one investor that he'd been conned. He blew the whistle, and the OPP moved in to investigate, followed closely by Lindquist Holmes.

"In order to get a fraud conviction," Don Holmes explains, "we had to prove that the money didn't go where Foster said it was going. It didn't matter whether the schemes, the gold bullion and the Mafia bonds and all the rest, were legitimate or not. What was important for us was to show the courts that Foster kept money for his own personal gain. That was tough, because hardly any of the money, not a tenth of it, ever went into a bank account that we knew of. It was in cash. But we dug around and found four or five concrete instances where Tony slipped up and accepted payment by cheque. Each of those cheques created an audit trail that we could follow in and out of a bank account. We could show the specific use of those funds, and that was the key to the case."

A cheque for five thousand dollars from an investor named R. J. Yohn was found to have been deposited in the name of Helen Foster, Tony's wife, at a bank in London. More investigation revealed that Tony had signing power for the account. A deposit slip indicated that he put one thousand dollars from the Yohn cheque into the account, taking the other four thousand away in cash. The bank statement showed that cheques signed by Foster were shortly thereafter drawn on the account to pay amounts to Ginger's Bath & Boutique, Chargex (now Visa), Guildwood Lighting Ltd., the Military Book Club, National Car Rental, Leo Goodman Investments, and the Provincial Court. ("The gall of the man," Holmes says. "He used scam money to pay a parking ticket.")

To nail down the point – that Foster had used the Yohn money for his own purposes and not for the purposes of the alleged investment – Holmes took two more steps. He asked for invoices from each of Ginger's Bath & Boutique, Chargex, and the other payees. Sure enough, Foster had owed money to each. Next, Holmes turned to the books of an outfit called Midair, the company that Foster incorporated for his crop-dusting operations and for his other, less-reputable enterprises. Holmes compared items from the Helen Foster account with the Midair records for the same time period. If any item from the account matched with a Midair item, then Holmes allowed it as an expense that was in furtherance of the alleged investment. But few items coincided. The majority remained as Foster's personal expenses, unless he could explain them. As it later developed at his fraud trial, he couldn't.

Holmes followed the same laborious procedures on other investors' cheques – one for forty thousand dollars, another for fifty thousand – that Foster deposited to an account in his own name at a branch of the Unity Bank in Toronto. He analysed the account, followed the routes that the money took out of the account, and matched the expenditures against the Midair records. The result? Foster had kept substantial sums for his own gain.

"It was proving a negative," Holmes says, "proving that the money hadn't gone into the various investment schemes. The actual work was tedious, but it was still exciting to follow a path for months and end up with an answer that pinned Tony."

Holmes presented an analysis of Foster's finagling at a trial in Woodstock, Ontario, in 1979. The jury accepted Holmes's deductions, found Foster guilty, and Judge Chester Misener sentenced him to four years in Kingston.

That wasn't the end of Tony Foster's story. In the penitentiary, he suffered a heart attack and underwent triple-by-pass surgery. When he was released on parole and moved to Halifax, he wrote a book about his experiences. The book, entitled *By-Pass*, was lively and exciting (and dismissed Don Holmes's investigation and the Woodstock trial as a "judicial farce"), and it marked the beginning of Foster's new career as an author. In his subsequent literary life, he wrote books that he seemed especially qualified to write. Tony Foster wrote crime thrillers.

By the early 1980s, Lindquist Holmes had hit its stride. The firm operated out of two floors of a building on Wellington Street East in downtown Toronto and employed thirty-five accountants and support personnel. Its offices featured – along with the requisite adding machines, computers, and word processors – a pool table. Bob Lindquist and the others used to gather around the table, cues in hand, to conduct business sessions. But as much as anything, the pool table was a symbol of the sense of fun and swagger that these guys brought to their brand of accounting, the forensic brand.

The firm continued to handle criminal investigations, working in tandem with fraud cops and Crown attorneys. The Argosy case was one of theirs, an investigation by Lindquist Holmes into officers of an investment company called Argosy Financial Group, who took sixteen hundred investors to the cleaners to the tune of $27 million. And the firm helped put Helmuth Buxbaum behind bars. He was a millionaire nursing-home owner from London, Ontario, who hired hit men to murder his wife. One of the hired killers confessed to the cops that Buxbaum had paid him specific sums of money on four specific days to finance the hit. It was Lindquist Holmes's task to analyse Buxbaum's bank accounts, automatic-teller withdrawals, and credit-card statements in order to establish that Buxbaum had put himself in sufficient funds to pay the hired killer in the amounts the killer named on the days he named. The graphs and charts that the Lindquist Holmes accountants displayed in court for the jury aided in paving the way to Buxbaum's conviction. He got twenty-five years.

But the nature of forensic accounting, more especially the nature of the clients, was changing for Lindquist Holmes, and the company found itself acting less often for the cops and more often for private companies. These were companies that needed expertise in fidelity-bond insurance disputes, in assessing the honesty of claims for inventory losses, in reconciling financial conflicts in franchise operations, in evaluating damages for patent infringements. Then there were the companies that suspected they were the victims of frauds perpetrated by employees, by customers, or by rivals. They hired Lindquist Holmes to produce the paperwork that documented whatever hanky-panky was going on. With the accountants' report in hand, the companies could follow their own course of action, maybe turn over the whole package to the police for prosecution, maybe seek a return on pilfered funds by suing in the civil courts, or maybe just install corporate controls that would head off future thefts. For the Lindquist people, it was still forensic accounting, but it was different.

Lindquist Holmes was changing, too. In 1985, it merged with one of the Big Six among Canadian chartered-accounting firms, Peat Marwick. The motive behind the union for Lindquist Holmes was to give itself national exposure and national clients. Peat Marwick, for its part, was just keen to get in on this hot new forensic end of the business. The merged firm grew even larger, the very biggest of the Big Six, with another merger in 1989. This time Peat Marwick took in Thorne Ernst & Whinney and became KPMG Peat Marwick. The firm was by now huge in size, in reach, in services, in number of clients – and the old Lindquist Holmes gang wasn't altogether comfortable with the new scale of things.

For one thing, the forensic guys kept running into conflicts of interest. They would be carrying out an investigation on behalf of a corporate client, perhaps one of those complex fidelity-bond deals, and they'd find another client of KPMG Peat Marwick on the opposite side of the dispute. Since accountants from the same firm couldn't ethically act on both ends of a potentially litigious matter, more often than not the forensic accountants would have to bow out. "We lost millions of dollars in fees," Lindquist says.

And for another thing, the Lindquist group missed the swagger of the old days. True, there were some cases that had the familiar thrill. One of those came in March 1990, when the new Romanian government retained them to track the hundreds of millions of dollars that the deposed and deceased dictator Nicolae Ceausescu had salted away in foreign accounts. The hunt led the accountants to Bucharest, Switzerland, Cyprus, and Austria, and past mysterious forces apparently intent on throwing them off the scent, before they finally and triumphantly turned up the loot. But the Romanian case was among the exceptions. Things had grown more tame. The pool table was gone (it ended up in Don Holmes's basement). And so was much of the sense of playing detective.

~

On a morning in December 1986, reading the *Globe and Mail*, Bob Lindquist's attention just naturally gravitated to a story about scandal and corruption. The dateline was Trinidad, where, the story said, an election was coming up. The story went into detail about a cloud of disgrace that hung over the party in power, about kickbacks and bribes, about a former Trinidadian named John H. O'Halloran, who had died in Toronto leaving behind many unanswered questions and much unaccounted-for cash. Some people in Trinidad, according to the story, people in the opposition party who hoped to come to office in the forthcoming election, were wondering where all the missing money was and whether they could ever recover it.

Right up my alley, Lindquist thought when he finished the story. He put together a package that outlined the Lindquist Holmes background and services, and mailed it off to Trinidad.

It took a year. It took the election in Trinidad of the new party, the National Alliance for Reconstruction, and the appointment of Selwyn Richardson to the post of attorney-general. And it took the fortunate coincidence of another forensic-accounting job in Trinidad that sent Lindquist to the island. But in late 1987, Lindquist and Richardson held their first meeting, a chance for each to size up the other. Lindquist decided that Richardson was entirely on the level in his pursuit of the O'Halloran loot. And Richardson recognized that he needed Lindquist in the worst way.

"I had been fighting this O'Halloran thing since 1977, when I was attorney-general in the previous government," Richardson said some years later. "But without the accounting side of it, I couldn't get anywhere."

After the meeting, and back in Toronto, Lindquist prepped himself for the investigation that lay ahead. He read a couple of dozen books about Trinidad's history. "By the time I finished," he says, "I pretty well knew who all the key political players were in the island's past thirty years." In Trinidad, Richardson combed

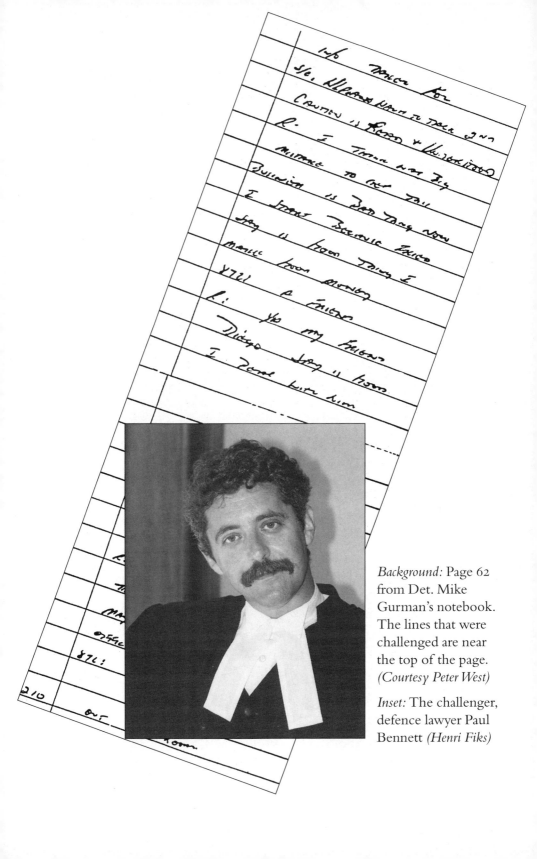

Background: Page 62 from Det. Mike Gurman's notebook. The lines that were challenged are near the top of the page. *(Courtesy Peter West)*

Inset: The challenger, defence lawyer Paul Bennett *(Henri Fiks)*

OPP officer Jim Eadie's own photographs, taken during his investigation.

(Top) The site of the robber's footprint in the snow. (Middle): Eadie's sulphur cast of the footprint. The investigators carried this photo with them. (Bottom): The sole of the Nike recovered from the Footlocker store.

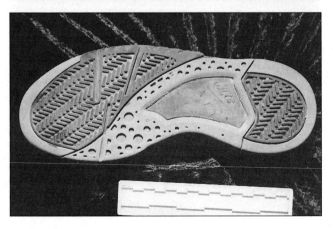

Forensic accountant Bob Lindquist

The team that cracked the Johnny O case:
(left to right) Bob Lindquist, Selwyn
Richardson, and Bill Horton.

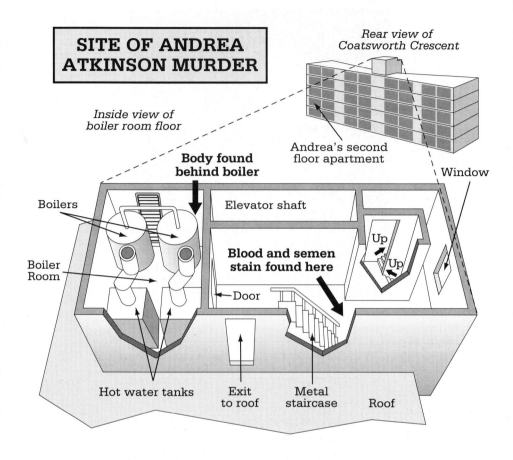

SITE OF ANDREA ATKINSON MURDER

Rear view of Coatsworth Crescent

Inside view of boiler room floor

Body found behind boiler

Andrea's second floor apartment

Window

Boilers

Elevator shaft

Boiler Room

Blood and semen stain found here

← Door

Up

Up

Hot water tanks

Exit to roof

Metal staircase

Roof

(Illustration by Andrew Smith Graphics, adapted from *Toronto Star* drawing)

Johnny Terceira being taken into custody for
the murder of Andrea Atkinson by (left) Det.
Tom McNamara and (right) Det.-Sgt. Rick
Gauthier (Richard Lautens/ *Toronto Star*)

Leo Adler, defence counsel for Johnny Terceira

THE DNA PROFILING PROCESS

(Drawing supplied courtesy of the Centre of Forensic Sciences)

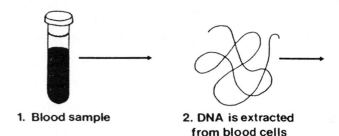

1. Blood sample

2. DNA is extracted from blood cells

11. The X-Ray film is developed to make visible the pattern of bands which is known as a
DNA PROFILE

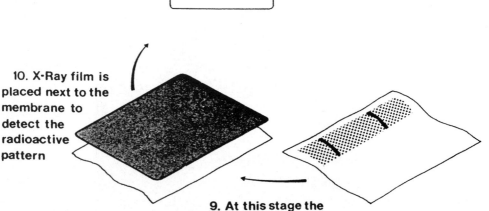

10. X-Ray film is placed next to the membrane to detect the radioactive pattern

9. At this stage the radioactive probe is bound to the DNA pattern on the membrane

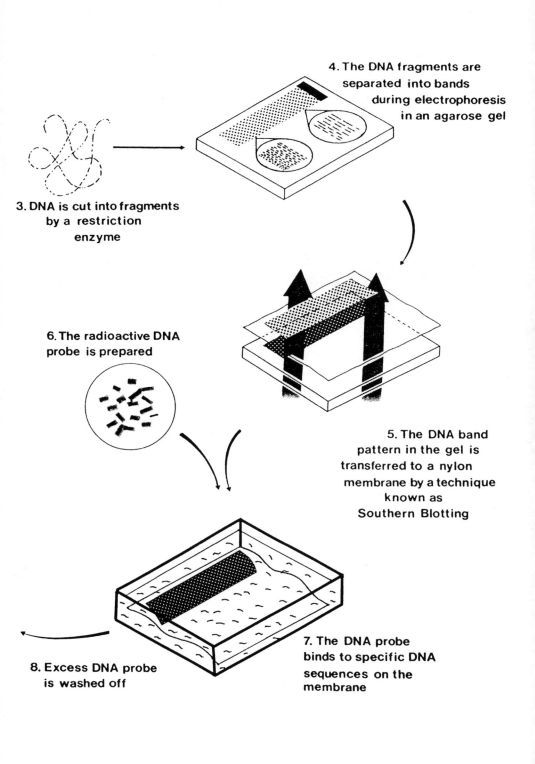

4. The DNA fragments are separated into bands during electrophoresis in an agarose gel

3. DNA is cut into fragments by a restriction enzyme

6. The radioactive DNA probe is prepared

5. The DNA band pattern in the gel is transferred to a nylon membrane by a technique known as Southern Blotting

8. Excess DNA probe is washed off

7. The DNA probe binds to specific DNA sequences on the membrane

"I guess it must be in the genes." Guy Paul Morin (right) remains poker-faced after cracking up his defence counsel, James Lockyer (left), and others at the press conference following his acquittal on murder charges. (*Globe and Mail*/Tibor Kolley, courtesy James Lockyer)

through his O'Halloran files and assembled about twenty cases of Johnny O's malfeasance, cases in which Richardson was certain large amounts of money had been diverted to O'Halloran's own pockets.

In further meetings between the two men, and in much correspondence, Lindquist analysed Richardson's paperwork and eventually settled on three cases out of the twenty to pursue, three in which he decided a crime had been committed and figured there was a fair chance of chasing the money and realizing some return for Trinidad.

The three were these:

A series of bribe payments totalling $575,000 made in 1977 by the big American aircraft company McDonnell Douglas of California to a Trinidad businessman, who was probably fronting for O'Halloran, to secure the sale of three DC-9s to Trinidad's national airline.

A bribe of almost $1.5 million paid to O'Halloran by a construction company that won the bid to build the Caroni Racing Complex outside Port-of-Spain.

And, finally, a series of kickbacks, possibly totalling in the millions, funnelled to O'Halloran by a Texas oil company, Tesoro Petroleum Corp., which acquired a 50-percent partnership in Trinidad's oil rights in 1968, a year when O'Halloran was the island's minister of petroleum.

Over the following two and a half years, Lindquist burrowed into the three cases. The three tended to feed off one another. A small fact picked up in one case would provide a key point of departure in another. Different characters turned up in each case, but inevitably they had in common connections to John O'Halloran. Lindquist went searching for the connections, for the small facts. His objective in all of this was to put together material that was persuasive enough to take to court. No parties in either of the three cases were going to cough up any money. They'd have to be named in lawsuits. Lindquist's task was to figure out who to sue and for how much. And, one more thing: he'd have to provide the evidence to win the lawsuits.

Back in the early 1980s, Selwyn Richardson had actually made some significant yards in the McDonnell Douglas bribery case. McDonnell Douglas itself had voluntarily owned up about the bribes to the U.S. Securities and Exchange Commission, confessing that, on sales of the three DC-9s to the British West Indian Airways for $27.5 million (U.S.), it had delivered four separate cheques totalling $575,000 to Navarros & Company Ltd. in Trinidad. According to McDonnell Douglas's written statement, given to the SEC in July 1980, "a designated adviser" and "a high official" of the government of Trinidad told MDC that, if it hired as its representative a firm named by them and paid a commission suggested by them, MDC "would be favored in the sales competition." The firm was known to be Navarros & Company, but McDonnell Douglas wasn't saying who the "designated adviser" and the "high official" were. Even without the names, Richardson, as attorney-general, had pushed ahead with criminal charges against the man who ran Navarros, Fernando Navarro. Richardson felt certain that Navarro had been a conduit to get the bribe money to O'Halloran, but, if he couldn't nail Johnny O, he'd at least go after his front man, Navarro.

O'Halloran had other ideas. Knowing that the key witnesses in the Navarro prosecution were the pair of McDonnell Douglas officials in California who had handled the bribe payments, he set about throwing a scare into the two Americans. First he floated rumours of violence that would occur to the men if they should leave the safety of California to testify in Trinidad. Then he arranged for a Trinidad government official to write to the two, promising – in frighteningly ambiguous language – that, while on the island, the Americans would "in no way be embarrassed either personally or by reasons of their corporate associations, it being understood that the normal laws of the country will apply (e.g., speeding, improper parking, currency violations, drugs, etc.)." By now, the McDonnell Douglas guys, though still game to testify, were really looking over their shoulders.

"They made it a condition that during the trial, they'd never have to stay overnight in Trinidad," Selwyn Richardson says. "They flew in from Miami or Barbados every morning. I picked them up at Piarco Airport by helicopter, and I took them back at the end of each day. That's how scared they were."

At the trial, the McDonnell Douglas officials did not reveal the names of the mysterious people they'd dealt with on the bribes, "the high official" and "the designated adviser." But their testimony helped to convict Fernando Navarro, who was fined $2,784,150 in Trinidad dollars. That looked like progress. The trouble was, it didn't last long. Two years later – after Richardson had quit as attorney-general and left the government – the fine was reduced to chicken feed, four thousand Trinidad dollars. The message was that John O'Halloran and friends still called the shots in Trinidad.

Still, from Bob Lindquist's standpoint, one very useful piece of information emerged from the Navarro prosecution. McDonnell Douglas had paid its bribes in four cheques. The first three went into a Navarros & Company account in Caracas, Venezuela. The fourth cheque, for the smallest amount by far, $12,500, was deposited to the account of 354233 Ontario Ltd., in a Toronto branch of the Royal Bank of Canada. Who endorsed the cheque? The president of 354233, John E. O'Halloran, the son of Johnny O. This was a significant piece of data, because John E. would be a natural target for any lawsuit trying to recover O'Halloran senior's ill-gotten gains. John E. appeared to Lindquist to have plenty of resources. He was a prosperous young entrepreneur with substantial interests in forty-eight Canadian companies. John E. was one guy to go after.

～

Lindquist approached the case of the McDonnell Douglas bribes from two angles, both designed to tie the money, Johnny O, and John E. into one tidy package. First, he needed to get from the close-mouthed McDonnell Douglas officials the names of the two people they dealt with in Trinidad. And, second, he wanted to establish links between both O'Hallorans and the rest of the bribe money, all except the $12,500 that had gone into the 354233 Ontario Ltd. account.

The first piece of business called for a trip to McDonnell Douglas headquarters in Long Beach, California. Lindquist took two allies with him. One was Selwyn Richardson. The other was Bill Horton, a crackerjack litigation lawyer from the Toronto firm of McMillan Binch; Horton would coordinate all the legal aspects of the entire O'Halloran investigation. In Long Beach, the three men met with Robert Baird, McDonnell Douglas's director of national sales for Latin America and the Caribbean. Prying information out of Baird was like pulling teeth. This was no surprise, since Baird was the guy who had physically handed over the bribe money in Trinidad, and he wanted to shake himself free of the whole unsavoury mess.

Eventually, though, after Baird realized his three visitors didn't intend to leave California without answers, and after he brought in his own personal lawyer for protective advice, he named names. The mysterious "high official" he had dealt with in Trinidad was Francis Prevatt, who was no one less than the minister of finance in the government of the time. And the equally elusive "designated adviser"? He was John H. O'Halloran, Johnny O, Mr. Ten Percent.

Hell, said Robert Baird, did you expect it would be anyone else?

Back in Toronto, the business of fitting John E. O'Halloran, the son, further into the McDonnell Douglas picture was a matter of tedious paperwork. Lindquist had no trouble obtaining the stacks of documents that laid out McDonnell Douglas's bribe payments; these had become a matter of public record in the earlier prosecution of Fernando Navarro. Lindquist also got his hands on John E. O'Halloran's financial records in Canada; this came about as a result of a judicial order that Bill Horton, citing Trinidad's interest in pursuing Johnny O's dips into the country's till, obtained from the Supreme Court of Ontario, an order that froze John E.'s assets and required full disclosure of his business interests. Now the trick for Lindquist was to see if there were hookups between the payment of the bribes and the arrival of new funds in John E. O'Halloran's bank accounts. In this, Bill Horton, for one, was positively dazzled by Lindquist's performance.

"There were two deposits that matched the time frame," Horton remembers, "but not the amounts. I would have gone past them, but Bob immediately thought to check the conversion rate from U.S. to Canadian funds on that particular date. When he did that, the numbers matched. That may seem obvious in retrospect, but when you're looking at incredible masses of numbers in hundreds of pages of documents, to pick out those two numbers and make them meaningful is an art."

The two numbers drew John E. deeper into the plot.

Lindquist uncovered another connection between O'Halloran junior and his father's money when he got into the case of the racetrack-construction bribes.

Johnny O, in his capacity as chairman of the Trinidad and Tobago Racing Authority, had awarded the contract for building the Caroni Racing Complex to a Texas-based company called the Sam P. Wallace Overseas Corp. To demonstrate its undying gratitude, the Wallace company slipped O'Halloran a series of cheques that added up to $1.39 million in U.S. money.

After Trinidad Prime Minister George Chambers, successor to the suddenly deceased Eric Williams, cancelled the Caroni project in 1981, word of the bribes from Wallace to O'Halloran reached the media. Not bribes, Johnny O insisted in interviews, merely political contributions to his party, the party in power, the glorious People's National Movement. Why, Johnny O went on, he had himself deposited the $1.39 million in the PNM's very own treasury. By the time the press, and the police, saw through that pack of lies, O'Halloran was long gone, decamped to Toronto, and he was never prosecuted for the bribe-taking. Nor were the bribes recovered.

Now enter Bob Lindquist.

On one of Lindquist's investigative trips to Trinidad, he asked to be put in touch with the police official who had handled the abortive Wallace–O'Halloran inquiry. This was John Kingston, who held the rank of assistant commissioner. Kingston made Lindquist welcome to the file he had put together seven or eight years earlier. Inside, rather to Lindquist's astonishment, he found the cheques that the Wallace company had delivered under the table. They were made out to an outfit named the Caribbean Contracting Co., which O'Halloran had set up for the purposes of receiving his bribes. Lindquist sifted quickly through the cheques, hundreds of thousands of dollars' worth of them. Some of the cheques, Lindquist noted, had been deposited in Panama banks, some in a bank in the Grand Cayman Islands, and some – and here was where Lindquist realized he was coming up aces – in a Toronto branch of the Royal Bank of Canada. Lindquist added up the Royal Bank cheques. The sum was $636,000 (U.S.). He turned over the cheques. Each was endorsed for deposit by two people. And one of the two signatures on the back of each cheque belonged to John E. O'Halloran.

"There it was, all laid out," Lindquist says. "The signatures connected the son directly to the father's money."

The most spectacular of the John H. O'Halloran scams, and the one that resonated most deeply in Trinidad's history and economy, was the one that turned on oil and the Tesoro Petroleum Corp.

Up until 1968, British Petroleum Corp. owned and managed

almost all of Trinidad's vast off-shore oil resources. But in that year, 1968, two events conspired to place oil ownership in Trinidadian hands. One event was the rise of nationalism on the island. The other was the slump in world oil prices, which made BP entirely amenable to bowing out of the Trinidad oil business. The departure of BP came at a price, of course: $20 million in American money. Trinidad borrowed that sum, handed it to BP, and bid them adieu.

Nobody in Trinidad had the expertise to run an oil industry, and it was expected that the government would strike a bargain with one of the other heavyweights in the field – Shell, Mobil, someone multinational – to handle the technical end of the business. But John O'Halloran, minister of petroleum in the Eric Williams government, had other ideas. He brokered an arrangement with an entirely obscure oil company called Tesoro Petroleum Corp., which operated out of Texas – Johnny O seemed to have an affinity for slick Texans – and it received a deal from Trinidad that seemed to have been made in con man's heaven. Tesoro was charged $10 million for a 50-percent share in Trinidad's oil, for which Trinidad had just paid $20 million, and Tesoro was required to put up a mere $50,000. The rest of the $10 million would come out of future profits. Tesoro was laughing.

The deal turned into one of the steals of the century when oil prices skyrocketed in the 1970s and into the 1980s. As Trinidad's oil revenues hit the $3-billion mark in 1982, Tesoro progressed from small and obscure to large and prominent (former U.S. president Gerald Ford sat for a time on the company's board of directors). Trinidad bought out Tesoro in 1985 for $200 million, not bad on an original 1968 investment of $50,000, but by then the oil market had crashed, and Tesoro had already made its fortune.

It seemed certain that John H. O'Halloran had made his fortune out of the Trinidad oil boom, too. Johnny O was the man who had installed Tesoro in the position from which it could rake in the enormous profits, and, since Mr. Ten Percent had never

made a move without realizing his share of the booty, there had
to be O'Halloran oil money stashed away somewhere. But where?
How could Trinidad recover the money – or even some of it?
Where did one start looking?

One place, as Bob Lindquist discovered, was in the newspapers.
It seemed that, in 1987, disgruntled Tesoro shareholders in the
United States had brought a civil suit against the company, claim-
ing a cool billion dollars in damages. The shareholders alleged that
the people running Tesoro had been guilty of securities fraud and
various other racketeering offences that had cheated the shareholders out of their rightful dividends. All of this was reported
in press clippings that a man named Karl Hudson-Phillips had
saved. Hudson-Phillips was a former Trinidad cabinet minister
and a long-time buddy of Selwyn Richardson. He made the clippings available to Lindquist, and it was these clippings that yielded
a vital lead in the Tesoro–O'Halloran case.

The Tesoro shareholders' suit came on for trial in San Antonio,
Texas, in late 1987 before a judge who gloried in the name of
Hippo Garcia, and, although the case was decided in favour of
Tesoro, and although it didn't directly concern Tesoro's activities
in Trinidad, many juicy Trinidad-related titbits emerged from testimony at the trial. For example, there was the blonde prostitute
whom Tesoro provided for George Chambers in 1974. Chambers,
later to become Trinidad's prime minister, was at the time minister of finance and a proponent of a tax program that would have
cut into Tesoro's profits. After the blonde prostitute's ministra-
tions, which Tesoro charged on its books to "consulting services
rendered," Chambers, who could apparently be bought cheap,
changed his stand on the tax program. That episode struck
Lindquist as amusing in a titillating sort of way, and there were
other, similar, examples. The trouble was that none of them,
though they demonstrated the corrupt mindset at Tesoro, tied the
petroleum company to John H. O'Halloran.

That wasn't true, Lindquist suspected, of one other piece of information that the trial in San Antonio disclosed. This concerned a former Trinidad public servant named John Rahr. Rahr had played an official role, presumably as a public servant, in the original negotiations that had brought Trinidad and Tesoro into its oil partnership in 1968. A year later, between July 1969 and January 1970, according to testimony at the 1987 trial, Tesoro had made payments to Rahr that totalled $2 million (U.S.). Tesoro listed the payments in its records under that old favourite, "consulting services."

Lindquist reasoned that Rahr wasn't a sufficiently major player in the oil scam to deserve such a hefty kickback. Two million dollars was more on the Johnny O scale, and Lindquist saw Mr. Ten Percent's fine hand somewhere in the Tesoro payments – probably on the receiving end.

"John Rahr is the key," Lindquist said to Selwyn Richardson and Karl Hudson-Phillips. "We've got to find John Rahr."

Lindquist loves documents. He speaks about documents in figures of speech and metaphors of his own invention.

For example: "I relate to documents the way Linus relates to his blanket," he says. "They make me feel secure and comfortable, because I know, if the documents exist, so do the answers."

Or: "Documents talk as long as you know their language."

And Lindquist has developed special rules that define his approach to documents. Here are three of the rules:

1. Look at every single thing on a document, no matter how insignificant or trivial it seems. *Especially* the seemingly insignificant. Handwriting, for instance.

2. Always turn a document over and examine the back.

3. Commit everything you see to memory.

In the O'Halloran–Tesoro case, Lindquist had documents from many sources to scrutinize, turn over, and memorize. He had the documents from John E. O'Halloran's businesses and bank accounts that the order from the Supreme Court of Ontario had freed up. He had the documents that Selwyn Richardson had accumulated over the years. And he had boxes of documents concerning Johnny O that the Trinidad government and police had stuck away in an old warehouse in the early 1980s. The latter proved a little tricky for Lindquist to handle. He was used to getting his hands dirty in searches through dusty warehouses. But he wasn't used to prowling through a warehouse, like the one in Trinidad, where snakes had built their homes.

Nevertheless, snakes and all, Lindquist searched on. In the Trinidad warehouse, he came across a virtual paper biography of John H. O'Halloran. Income-tax returns, minutes of cabinet meetings in which O'Halloran had participated, Johnny O's cancelled passports. Lindquist read everything. He read stuff that seemed inconsequential. He read that Johnny O's mother's maiden name was Bowen. That was in one of the cancelled passports. Bowen. Lindquist stored the name in a corner of his mind.

In Toronto, Lindquist went at the documents furnished by John E. O'Halloran with the same single-mindedness. One set of papers seemed particularly intriguing, papers about a bank account in Amsterdam. The account held $1.7 million in U.S. funds. It was in a company name. The name meant nothing to Lindquist. He checked the company's signing officers. There were two of them. John Fleet and John Bowen. Hold on. Where had Lindquist seen that name before? Sure, it was Johnny O's mother's maiden name, from the passport. And that wasn't all. Lindquist looked at John Fleet's signature. The handwriting rang a bell. Of course, it was the same handwriting that appeared on the endorsements of cheques that Lindquist had seen earlier, the McDonnell Douglas cheque for $12,500 that had gone into the John E. O'Halloran account, 354233 Ontario Ltd., and the Sam P. Wallace cheques for $636,000 that had gone into the Toronto branch of the Royal Bank. The handwriting was John E.'s. He was "John Fleet." Johnny O was "John Bowen."

"The money in the Amsterdam account was dirty money," Lindquist says. "They proved it, the two O'Hallorans, by not using their real names."

Karl Hudson-Phillips, the former cabinet minister, tracked down John Rahr, the former civil servant. Rahr was living in exile in England, and Selwyn Richardson hopped on a plane and forced a meeting with him in London. For Richardson, expecting Rahr to spill at least some of the beans about the Tesoro kickback scheme, it was an encounter of deep frustration. Rahr was elderly, seriously ill, and determined to be elusive on the subject of John H. O'Halloran.

"After several hours of Rahr's rambling talk, I realized all I was getting was an evasion," Richardson says of the meeting. "But at least I left him with one thought. I told him that he couldn't be far from his maker, and that surely he'd want to meet him with a clear conscience."

The appeal to higher authority apparently had an effect, because, not long after Richardson's return to Trinidad, Rahr contacted him and suggested a second sit-down in London. This time, Lindquist accompanied Richardson, and at the beginning of the three-way conversation, Lindquist worked a small stratagem on Rahr. He carried with him a stack of documents from the Trinidad warehouse, which he plopped on a table in front of Rahr without saying a word. Maybe Rahr recognized some of the papers. Maybe he didn't. But that wasn't the point. What Lindquist hoped was that the presence of the documents would convey the message that he knew the whole Tesoro story, that Rahr would be merely confirming what Lindquist had already uncovered. This was, of course, far from the truth; Lindquist's knowledge was riddled with gaps that only Rahr could fill. It was all a ploy, the plopping of the documents in front of Rahr, and, as ploys go, it was an oldie, but it may have helped to prime John Rahr's pump.

Rahr began to talk, and what he told Lindquist and Richardson over the following few hours had the flavour, character, and moral nastiness of a chapter from an Eric Ambler novel.

Yes, it was true, Rahr said, that Johnny O had extracted a $2-million bribe from Tesoro. And, yes, it was he, John Rahr, who had acted as the bribe's facilitator.

Rahr, who must have been a novel sort of civil servant, had been secretly retained by Tesoro in 1968 to lobby on its behalf in acquiring the 50-percent interest in Trinidad's oil. After O'Halloran, as minister of petroleum, realized that Tesoro was a company he could do business with – the usual under-the-counter business – he approved the Texas outfit as Trinidad's oil partner. That was when John Rahr switched from lobbyist to facilitator.

To receive Johnny O's kickbacks, Rahr set up two entities. One was a company, called Merkol Establishment, in Liechtenstein. The other was a bank account in Merkol's name at Banque Populaire Suisse in Lugano.

In July 1969, Tesoro transferred $1.1 million from various New York bank accounts to an account in Curaçao. From there, the money moved to the Merkol account in Lugano.

At the time that all this rapid-fire money shuffling was going on, Rahr flew from Trinidad to Lugano by way of London. At Heathrow, as Rahr was stepping out of the VIP lounge, Johnny O materialized at his side.

Be alert, O'Halloran told Rahr, for instructions to redirect the $1.1 million out of the Merkol account in Lugano.

Then Johnny O faded into the Heathrow crowds.

"When I checked into Alitalia about a half hour before my flight," Rahr recalled for Lindquist and Richardson, "I was handed an envelope at the check-in desk addressed to me and marked 'Private and Confidential.' The contents were a Swiss bank number with a Swiss bank. Nothing more."

In Lugano, Rahr dutifully carried out the switch, transferring the money from the Merkol account to Johnny O's secret and personal account. Rahr didn't switch the entire $1.1 million. He held back $100,000. He kept that for himself; it was his facilitator's fee.

Six months later, Rahr negotiated the same process, this time escorting $950,000 in Tesoro bribe money into O'Halloran's Swiss account.

And in January 1972, he did it all again, $105,000 from Tesoro to Johnny O's hideaway Lugano account.

The kickbacks added up to $2,055,000, minus John Rahr's $100,000 slice, more than $2 million (U.S.) that Tesoro paid for O'Halloran's services in cutting them in for half of Trinidad's oil resources.

When Rahr finished telling this breathtaking tale, he asked one condition of Lindquist and Richardson. Rahr asked, this sick, elderly crook, that he be spared criminal prosecution. Lindquist and Richardson thought that would be possible. In return, Rahr said, he would repeat his story for the court record. And later he did, in early February 1989, sitting in a room at the Clifton Hotel in London, speaking into a videocamera, talking under oath, and taking his listeners once again through the story that joined Tesoro and O'Halloran in rich corruption.

Trinidad, under the guidance and counsel of Lindquist and of Bill Horton, the McMillan Binch lawyer, moved on two litigation fronts.

In Toronto, Trinidad sued to recover the bribes that they now knew Johnny O had received: $2 million from Tesoro, $575,000 from McDonnell Douglas, $1.39 million from the Sam P. Wallace Corp. The suit named eight defendants, but the number-one target was John E. O'Halloran. He was the defendant with the deep pockets and the direct connections to Johnny O's shenanigans.

In New York, Trinidad brought a $350-million claim against Tesoro Petroleum. This was an action under the Racketeering

Influenced Corrupt Organizations Act, the famous RICO statute
that had been used so effectively to battle the American mafia.
The suit also alleged that Tesoro had committed acts of fraud,
bribery, interference with contractual obligations, conspiracy, and
breach of fiduciary duty. These were tossed into the proceedings
just to demonstrate that Trinidad wasn't kidding around.

Despite the plethora of incriminating paperwork that
Lindquist had marshalled, despite John Rahr's damning little tale,
despite the matters of truth and justice that Trinidad could claim
on its side, neither lawsuit was going to be a piece of cake. That
was especially true in the United States. For one thing, the facts
of the Tesoro bribery case reached twenty years into the past, and
it was possible that Tesoro had a strong defence under the U.S.
Statute of Limitations. And for another, Tesoro started out as if
it intended to fight the litigation to the very death.

"We would go to meetings, and there would be twelve Tesoro
lawyers across the table," says Sheila Cheston, a Washington lawyer
whom Bill Horton retained to handle part of the American end
of things. "And at one point, I think six or seven months after
we began proceedings, the Tesoro lawyers said in court they had
already spent three million dollars in legal fees."

Still, it aided Trinidad's cause in the United States that
Lindquist, continuing to burrow away at the documents from the
Trinidad warehouse, was able to supply Sheila Cheston and the
other American lawyers with even more evidence of bribes that
Tesoro had distributed in Trinidad – in addition to the romp with
the blonde prostitute Tesoro arranged for prime-minister-to-be
George Chambers. In 1977, Lindquist revealed, Tesoro had cut
Francis Prevatt in for a payment of $120,000 (U.S.), discreetly
deposited in a Canadian bank. Prevatt was the Trinidad cabinet
minister, later chairman of the People's National Movement,
who had also been involved up to his ears with Johnny O in the
McDonnell Douglas bribes. Ben Primus, a Trinidad lawyer who
served as chairman of Trinidad–Tesoro Petroleum, the joint oil

venture, collected from Tesoro a "consulting fee" of anywhere from $500 to $1,250 in American cash every month for eight years. Even Trinidad's governor-general, Sir Ellis Clarke, came in for some Tesoro payola. Clarke, obviously a man of more refined tastes than Chambers, got an all-expenses-paid junket to a French château, which included as much wine as he could sip.

Under the onslaught of Lindquist's documentation, and after hard-nosed negotiations by the lawyers engaged on Trinidad's behalf, Tesoro in the United States surrendered in an out-of-court settlement. The amount Tesoro agreed to pay was nothing like the $350 million named in the lawsuit – that was an in-your-wildest-dreams bargaining number anyway. The settlement figure, reached in the spring of 1990, was $3.3 million (U.S.). Trinidad's lawyers were ecstatic.

"I think the odds were very high that if we had had to go to court," says Roger Witten, another Washington lawyer retained by Bill Horton, "that Trinidad would have recovered nothing and would have had a large legal bill to pay. To take a twenty-year-old case with a Statute of Limitations consideration and bring it to any result is a heck of a victory."

Events broke the same way at the same time in Toronto. John E. O'Halloran settled before trial, agreeing to pay Trinidad a total of $4 million in Canadian money (a sum that explicitly included the $1.7 million that the two O'Hallorans had squirrelled away under phoney names in the Amsterdam bank account). Bill Horton celebrated the result.

"We sued on bribes totalling four million U.S., and we won four million Canadian for a cost that ended up being about 10 percent of settlement," he says. "That's a spectacular result. From a legal perspective, it was most unlikely we could have recovered any more money based on the claim for profits."

On July 24, 1990, a few weeks after the settlements had been reached, Bob Lindquist stood in the Trinidad Parliament as Prime

Minister Arthur Robinson revealed to the House the details of the John H. O'Halloran scandal and of the resolution that Lindquist and company had worked with such finesse to win.

"The results we achieved," Robinson said, "were truly historic. We are the first nation to bring a case of bribery in a United States court against a United States company and recover. We succeeded in obtaining the facts, particularly of the cover-up by the former government. The result is a triumph for morality."

After the speech, Lindquist hung around long enough to accept congratulations, then caught a plane home to Toronto. Four days later, on July 28, a band of armed Trinidadian rebels swooped on the Parliament Building and took it hostage, along with all the cabinet ministers on the premises. The rebels were Muslim, led by a semi-fanatic named Abu Bakr. His beef was that Prime Minister Robinson and his government were as corrupt and irresponsible as the former regime, the PNM bunch that Robinson had defeated. It may have been that Bakr was specifically urged to violent action by what he perceived as the paucity of the recovery in the John H. O'Halloran case – a mere $8 million, when everybody in Trinidad suspected O'Halloran had looted billions.

In any event, within the barricaded Parliament, Bakr demanded that Robinson hand over power. Robinson demurred. Bakr ordered one of his followers to shoot Robinson in the foot. The follower obliged. Now, said Bakr, shoot this other fellow in the same place. Bakr was pointing at the minister of health, Selwyn Richardson. The follower drilled Richardson, a hero only four days earlier. Neither man, Robinson or Richardson, operating on one pedal extremity each, would give in to Abu Bakr.

Outside, in the streets of Port-of-Spain, Bakr's supporters demonstrated, rioted, and looted. The turmoil lasted a few days before police and army forces subdued the rebels, liberated Parliament, and tended to the two hobbled leaders. The toll had been frightening, thirty-eight Trinidadians dead, more than three hundred injured, hundreds of thousands of dollars in property damage. But Abu Bakr's rebellion was quelled, and the government shook itself and returned to power.

In 1991, Bob Lindquist decided to split from KPMG Peat Marwick, taking with him most of his original associates, except for Don Holmes, who became head of forensic accounting at another firm, Ernst & Young. The new outfit, Lindquist Avey Macdonald Baskerville & Company, went international. With offices in four Canadian cities, they opened up in four more cities in the United States where, oddly, forensic accounting was a less-well-known and rather underpractised profession. Lindquist packed up his wife and three children and moved to Washington, D.C., to run the American operation, to spread the forensic gospel, and to pick up business. And the business was more like the sort that it had been in the beginning, back in the mid-1970s, heavy on investigation, tilted to good-guy-bad-guy stuff.

"It's like when I was racing cars," Lindquist says, still soft-spoken but allowing a little glee to show through. "I'm in risk situations, but that's okay. It's fun. What this work is, it's very, very neat stuff."

A few years later, long after the events in Trinidad of July 1990, Bob Lindquist was asked whether, even in retrospect, he feels a shiver of apprehension over his near encounter with the Muslim gunslingers. It could have been he who took a shot to the foot. Or worse.

"Me? The *accountant?*" he says. "When one group of people goes after another group with violence in mind, they *never* think of the accountant."

Even a forensic accountant?

Hair, Blood, Semen, DNA:

The Case of the Perfect Science

ANDREA ATKINSON, SIX YEARS old, dressed herself at seven o'clock in the quiet of a Sunday morning in October 1990. She was a pretty little girl, with tangled blonde hair, blue eyes, and a wide mouth that, when she smiled, brought out something in her expression that was almost adult, almost alluring. She dressed carefully, stylishly. She put on navy-blue leotards over her panties, a grey T-shirt that read "Super Star" across the front in pink trim, a grey dress in a Barbie motif, white running shoes, and an orange plastic bracelet on her tiny wrist. She looked adorable.

Her mother's boyfriend was dozing on the sofa in the apartment's living-room. His name was Doug Heinbuch, a macho sort of guy who worked in construction, and, even though Andrea's mother had been dating him only since Labour Day, just six weeks, Andrea had learned to call him Dad. On this morning, Andrea and "Dad" watched cartoons on television for almost an hour. Then Andrea grew restless. She went out to the kitchen and ate cereal and drank a big glass of milk.

Andrea's mother was stirring by now. Ruth Windebank — it was her maiden name — had separated from Andrea's father, Terry

Atkinson, four years earlier, and neither she nor Andrea had seen Atkinson for a year and a half. Ruth thought at one point that Andrea was so hurt and puzzled by the absence of her father that she put Andrea in counselling at the Toronto East General Hospital.

Ruth lived on public assistance, on mother's allowance, in subsidized housing in the CityHome complex at 33 Coatsworth Crescent in the east end of Toronto. She talked of how she "street-proofed" Andrea, how Andrea was her "best friend," how Andrea was "an Aquarius, you know, *creative*." Ruth wrote poetry. She talked with the confidence of a panellist on the Oprah show.

At a couple of minutes before nine, Andrea told her mother she was going to call on her friend Candace Burkett. That was okay by Ruth. Andrea was used to roaming the five-storey building, visiting other tenants, making the place her playground; she wore a little whistle and a key to the building's front door on a shoelace around her neck. Besides, Candace Burkett lived just down the hall from the Windebank apartment on the second floor.

Andrea gathered up the bundle of collector cards of her favourite rock group, New Kids on the Block, shrugged into her bomber jacket, brilliant in pink, white, and green, and headed for the door.

"Have fun, eh," Ruth called after her.

Andrea went past Candace Burkett's apartment without stopping. At least, Candace's father, Frank, heard no knocking on the door at 9 A.M. Rose Kelly heard Andrea knock on *her* apartment door. This was just after nine. Andrea wondered if Rose's granddaughter could come out and play. Rose said it was too early and shut the door. Another tenant, Rosemarie Lornegard, looked through the window from her first-floor apartment at 9:10 and saw Andrea outside. Andrea waved to her. Lornegard waved back. Everybody in the building knew Andrea. A few minutes later, Regina Boudrea, another tenant, noticed Andrea at the rear of the apartment building. Andrea was alone, just looking for someone to play with her.

After that, after 9:15, no one saw Andrea, not for sure. A couple of people later said they thought they had noticed her around the building that morning, but they were apparently mistaken. Andrea didn't seem to be anywhere. Life went on in the Coatsworth apartment building, but Andrea Atkinson took no visible part in it.

Ruth Windebank went looking for her daughter at 11:30 to ask Andrea what she'd like for lunch. She knocked on Frank Burkett's door. Burkett said Ruth was the first person who'd come calling all morning. He hadn't seen Andrea. Ruth tried other apartments. She went outside and shouted Andrea's name. There was no answer. Doug Heinbuch hollered in his deeper, louder, voice. Nothing. Ruth went back to the apartment and smoked a cigarette. At one o'clock, she dialled 911 from a neighbour's phone.

Acting Superintendent Robert Yates of Metro Police's 55 Division was summoned at mid-afternoon on that Sunday, October 14, to assume a command role in the hunt for Andrea Atkinson. Yates ordered a Phase 3, police code for an all-out search, and, over the following nine days, Yates stayed on the job from six in the morning until midnight of each day. He commanded seventy-seven police officers in the search, a canine unit, and a helicopter on loan from the Sûreté du Québec that was equipped with an infrared camera that could pick up the heat of human forms hidden from sight in bushy terrain. Hundreds of citizen volunteers joined in the hunt, ninety students from a law-enforcement course at Humber College, parents of kids from Andrea's grade-one class at Earl Haig Junior Public School, strangers, friends, and Terry Atkinson, Andrea's father. Crews from the Metro Works Department splashed into storm sewers in the neighbourhood, the Police Commission offered a reward of $50,000 for information leading to the arrest and conviction of anyone who might have made off with Andrea, and police set up a command post at Todmorden Mills in the wooded Don Valley, northwest of the Coatsworth building.

Ruth Windebank stuck to her apartment. She wasn't sitting by the phone waiting for word about Andrea; Bell Canada had shut off service four months earlier for non-payment of bills. Ruth stayed in to avoid the media swarm outside the building, the TV cameras and reporters and still photographers. But on Tuesday, a little over forty-eight hours after Andrea disappeared, she and Doug Heinbuch invited the media into the apartment for what she announced was a press conference. People from the newspapers, radio, and television came and took note of Andrea's precious store of toys, the Fisher-Price stove in her bedroom, a drawer heaped with little purses, pictures on her wall of Tom Cruise, Bon Jovi, and Minnie Mouse, a corner of the living-room lined in Barbie dolls, all with blonde hair, some missing an arm, a leg. The TV footage, showing the Barbies, the closet of stuffed toys, had the effect of making the little girl who had played with them, the little girl who wasn't there, seem naked and vulnerable.

At her press conference, Ruth smoked, giggled nervously, talked in quick bursts. Maybe she wasn't an Oprah person after all, not cool, not media hip. She offered extra audiotapes to reporters whose recorders might run short. And she offered a theory to account for Andrea's disappearance.

"I think somebody wants a child real bad," she said, "and if I was that person and I was a little off-balance, didn't have kids of my own, Andrea's the little girl I would want to grab."

The Homicide Squad got into the picture early. There was no body, no suggestion yet of a death, but by Monday afternoon, the day after the disappearance, one team from Homicide's complement of thirty-two officers was nosing around. These were two guys, Rick Gauthier and Tom McNamara, who were new to

Homicide. They had been together just a little over a year, but they'd had a hand in sleuthing several difficult killings – the rape and strangulation of a street woman in the Parkdale district, the stabbing of a young man in the middle of New Year's Eve celebrations on Yonge Street – and both detectives were looked on as comers on the squad. The man who picked Gauthier for Homicide said, "Rick's a natural at this." The man was Deputy Chief Dave Boothby. In late 1994, Boothby, a Homicide graduate himself, was named chief of the Metro Police Force.

Gauthier and McNamara checked out Ruth Windebank. It seemed cruel to hit on the mother, but the detectives were operating on the premise that Ruth could have connections to people who might find reason to harm her or her family. And besides, some things about Ruth came across as slightly wingy; she had a mother and six brothers, but hadn't seem them in years, and the first news *they* had of her, the first they knew she lived on a street called Coatsworth, came in the ghastly stories on TV. Gauthier and McNamara questioned Ruth late on the Monday night. Had Ruth ever worked as a prostitute? Did she use drugs? Owe any large debts? How many guys had she had relations with in the past couple of years? What were their names? Ruth seemed clean. She wanted to take a lie-detector test. She felt humiliated.

All the Coatsworth apartment residents were new to the neighbourhood. So was the building. So was Coatsworth Crescent itself. The area, which covers an acre or two, was cleared out in the late 1980s, the small working-class bungalows that had stood since the First World War had been torn down, and, in their place, the provincial and city governments had put up a CityHome housing project on a curving crescent. The north side of Coatsworth is given over to townhouses and fourplexes, while the apartment building, number 33 Coatsworth, takes up the entire length of the south side. The building has a determined, stubby look, as if it were constructed of Lego blocks. But the architects and designers gave the complex many dashes of colour – tan brick, low green shrubs, and evergreens in the large front courtyard, vivid blues in the play area at the east end. And, all in all, at least in the early years, Coatsworth was resisting the grey, defeated feel of much of the public housing in Toronto.

During the search for Andrea Atkinson, the police made five official sweeps through the apartment building. They checked hallways, stairwells, elevator shafts, and they toured each tenant's apartment, five times for every apartment. "They looked in my freezer," one tenant said, "under my bed, in my microwave." In this thorough fashion, the cops covered all five floors. That was admirable. It also turned out to be a terrible mistake, since, strictly speaking, the apartment building had *six* floors.

The sixth floor consisted of just one small clumpy rectangular block, flush to the front edge, rather like the ultimate piece of Lego at the crown of the structure. A door from the fifth floor led up a short flight of stairs to this final set of rooms. At the top of the stairs, there were two rooms with cement floors. The first, an anteroom, contained a window and, on the west wall, a set of metal stairs that ended in a door to the roof. Across the anteroom, in its north wall, was the door to the boiler room beyond. Smaller than the anteroom, it housed two large boilers and two equally large hot-water tanks. A block on the roof held other equipment – an electrical panel that controlled the fire-alarm system, the elevator hoist that lay behind the east wall of the anteroom – and all of this, the boilers, the alarm system, the other equipment, made the small sixth-floor block a working hub of the apartment building.

But not one police officer in the days of the methodical Phase 3 search for Andrea ever walked up the stairs to examine this sixth floor.

Police Chief Bill McCormack later tried to paper over the omission. "The room was not searched for a specific reason," he said at a press conference on December 3, more than a month after

Andrea vanished. That cryptic remark was all that McCormack offered, as if the explanation hinged on some deep and for-police-eyes-only information too rarefied to be trusted to ordinary citizens. The "specific reason" was never referred to again. It probably never existed, and, in the end, Acting Superintendent Robert Yates, the man who had devoted eighteen-hour days to the search for Andrea, was the guy who, in public, was hung out to dry over the matter of the sixth floor that was ignored. This would come two years later, when Yates was compelled to say in court, "The bottom line is we failed to search the room. It was our responsibility to do it, and we didn't do it. On behalf of the Division, I apologize."

"Did you ever look *up?*" Yates was asked by a lawyer. "You mean to say you never saw the *top* of the building? The *room* up there?"

"Obviously, sir, yes," Yates answered bravely and sheepishly. He *saw* the room. He just never inquired whether anyone had *searched* it.

Robert Yates had retired from the police force by this time. He had moved far away, out west to British Columbia.

He was probably glad to be far from the scene of the Atkinson case, because it was in the boiler room of the sixth-floor block in the Coatsworth Crescent apartment building that somebody, not a police officer, finally found Andrea's raped and murdered body.

Lake Persaud was CityHome's on-site chief at the Coatsworth apartment. His title was building superintendent. But Persaud was out of the city on holidays on the Sunday Andrea disappeared, and, since he didn't return until later in the week, he had little role in the search. He also had an alibi when the trouble came down.

In Persaud's absence, the assistant superintendent, Howie Schmidt, was in temporary charge. Schmidt was a chunky guy, close to forty, with a buccaneer's moustache and a chip-on-the-shoulder attitude. He lived alone in an apartment on the fifth floor of Coatsworth. He knew Andrea, and he *really* knew Ruth; the two had had an affair a few months earlier, a romance that was broken up, Schmidt said, by too much drinking on both sides. Booze was what kept Schmidt out of the drama over Andrea on Sunday afternoon. He was tending to a massive hangover he'd acquired at a party in another part of the city the night before. He'd also picked up a cut on the nose when a fellow guest punched him out. Even if he was in temporary charge of the building, Howie Schmidt just felt like lying low on Sunday.

Next day, Monday, back on the job, Schmidt made a quick trip to the roof during his coffee break. He later insisted he had no special reason for choosing the roof; he was just taking his break up there, smoking a cigarette, looking down at all the cops milling around the neighbourhood. To reach the roof, Schmidt had to open the door to the stairs that led from the fifth floor to the block on top of the apartment building. The door was locked. It was always locked. Schmidt had a key to it. So did Lake Persaud and the three people who worked as cleaners in the building.

Schmidt unlocked the door and climbed the stairs to the ante-room. Right away, on the anteroom floor, something caught his eye. It was round and orange, maybe a ring. He didn't pick up the ring. He stared at it, and he thought maybe the ring was Andrea's. Maybe, lying on the floor like that, it meant, Jesus, she was up *here*.

Schmidt crossed the floor to the boiler-room door. It was kept locked, too. The same key that opened the lower door unlocked the boiler-room door. Schmidt unlocked the boiler room, pushed the door back about a foot and a half, and peeked in. He just took a glimpse, nothing more, and all he saw in there were the boilers and the water tanks. That was it. He shut the door and relocked it. He felt relieved.

When Howie Schmidt came down from the sixth floor, he didn't say a word to the police about his trip to the block of rooms upstairs. He didn't say a word about the *existence* of the block of rooms on top of the building.

"*They* were doing the search," Schmidt said much later by way of explaining his silence, the chip teetering on his shoulder. "It was up to *them*."

In fact, two whole years went by before Schmidt thought to tell anyone about seeing the "ring" on the anteroom floor that Monday. By then, the police had long since found the orange object for themselves. It was Andrea Atkinson's plastic bracelet.

Two more people visited the sixth floor on the Monday after Andrea's disappearance. They were two of the three cleaners in the building, Phil Payne and Elese Roberts. Neither had entered into the excitement over the little girl's vanishing on Sunday, Roberts because she was off duty and at home, Payne because he'd arranged for the third cleaner, Johnny Terceira, to work his weekend shift while he went to a wedding in Oshawa. The wedding was held on Saturday night, but Payne expected to knock back a few celebratory drinks – and he did, a whole forty-ouncer of rye whiskey – and planned to stay over in an Oshawa hotel for Sunday-morning recuperation.

By Monday, Payne was back in the Coatsworth building, and he and Elese let themselves into the sixth-floor anteroom. They were there for the reason that had apparently drawn Schmidt two hours earlier, a break from work, curiosity, a good place to watch the cops. Payne pushed open the door to the roof and walked to the edge. Elese hung back at the roof door. She was frightened of heights. From their two different vantage points, they stared at the police action down below for ten or fifteen minutes.

Back inside the anteroom, the two lingered a little longer, feeling slightly spooked by events, the missing girl, all the cops around the place.

"She couldn't be up here, could she?" Elese said. "In there? In the boiler room?"

"If she's in there," Payne said, "I'll shit."

Payne unlocked the boiler-room door and peered in. He didn't step inside the room, didn't hold the door open for more than a few seconds. "There isn't nothing here," he said.

He locked the door, and the two hurried away from the sixth floor. They hadn't seen a body, hadn't noticed anything suspicious, not even the orange plastic bracelet on the floor of the anteroom.

But Elese Roberts couldn't shake an eerie sensation.

"You know," she said a day or two later to the other cleaner, Johnny Terceira, "I can't get over the feeling I got she's still in the building, that little girl."

"No fuckin' way," Terceira said.

Roberts and Payne, like Schmidt, mentioned nothing to the police about the sixth-floor rooms. It just didn't occur to them. That was how they later explained their silence on the point. For that matter, it apparently didn't occur to Terceira either.

Late on the morning of Tuesday, October 23, nine days after Andrea disappeared, nine days of police searching and investigating, a CityHome supervisor, John Clarke, stopped by the Coatsworth apartment building to pick up an employee he'd sent around earlier to inspect the building's emergency lighting system. Clarke couldn't immediately find his employee, and he asked Elese Roberts to help him track down the man. Roberts suggested they look in the rooms on the sixth floor. There was lighting equipment up there. Roberts, using her key, opened the door from the fifth floor and led Clarke to the stairs.

"What's the smell in this place?" Clarke asked. The two had reached the anteroom. "It's foul, whatever it is."

"I haven't been up here in a while," Roberts said. "Yeah, the stink's awful."

"Like sewer gas. It smells to me like something's leaking. Sewer gas, maybe."

Roberts unlocked the door to the boiler room. Inside, on the left, were the two large square boilers, and on the right, the two large hot-water tanks. Roberts, standing in the doorway, glimpsed something in front of her, something that warned her away from the room. It was a long stain, running from under the boiler on her immediate right, the boiler closest to the door, to the drain near the centre of the floor. The stain was faint and pinkish.

Roberts moved back, out of the doorway.

"Listen, why don't you look in there?" she said to Clarke. "I don't like this."

Clarke stepped into the boiler room and, stooping over, peered under the near boiler.

"A flash of colours hit me," he said much later. "It seemed to be a bundle. Two colours stood out, mauve or pink and turquoise or green."

That's what John Clarke said much later, when he'd had time to reflect. What he said at the moment he looked under the tank was something less analytical and more instinctive.

He said, "Oh my God, it's the little girl!"

Phil Sudeyko and Rick Bunting work with tweezers. Both men are detectives with the Metro Police's Forensic Identification Unit. Their job is to handle the picky stuff at a homicide scene, to go over the area around a body on the lookout for tiny clues, for any item the killer might have left behind, a hair, a fragment of clothing material. They collect the clues and pass them on to the people at the Centre of Forensic Sciences for deep analysis. Up on the sixth-floor block at 33 Coatsworth, the clue-gathering called for much, much tweezer work.

Sudeyko and Bunting arrived at Coatsworth by 1:30 P.M., a little over an hour after John Clarke came across Andrea Atkinson's body. Bunting was the cameraman of the team, and he videotaped the crime scene from the fifth-floor door, up the stairs, across the anteroom, into the boiler room, where Andrea's body lay half-hidden behind one boiler. After that, Bunting lit the anteroom with low-lying lamps that beamed across the floor, then took still photographs from the same worm's-eye level. The idea was to pick up on film any disturbance in the dust, shoeprints, scuff marks. Clues.

Bunting did his photography from inside an area he had marked off with yellow tape. The tape ran along the floor parallel to and three or four feet out from the room's west wall. The police called this the contaminated area. It defined the free space around the edges where anyone coming into the room could step. No cops, except Bunting and Sudeyko, could stride around the rest of the anteroom, disturbing the dust, enlarging the contaminated area, putting their size twelves on top of small articles that might be clues.

Of course, before Sudeyko and Bunting even got to the scene, other people, rushing to the sixth floor in the first thrill and horror of discovering Andrea's body, had already trampled the two rooms. Terry Denvir and Derek Flatman, the two young constables on duty in the apartment building at the time John Clarke found Andrea, the two to whom Clarke reported his grisly news, had both trotted through the rooms. The detectives from Homicide, Rick Gauthier and Tom McNamara, had walked the two rooms. Lake Persaud, for heaven's sake, the building superintendent, had got his feet on the scene. All of them, especially the senior police, minded where they stepped, but the whole area had become at least slightly contaminated during the period before Sudeyko and Bunting got down to their work's fine strokes. Oh well, they took the crime scene as they found it.

At 3:35 P.M., Sudeyko and Bunting laid a ladder horizontally across the floor of the anteroom. The ladder was their operating platform, a way of keeping their feet off the floor. They stretched themselves prone on the rungs, and went on the hunt for hairs, fibres, and whatever else the anteroom might yield. This was eyeball-intensive labour. Each guy would spot a hair or zero in on a fibre, devilishly minuscule damned things. Then he'd snaffle it with his tweezers, drop it in a folded piece of paper, seal the paper in an envelope, and mark the envelope with an exhibit number.

The work wasn't as cut and dried as it might seem, not as *final*. For instance, Sudeyko and Bunting couldn't always be sure which items they tweezed, so alike to the eye, really were hairs and which really were fibres. They marked the envelopes "hair" or "fibre" or "hair/fibre," but left it to a trained expert, the hair-and-fibre specialist at the Centre of Forensic Sciences, to sort out the true identification.

Then there was the smear on the floor, what looked like blood or blood mixed with some other fluid. It was better for now to work around the smear. Test it later. Or pass on the job to the blood-and-semen guy from the CFS. Thank God for the orange bracelet. No problem there. It was just sitting on the floor near a wall, waiting to be found. It was once precious, this bracelet, to the little girl who wore it. Now she was dead, and it was a forlorn piece of plastic in the dust of the floor. Sudeyko placed it in an evidence envelope.

Sudeyko and Bunting worked the anteroom in a U, starting from the north wall, moving south in a loop that took them back north to the threshold of the boiler room. By 6:05 P.M., they hadn't finished with the anteroom floor, not by a long shot. More hairs and fibres lay there for their tweezers to seize, but that could wait till the next day and the days after. It was time to get to the boiler room, get at Andrea. The pathologist would want the body out of there. He'd already come by late in the afternoon. Dr. Noel McAuliffe, an Irishman from County Cork, was now the number-one pathologist at Ontario's Forensic Pathology Branch. He said he'd be doing the autopsy on Andrea Atkinson's body next morning at the Coroner's Building on Grenville Street.

The body was in a space between a boiler and the wall. It seemed to be not so much forced into the space, not stuffed into it, but more as if it had been discarded there. Whoever did the discarding had put Andrea down on her left side. Then the person had tucked the little girl's upper body into the bright pink, white, and green bomber jacket. The sleeves of the jacket had been pulled inside out. Andrea's other clothes were more or less in place, though the navy-blue leotards had been folded down just over her hips, and her T-shirt, the one with "Super Star" in pink, rode up on the left side of her torso. Both shoes were on her feet. It was Andrea Atkinson in the space behind the boiler, but an Andrea that was nine days dead, bloated and decomposing into a horror-movie caricature of herself.

Sudeyko and Bunting didn't go immediately to the body. They worked over the room first. It was excruciating in there, at a temperature of thirty-two degrees Celsius, the air thick with the putrefaction of flesh, the small dead body close by the men, in sight each time one of them faced in its direction.

Sudeyko and Bunting gathered some obvious stuff off the floor. A cigarette butt. Some cards scattered close to the body. Those made a sight to bring tears to the eye, Andrea's cards, the New Kids on the Block collection. She'd left home clutching them nine days earlier. They were still with her. The two detectives picked up the cards with tweezers and filed them in the usual evidence envelopes.

Then, given the narrow confines of the boiler room, rather smaller than the anteroom, the detectives decided to do a static lift on the floor. They spread a large piece of Mylar over the section of the floor between the boilers and the hot-water tanks. Mylar is a brand of polyester film, and when Sudeyko and Bunting gave it an electrical charge, the sheet sucked up hairs, fibres, the outlines of footprints, and anything else that was resting on the floor's surface. Once the Mylar had done its task, the two men wrapped it in a clear plastic sheet and lugged it out of the room for later examination. It was hot, dusty, tedious, tiring work, and when the two finished, shortly after 10 P.M., the body-removal people had arrived. It was time for the grimmest job of all.

The body-removal people weren't actually going to do what their name implied: lift Andrea's body out of the boiler room and take it away. They'd carry it down from the sixth floor, all right, and drive it off in an ambulance. But it was Sudeyko and Bunting who would handle the horrible touching and manoeuvring in the boiler room. They put on special gear that the body-removal people had brought for the purpose: white cloth suits with hoods and gloves. Then the two men, looking like NASA technicians, squeezed around the boiler in position to raise the body. They considered for a moment whether they should first examine Andrea's clothing for hairs, fibres, clues, but decided the tiny area was too cramped for efficiency. That examination would come a little later at the morgue.

Sudeyko began the removal operation by lifting the pink, white, and green jacket from where it had been folded over Andrea's upper body, and sliding it into the foot of the body bag that the body-removal people had supplied. The bag was also white, and it was in a child's size. Then, gingerly, awkwardly, Sudeyko and Bunting raised Andrea from behind the boiler. She was almost weightless. Gently, the two detectives fitted her into the body bag and, pulling up the bag's zipper, closed her out of sight. Sudeyko marked the bag with an exhibit seal.

The two of them carried the bag out of the boiler room. Somehow the balance of the bag didn't feel right. Or maybe neither guy had the correct grip on it. They stopped, lowered the bag to the floor, and regrouped. A drop of bloody liquid fell from the bottom of the bag. What the hell was this? As they inspected the bag, it was clear the bloody stuff hadn't leaked *through* the bag. It must have been picked up in the loading and lifting of the body. And thank God it had dripped onto the floor in the anteroom's contaminated area. It wasn't a clue – it was an *accident*. The two guys made notes of what had happened. Nobody wanted a screw-up on this case.

Sudeyko and Bunting transferred the bag to a stretcher, and somebody threw a blue blanket over the bag. Down at the entrance to the apartment building, there were sixty or seventy people standing around, tenants, press, neighbours, all of them silent. They watched as an ambulance took Andrea Atkinson's remains and drove them off to the morgue, in the Coroner's Building downtown.

A few hours into the morning on October 24, at 1:56 A.M., Phil Sudeyko showed up at the morgue. He was there to inspect the outside of Andrea's clothing for hairs and fibres before Noel McAuliffe began the autopsy later that morning. Sudeyko broke the seal on the body bag, unzipped it, made an eye check of the leotards, the T-shirt, the jacket, and decided this was a job for the Luma-Lite.

The Luma-Lite, invented in the late 1980s by John Watkins, a scientist at the National Research Council in Ottawa, is a portable high-intensity laser that can fluoresce everything, from fibres to bloodstains to fingerprints. It packs amazing power. In one British Columbia case, the RCMP thought they had success-fully tracked a hit-and-run driver whose car had killed a woman. But the suspect had washed and waxed his car before the Mounties reached him. The car seemed clean of incriminating traces until the RCMP Identification officer trained a Luma-Lite on the vehicle. It picked up a thread of synthetic material, no more than two millimetres long, stuck in a minuscule nick on the car's front grille. The thread was a match to material in the dead woman's clothing. Thanks to the Luma-Lite, the Mounties got their man.

Phil Sudeyko had brought Dick Wiszoiwski to the morgue with him. Wiszoiwski was another detective from the Forensic Identification Unit, and he was a whiz with the Luma-Lite. He got down to cases with the portable Luma, and, over the next hour or so, the detectives picked off Andrea's clothing at least one hair and many, many fibres. Sudeyko filed the new stuff in exhibit envelopes, and at 3:03 A.M., he zipped the body back in the body bag, resealed it, and returned it to the refrigerated locker marked with Andrea Atkinson's name.

The autopsy began at 10:50 A.M. on October 24, and Andrea drew a full house. The two Homicide detectives were there, Rick Gauthier and Tom McNamara. So were Sudeyko and Bunting. A scientist named Jim Crocker came over from the Centre of Forensic Sciences. And McAuliffe, the pathologist, had four assistants in tow. One of them was Dr. Barry Blinkerstop.

For the early part of the autopsy, Blinkerstop and Sudeyko worked in tandem. Blinkerstop removed Andrea's clothes. Sudeyko received delivery of them. The shoes, leotards, T-shirt, underwear, all of it, all that was on Andrea's body, including the shoelace holding the whistle and key – Blinkerstop took them off and handed them to Sudeyko, who put them in paper bags. Later, Sudeyko walked the bags of clothing a block north to the Centre of Forensic Sciences, where he hung the clothes in a special room, the centre's drying room. Andrea's clothes needed to dry. They were soaked in her bodily fluids.

The clothes weren't all that Sudeyko took away from the autopsy. He also took hair samples that Blinkerstop pulled from Andrea's scalp, prints of Andrea's fingertips on both hands, fingernail clippings from both hands, and swabs from Andrea's mouth, vagina, and anus. And he took two loose hairs that Noel McAuliffe found on Andrea's body at the start of the autopsy, one hair stuck high on the left thigh, the other matted on the right thigh. Sudeyko packed the hairs and everything else in exhibit envelopes for his delivery run to the CFS.

Parts of Andrea's body, as McAuliffe noted for all present, were squishy with decomposition fluid. This fluid consisted of bacteria, blood, fat, muscle, and skin all turning into liquid in Andrea's decaying body. Over the days in the hot boiler room, blisters had formed on the outside of the body. Some of the blisters had broken and released streams of the fluid. That was what the cleaner, Elese Roberts, had spotted on the floor of the boiler room on the day she and John Clarke found Andrea's body, the dried pinkish rivulet of decomposition fluid that had flowed from the body to the drain.

But, for all the ghastly condition of Andrea's body, the bloating and decomposing, McAuliffe could still track the damage that had been inflicted on it. The vagina, he pointed out, had a tear in it that measured from one to two centimetres long. The tear extended backwards towards Andrea's rectum, and it was, McAuliffe said, "a traumatic tear." What did he mean by that term? He meant that "it's an injury a blunt force causes." Something, a grown man's penis, maybe, had pounded into the little girl's vagina. It left the vagina, McAuliffe estimated, "enlarged by twice its normal size."

But it wasn't the blow to the vagina that caused Andrea's death. Nor was it the broken bones that they found in Andrea's skull that had killed her. McAuliffe was inclined to think, judging from the lack of bruising under the scalp, the lack of bleeding under the skull, that the breaks in the skull bones had happened after she was dead, that the pressure built up by interior gases had erupted and cracked the skull at its growth points, at the points in Andrea's skull that were waiting to accommodate her brain when she became older and her brain grew in size. The skull fractures didn't kill Andrea.

What did?

Asphyxia, McAuliffe said. She'd suffocated. She'd stopped breathing. But McAuliffe couldn't say how that happened, couldn't figure out for sure what caused the asphyxia. It wasn't the shoelace around her neck, the one that held the key and whistle. The skin under the lace showed discolouring, but that didn't necessarily mean the lace had been used as a ligature to strangle Andrea. McAuliffe was more inclined to think that the swelling of the body over its nine days in the boiler room had caused Andrea's neck to press into the lace. That's what brought on the discolouring.

Many things about Andrea's condition pointed to her violent death by asphyxia: the tongue clenched between her teeth, the congested sinuses, the completely emptied bowels. But *how* did she stop breathing? Why? Was she smothered? Or choked? Or throttled? By a hand at the throat? Or by something else, such as a piece of clothing pushed into her face until she was forever still?

"I believe Andrea Atkinson's death was due to asphyxia," Noel McAuliffe said, "but the method the killer used I can only speculate [on]."

Metro Police 55 Division isn't far from the Coatsworth apartment building, just over on Coxwell Avenue and south. That was where, on the two days after Andrea's body was found, the detectives from Homicide, Rick Gauthier and Tom McNamara, backed up by four or five colleagues, interviewed men whose names had already surfaced in the case, guys who lived or worked in the apartment building. Once again, Howie Schmidt told the cops about his Sunday-morning hangover from the party at which the other guest bopped him in the nose. And Phil Payne repeated his tale about the wedding and the forty-ouncer of rye whiskey. This time the detectives put the stories in writing and asked each guy – Schmidt, Payne, Doug Heinbuch – to read and sign his statement.

"Something else you can help us with," the detectives said to each. "This is a six-year-old girl that's been brutally murdered. Don't ever forget that. And you can help us find the bastard who did it. All we want is a sample of your blood. Samples from your hair, too. It's painless, don't worry about that, but it'll clear certain things up. Eliminate people from being suspects, you understand? It's strictly voluntary on your part. Up to you."

Everybody who was asked gave blood and hair. There was a system to the procedure. The cops would ruffle a guy's scalp, loosening hairs, then run a comb over the scalp to pick up the loose hairs. To ensure they got some hairs with the roots attached, the police would also just plain yank a sampling of the scalp hair. Next, the guy – Schmidt, Payne, Heinbuch – would lower his pants and underwear and allow a cop to comb and pull some pubic hairs. The analysts at the Centre of Forensic Sciences, who eventually examine such hairs, prefer that, in cases like this, the police bring them about eighty scalp hairs and twenty-five pubic hairs from each man. The cops don't always remember to go for that many hairs, but with Schmidt, Payne, and Heinbuch, they got generous enough samples.

As for the blood, the cops pricked each guy's finger and soaked small quantities into pieces of gauze. These are called blood suspensions. Later on, Howie Schmidt's blood suspension proved to be too weak for definitive testing, and a police detective drove Schmidt to a hospital, where a nurse ran a needle into Howie's vein and took a whole blood sample. Also later on, in the first week of November, the police took samples of another bodily fluid from each man. This time, it was saliva.

Johnny Terceira, the third Coatsworth cleaner, had also wiped himself out on booze on the Saturday night before Andrea disappeared. Det. Gary Atchison interviewed Terceira, and Terceira told a tale of consuming alcohol, and drugs, too, in staggering quantities.

Terceira said he started Saturday evening with six beers and a couple of joints of marijuana at home. He lived with his mother, grandmother, sister, two brothers, and one brother's girlfriend on Beaconsfield Avenue, a heavily Portuguese, working-class neighbourhood in Toronto's near west end. From home, Terceira had ridden the streetcar a few blocks to one of his favourite hangouts, Diane's Café at Queen and Manning. John the Bird was there, a pal, though Terceira never mastered John the Bird's last name. The two guys ordered drinks. Terceira had seven or eight beers and, somewhere in there, he downed a shot of Tequila and smoked a joint.

About 12:30, Terceira and John the Bird left Diane's and drove in another guy's car to a house where crack was going around. Terceira smoked a quarter gram. Later, finally back home, at 5:30 in the morning, he felt like something cool to level the crack. He looked in the fridge. Ah, a cold beer. The first one tasted like more, and he didn't stop until he'd finished six beers.

It was light out by now, seven o'clock, the hour that Terceira was supposed to report to Coatsworth, subbing for Phil Payne. He changed his clothes, put on blue sweatpants, a red lumber shirt, and construction boots, and took the bus – the subway didn't run until nine on Sunday – across town to Coatsworth.

Maybe it was Johnny Terceira's youth that kept him on his feet; all that alcohol and crack, no sleep, and he was still moving. He was eighteen years old, a small, prettyish boy, with masses of black hair. Experience with the hard stuff helped, too; he'd been a drinker since he was ten years old and he got seriously into drugs at fifteen, into hash, cocaine, marijuana. Not a day went by now that he didn't smoke up, didn't drink some beers. His father before him was an alcoholic. Johnny hadn't seen the old man in years.

But, that Sunday morning, Terceira's body wasn't entirely immune to the previous hours' debauch. He told Det. Gary Atchison that he threw up at work. He said he got a 7-Up out of the machine at the Coatsworth apartment, then, he said, he "started puking." As Terceira told the story, he grinned and shrugged at Atchison. The detective nodded. He thought Johnny was probably a nice enough kid, a little wild, but likeable.

Terceira said that, on the Sunday morning at Coatsworth, he tried to handle some work, picking up papers in the playground, checking out the laundry room for cleaning. But mostly he just felt lousy. As a matter of fact, he said, the crack from the night before was making him "depressed and spaced out." There wasn't much happening around the building anyway, not much work to do, not many people in sight. He didn't talk to anybody. Sure as hell he didn't see the little girl, Andrea. He threw up again and decided the hell with it, he was going home. It was about 9:30 A.M., and Terceira reached his house, after a stop along the way for a coffee, and after riding the subway and bus, just before 11:00. He spent the rest of the day dozing, drinking Coke, and watching cartoons on TV.

Atchison asked Terceira about the boiler room on the sixth floor.

"I been up there once in my life that I remember," Terceira answered. "This was like a week before the little girl was missing. A week before any of that happened."

Would Terceira give the police samples of his blood and hair (and, later, of his saliva)?

The kid grinned. "No problem."

Gary Larson cartoons are pinned to the wall of Jim Crocker's work space on the third floor of the Centre of Forensic Sciences. One cartoon shows a medical examiner leaning over a body. The examiner is surrounded by other guys in white smocks, and he's telling them, "Off hand, I'd say a blunt instrument did the job." The body is lying in a bowling alley.

Crocker is a senior forensic analyst in the CFS's biology section. His specialty is trace evidence. That means he knows just about everything worth knowing in the realm of hair and fibres. He's a good-natured, avuncular man. He brings amazing concentration to his work and produces astounding results, but he doesn't appear to take himself particularly seriously. He's just the sort of fellow you'd expect to decorate his office with Gary Larson cartoons.

The cops were quick to let Jim Crocker know his services

would be in heavy demand in the Andrea Atkinson case. Phil Sudeyko and Rick Bunting, Crocker was told, were gathering hairs and fibres in big numbers. So, just to put himself in the picture, Crocker attended Andrea's autopsy on Thursday morning, the twenty-fourth, and the next morning, he went up to the Coatsworth building to examine the crime scene. Before he left the CFS for Coatsworth, Crocker had a chat with Keith Kelder, another member of the biology section, an expert in blood and semen. Kelder asked Crocker to get the lay of the land for him, too. What was the blood and semen situation at the crime scene?

Crocker spent three hours in the anteroom and boiler room on the sixth floor. Sudeyko and Bunting were there, still collecting hairs and fibres, still combing the rooms for fine clues. Crocker worked alongside them, keeping busy. He got down on his hands and knees and surveyed the anteroom in the illumination of the oblique lighting. He was trying to form some notion of how dirty the cement floor was (quite clean, as a matter of fact), how widely the hairs and fibres might be spread (all over the place), what the number of extraneous hairs might be, hairs that had simply dropped off the clothing of cops and others who had walked through the rooms, hairs that would turn out to have no connection whatsoever to the case (probably a great many of those).

Sudeyko and Bunting asked Crocker to take a look at some scuff marks on the anteroom floor. Could they be parts of shoeprints that might point to someone? Possible clues? Crocker had brought along a portable stereomicroscope, in effect a powerful microscope, and he studied the scuff marks. Nope, he said after a while. No residue there, nothing in these marks that could lead anywhere interesting.

Next, Crocker tended to his errand for Keith Kelder, and here he set in motion a series of events that became crucial in the resolution of the entire Andrea Atkinson case. Sudeyko and Bunting pointed out to Crocker the smear on the anteroom floor, the one they'd noted on their first sweep around the room two days earlier. The smear was very small, greyish, and about three or four feet in front of the metal stairs that led up to the roof door. The first thing Crocker noticed, by the by, was that two hairs were stuck to the smear. One looked chewed up – insect damage, no doubt. That hair would be useless. Maybe the other would hint at something revealing. Then it was on to the tests for blood and semen. These were very preliminary tests, nothing definitive, just something to indicate what sort of action Keith Kelder could expect. Using chemicals and other materials that Kelder had supplied, Crocker treated a tiny corner of the smear for blood. The test came up positive. Then he got out another piece of equipment, an ultraviolet light, and aimed it at the smear. Something on the floor fluoresced. That might indicate the presence of semen.

Blood *and* semen?

Crocker went back to the CFS and reported his finds to Kelder.

Keith Kelder is a tall, slim, fair-skinned, balding man. His eyes, above dark circles, are set fairly deep in his head, and give off an air of assurance. There's no pedantry to Kelder, but he's a very positive man, positive about himself and his science.

As soon as he spoke to Jim Crocker on Friday afternoon, Kelder hurried to the anteroom on the sixth floor of the Coatsworth building. Detectives Sudeyko and Bunting directed him to the famous smear. Kelder bent down, studied the floor, and thought, wait a minute, there were actually *two* small smears or stains here. One was greyish, okay, and the other, close to the first but distinctly different, was much more red in colour. He tested the greyish smear for semen. It registered negative. Nothing surprising about that. Jim Crocker might have suspected the presence of semen because something on the floor fluoresced under the ultraviolet light, but ultraviolet light can make other materials fluoresce too.

Kelder switched his attention to the second, redder, stain and set out to test it for semen. First he let a drop of distilled water fall into a small piece of filter paper. He gently dabbed the dampened paper into the bottom-left portion of the stain. That gave him a smudge of stain on the paper. He rubbed the paper with a tiny amount of reagent. A reagent is a substance used to produce a chemical reaction. In this case, the reagent was a benzamine, which detects acid phosphatase, which is an ingredient of semen. When Kelder rubbed the reagent across the filter paper with the bit of stain on it, the paper turned a purple-blue shade. Bingo. That colour change meant the stain was positive for semen. Kelder's heart beat a little faster. He tested the stain for blood. It came up positive, too. The stain was weak on blood, not much of it, but the semen, on the contrary, seemed to be strong and in good supply.

"Right there, at that point, I stopped what I was doing," Kelder said later. "Foremost in my mind was, let's go back to the lab and get some idea about how best to sample the semen and preserve it for DNA. Semen is rich in DNA, and from this particular semen, we could get a profile of the man who left it. I knew I had something significant."

It was the first time in the Andrea Atkinson case that somebody had solid reason to think in terms of DNA. Kelder and other people at the CFS had *thought* about DNA, *speculated* about it, about the chances of using it as a tool in the sleuthing. But that was just conjecture, theory, blue-sky stuff. Now, with Kelder's find, he figured they were moving into reality, and if he was right, this would be the centre's first major DNA case.

It was late on Friday afternoon when Kelder finished at Coatsworth, and Monday morning rolled around before he had a chance to confer with Pamela Newall. She was the head of the centre's DNA unit, and she shared Kelder's heightened sense of anticipation over the DNA possibilities in the Atkinson case. There was nothing particularly exotic or even tricky about the method

Kelder and Newall decided on for taking up the semen from the anteroom floor. It was just a matter of being careful and cautious and not blowing a good thing now that it seemed so close.

Back at Coatsworth later Monday morning, Kelder got out a simple Q-Tip, a swab, and crouching down, steady of hand, he rubbed the swab across the stain from end to end. When he finished, he placed the swab in a sterile container and got out a second clean Q-Tip. He repeated the rubbing process on the semen stain until nothing remained of it. It was all on the swabs in the containers. Kelder went back to the centre carrying the precious store of semen. The DNA unit would be pleased.

On that Monday afternoon, and over the following couple of weeks, Kelder and his associates in the blood-and-semen section worked their own bag of tricks on a tiny portion of the semen from one of the swabs.

To begin, Kelder subjected the semen to blood testing. It's a property of semen that it can reveal the blood type of the man who ejaculated it. Is the guy blood type A, B, AB, or O? The semen might tell. When Kelder put the semen in the stain to ABO testing, it registered O.

But there was a complication. The semen in the floor stain was mixed with blood. There was not much blood, very little in fact, not even enough for any kind of helpful analysis. Still, the blood raised a conundrum. Suppose the blood was Andrea's, a conclusion that seemed entirely logical, if not a sure thing. Kelder knew from Andrea's medical records that her blood type was O, but it wasn't known whether she was a secretor or a non-secretor. A secretor is a person who produces his or her ABO type in bodily secretions, in saliva, semen, and vaginal fluids; a non-secretor does not produce his or her ABO type in these secretions. Another fact is that, when bodily fluids from two people are mixed, vaginal fluids with semen for example, and if the vaginal fluids are from an O secretor, then the O secretor's fluids will mask the blood type of the man whose semen is in the mix if the man is a non-secretor. So, given that Andrea was an O, Kelder was led to two conclusions. If Andrea was a secretor, then the blood type of the man who left the semen could not be A, B, or AB; it could only be O. And if Andrea was a non-secretor, then the semen had to have come from an O secretor.

Now Kelder turned to the samples of blood that the cops had brought in, samples from the men at the Coatsworth apartment building, and he put them through the ABO testing.

Howie Schmidt was a B.

Phil Payne was another B.

Doug Heinbuch was an A.

And Johnny Terceira was an O.

Next, Kelder tested the saliva samples from the Coatsworth men.

Schmidt was a B secretor.

Payne was likewise a B secretor.

Heinbuch was an A secretor.

And Terceira was an O secretor.

Thus, as far as Keith Kelder's tests were concerned, Schmidt, Payne, and Heinbuch were eliminated as suspects in Andrea's rape and murder. But Terceira, the O secretor, remained in the picture as a suspect. It was Terceira – or it was a man as yet unknown to Kelder and the cops.

Kelder and his associates did more testing, much more. Even before Kelder had lifted the stain from the anteroom floor on the Monday afternoon, he had studied it from every angle. He had put the ultraviolet light on it, and had concluded that the two fluids in the stain, the semen and the blood, were mixed before they hit the floor, and they arrived together in one small, ugly splat.

Then there were Andrea's clothes. At the CFS, Kelder examined them for semen stains. The clothes reeked of the little girl's decomposition fluids, which meant Kelder couldn't carry out the testing in the third-floor workrooms. "The smell would have grossed everybody out," he said. He took the clothes to the area the centre calls its bio-hazard rooms, a place where the smell could be contained from the rest of the building. And there, Kelder, alone with the awful odour, went at the clothes with a wet-press technique.

What he did was press sheets of wet filter paper into sections of Andrea's clothing, into her leotards, her panties, her jacket. The semen, wherever there *was* semen on the clothes, transferred to the filter paper. This transferring wasn't a process that was visible to the eye. But when Kelder treated the filter paper with the test reagent, the paper turned the familiar purple-blue in spots where semen was present. It seemed to be widely spread. There was semen on the back of Andrea's panties, both inside and outside; semen on the outer surface of her leotards at the back; semen on the lower half of her dress at the back, inside and outside. There was no semen on Andrea's shoes or jacket. And – this was disappointing to Kelder – there wasn't enough semen in all the clothing to test for ABO typing. But – and this was definitely *not* disappointing – there appeared to be sufficient semen, especially on the leotards, for DNA testing.

In yet another series of tests, Kelder examined the swabs that had been taken at the autopsy from Andrea's mouth, vagina, and anus. He was looking for semen. He found none. Whoever had raped and killed Andrea, it seemed, had not ejaculated in any of her bodily orifices. But he had sprayed her clothes with his semen.

Jim Crocker, the hair-and-fibre specialist, has a cute little analogy that he uses to explain the composition of a hair. A hair, he says, can be compared to a pencil. The root end of a hair, the part that comes out of the scalp or other area of the body, is like the eraser end of the pencil. The other end of a hair is sharp, like the point at the pencil's writing end. The outer layer of a hair, which is called the cuticle, is very thin, made of clear, overlapping cells. It's comparable to the paint on the pencil. Underneath the cuticle is a layer called the cortex. It contains the hair's pigmentation, and it's analogous to the wood in the pencil. The third and final element in a hair is the central cellular area, which is called the medulla. It's like the lead in the pencil.

The analogy works nicely as a way of understanding the hair's structure, but the real brain-teaser in Crocker's line of science comes when he goes about the business of comparing hairs from two different sources. All hairs, with their cuticles and medullas and cortexes, may be comparable to pencils, but coming to Crocker from the different sources, possibly from different bodies, they vary in ways that only an expert like Crocker can detect. The hairs may differ in degree of coarseness and in degree of curl, in pigmentation, in thickness and thinness, and in various other characteristics. Even hairs on the same scalp may show minor dissimilarities; for example, the pigment may be concentrated three centimetres from the end of one hair and five centimetres from the end of its neighbour. It takes someone with Crocker's trained and practised eye to work out the difference, to be able to declare, for instance, that the two hairs with the pigment concentrated at minutely different distances from their respective ends are actually microscopically similar. (No two hairs are ever identical. They are either different or they are "microscopically similar.")

Crocker's daunting chore in the Andrea Atkinson case was to compare two batches of hairs – those connected to the crime scene, and those collected from the suspects, from Schmidt, Payne, Terceira, and Heinbuch, plus the hairs pulled from Andrea's scalp during the autopsy. If possible, Crocker, in addition, was to pinpoint hairs from the first group that were microscopically similar to hairs from the second group.

He had dozens and dozens of hairs in the first group, the hairs tweezered from the cement floors at 33 Coatsworth by

Detectives Sudeyko and Bunting, the hairs found on Andrea's body during the autopsy, the hairs that Crocker himself lifted off Andrea's clothing when he, like Keith Kelder, examined the smelly garments in the CFS's bio-hazard room. He had almost as many hairs in the second group, the hairs that the cops had clipped, pulled, and yanked from the suspects. But at least, with the second group, he knew whose bodies the hairs came from. These were the "control" hairs, the ones that Crocker would compare with the "unknown" hairs from the floors and from Andrea's clothes and body.

Crocker's first step was to give each hair a check under his stereomicroscope. It was equipped with binocular-style eyepieces and showed the hairs in three dimensions. On this first check, Crocker kept the magnification on the microscope at a low power, because he was merely embarking on a preliminary run-through, reviewing the hairs for things like dirt, cosmetic treatment, bleaching, dying (Howie Schmidt, it happened, dyed his hair), and other more or less superficial characteristics.

That done, satisfied he had a rough idea of the sort of prospect he faced, Crocker set about the lengthy work of mounting the hairs on microscope slides. He didn't mount *every* hair. If he had, say, thirty hairs from Howie Schmidt, he would mount about fifteen of them, the fifteen that appeared to be in the best condition. Fifteen was a sufficient number to include, in comparison studies, all the characteristics of Schmidt's hair. The mounting was a three-step operation: place the hair on a microscope slide (one hair per slide), dab on a resin base solution, and cover the hair and solution with a thin piece of glass called a coverslip. The hair, sandwiched between two layers of glass, was now ready for inspection and comparison under the microscope.

The microscope was a double-barrelled affair, actually two microscopes connected by an optical bridge, so that Crocker could look at two hairs at once, a control hair under one lens and an unknown hair under the second lens. The microscope was also of the bright-field variety, meaning the entire area surrounding the hairs was lit up with light shining from below and through the hairs. And Crocker set the magnification on the microscope particularly high, up to four hundred times the real size of the hairs. That put the hairs, for Crocker's eye, on stage in every infinite detail.

Now Crocker began the labour of hair comparison. He would place an unknown hair under one lens, and under the other lens, he would place, for example, in sequence, the fifteen Howie Schmidt scalp hairs. He performed the same job for all the unknown hairs, measuring each against the scalp and groin hairs of Schmidt, Payne, Terceira, and Heinbuch. It was exacting labour, and it took a very long time, days and weeks.

"You can't do this work constantly," Crocker explained later. "You do a couple of hours, get up, change gears for a while, and go back at it again."

And there was something else that was consistently true in the art of hair comparison.

"If two hairs are different, you catch on fast," Crocker said. "If two hairs seem to be the same, you look and look and look, back and forth, back and forth, until you're totally satisfied. A negative conclusion takes ten seconds. A positive conclusion takes an hour."

The conclusions that Crocker ultimately arrived at, both negative and positive, about the hairs in the Andrea Atkinson case took in plenty of territory, and they included these:

Seven of the hairs, found by Sudeyko and Bunting close together on the anteroom floor near the foot of the stairs leading up to the roof, were from Andrea's scalp.

The hair that Noel McAuliffe, the pathologist, picked off Andrea's left groin during the autopsy was a limb hair, from somebody's arm or leg. Crocker had no limb hairs among his control group for comparison purposes. He didn't think it mattered anyway, since limb hairs are too small to reveal much information.

The hair removed from Andrea's right groin at the autopsy wasn't similar to any of the control hairs.

Seventy-four hairs collected from the floor of the anteroom and eight from the boiler-room floor didn't match any control hairs either. Nor did that concern Crocker. "People walk around all day with hairs on their clothes, shedding them as they go," he said. "Any person could have left the unidentified hairs, a policeman, an unknown man, anyone."

Crocker found six hairs on Andrea's T-shirt. Two matched none of the control hairs. Three were Andrea's. The sixth hair was microscopically similar to Johnny Terceira's scalp hair.

On the anteroom floor, slightly scattered, not in one spot, Crocker identified three pubic hairs as Terceira's.

And, again on the anteroom floor, two hairs, close together, were from two different identifiable sources, a scalp hair of Andrea's and a pubic hair of Terceira's.

"The Terceira hair on Andrea's T-shirt, that by itself wasn't enough to prove anything," Crocker said. "It could have been lying on the floor from some earlier time when Terceira walked through and the hair fell off his clothing and much later it was picked up on the T-shirt. The same applies to Terceira's other scalp and pubic hairs on the floor. The pubic hairs could have got on the outside of his pants and dropped off earlier. But the thing is that evidence of this nature gets to be cumulative. A hair on the T-shirt, more on the floor, pubic hairs, scalp hairs – the evidence begins to mount up."

Over the last days of October and into November, Johnny Terceira's life was pitched at a hectic level. Or maybe what he did and where he went was behaviour that had become routine for him. Most nights, he stayed out drinking and doing drugs until two or three in the morning. Some nights, he didn't go home at all. He bought a bundle of crack from a dealer in a government housing project near Queen and Bathurst. On two different nights, late, he let himself into a tony hair salon on Yorkville Avenue. Terceira had a key to the shop, because he worked there as a part-time cleaner. Cleaning had been his trade for much of the time since he dropped out of grade nine at St. Patrick's, a school for good Catholic boys. A pal of his named Coconut introduced him to an older man named Jesse Ramirez, who gave Johnny a job in the Ramirez cleaning firm, tidying up offices and stores after hours. Ramirez lived with his wife and two little kids at 33 Coatsworth, and it was he, considering Johnny a reliable worker, who recommended Terceira for the cleaner's job with CityHome. But on the two nights Terceira went into the Yorkville hair salon, he wasn't there to sweep the floors or empty the waste-baskets. He was stealing money. He needed the cash for his drugs.

The cops knew what Johnny Terceira was up to on these nocturnal excursions. They were just a step behind him most of the time, trailing him to the drug deal, to the hair salon, to the bars. Rick Gauthier and Tom McNamara, the Homicide detectives, had arranged for the surveillance on Terceira on October 26, the Friday when the two detectives, even before the scientific guys seriously pointed fingers in Terceira's direction, started playing all their hunches, including one that Johnny Terceira might be a solid suspect in Andrea Atkinson's rape and murder.

The philosophy behind Rick Gauthier's *modus operandi* in questioning suspects goes like this: "You have to get them to trust you. If they think you're lying, they won't tell you anything. You have to leave room for them to save face. Things often aren't what they appear on the surface, and they want to tell you they aren't the mad dog it appears."

So, on Tuesday, October 30, when Gauthier and McNamara brought Johnny Terceira into 33 Division for another round of questioning, the two detectives played good cop and another good cop. It was first names all round – Rick and Tom and Johnny

– and Gauthier and McNamara set out as if they were sharing confidences with Terceira. They floated the theory for him that maybe the killer was a paedophile, one of those sick guys who'd say the little girl led him on, that none of it was his fault, that it was *her* fault.

Terceira disagreed. He grew angry, almost in a temper, as he gave Gauthier and McNamara his own notion of the killer.

"It must've been somebody she knew," Terceira said. "They grabbed her and took her up there and maybe started. . . . I don't know. They probably molested her and stuff like that."

Gauthier wondered if Andrea would have cried out. Maybe screamed for her mother.

"That was the only person she knew," Terceira agreed. "I'm sure she must've called for her mom."

"Maybe," McNamara said, "the person involved put his hand over her mouth."

"Probably."

Terceira thought about it and turned angry again.

"Me, I'd like to get this guy alone," he raged. "I'd break his fuckin' face!"

Gauthier and McNamara kept the conversation going, leaking a little bit here, a little there, snippets of information that let Terceira know that these two cops thought *he* just might have had something to do with Andrea's murder.

Abruptly, Terceira's eyes filled with tears, his voice broke, he was crying.

"There's something I gotta tell you guys," Terceira sobbed. "I seen the little girl in the boiler room."

The story, as Terceira blubbered it, began with his admission that he used the stairway from the fifth floor to the roof as a regular hideaway to smoke joints. Once, twice a day, he'd slip up there and toke on some hash or marijuana. But two days after Andrea disappeared, the Tuesday, with cops crawling all over the building in their search for the little girl, when he went for his daily hit, he thought he'd better climb all the way to the top, up to the boiler room, out of sight. That was when he saw Andrea.

"Describe her, Johnny," Gauthier said. "What'd you see?"

"Blond hair and a blue face, man."

Then what did Terceira do?

"I just took off."

Terceira said he had a good and natural reason for not telling the police earlier about his discovery. It was because he'd have to explain why he was up in the boiler room in the first place, that he'd gone there to smoke dope. When CityHome heard about *that*, they'd fire him for sure. Terceira said he couldn't afford to lose his job. He needed the money to buy drugs! He couldn't *live* without drugs, man!

Gauthier and McNamara made understanding noises, and after a while, they typed up a statement incorporating everything that Johnny had said. Johnny signed the statement and left. A team of surveillance police stayed on his tail.

The analysis of fibres, the kind of intensive work that Jim Crocker performs, has a long and intriguing record in the solving of high-profile murder cases. It was fibre work that played a large part in nailing the infamous Atlanta serial killer of the late 1970s and early 1980s, and it was a Canadian fibre specialist who did much of the analysis that led to the killer's conviction.

Atlanta police knew they had something horrendous on their hands in the summer of 1979 when bodies began to wash up in the local Chattahoochee River. This grisly stuff went on for two years, bodies bobbing in the water, more than thirty of them before it was over, all of them boys and young men. The one consistent clue that turned up on many of the bodies, even on ones that were unclothed, was a series of similar fibres and animal hairs sticking somewhere to the corpses. Then, in the early morning of May 22, 1981, just after another body was dumped from a bridge over the Chattahoochee, the police nabbed a man named Wayne

Williams, who was driving away from the bridge. The police removed carpets, clothing, anything made of fabric from Williams's house and from his car, and the question they wanted the answer to was this: did the fibres recovered from the bodies in the river match fibres from material in Williams's house and car?

The man who furnished the final answer was Barry Gaudette, who was at the time the chief of the RCMP's hair-and-fibre section at its Ottawa laboratory. FBI scientists had already made a link between the two sets of fibres, those from the bodies and those from Williams's possessions, but they wanted Gaudette's opinion for two reasons. One was that many people in Atlanta, even cops, doubted the validity of fibre evidence, and a show of outside support from someone like Gaudette might counter the scepticism. And, two, the RCMP, having been at the business of fibre analysis since the 1930s, about twenty years longer than the FBI, enjoyed a high reputation in the field.

So Gaudette got busy at comparison in the Williams case. He concentrated, as had the FBI, on the five types of fibres recovered from two of the bodies. A couple of the fibres, Gaudette concluded, matched up to a yellow-green nylon rug on Wayne Williams's floor, another to a violet acetate bedspread in his bedroom. And the animal hair found on the two bodies matched up to the hair on Williams's German shepherd. Gaudette announced that it was virtually beyond question that the fibres on the bodies could have come from any other source than Wayne Williams's house. A jury convicted Williams of two murder counts.

When he turned to the materials from the Atkinson murder scene, Jim Crocker kept finding the same blue fibres. They were in the mix of hairs and other materials that Detectives Sudeyko and Bunting picked up with their tweezers from the anteroom and boiler-room floors. And they were on Andrea's clothes too, fibres that Crocker himself lifted off the jacket and leotards and other garments with clear cellulose tape. Actually, as Crocker studied all the findings under his microscope, there was not one kind of blue fibre but two similar fibres. One was medium blue and the other was a slightly darker blue. Both were acrylic.

There were other sorts of fibres on the floors, other colours, other materials. But none of them turned up in the same numbers as the blue fibres. And it was almost exclusively these ubiquitous blue fibres that covered Andrea's clothes. Crocker mounted forty-two of the blue fibres that he took off Andrea's jacket, ten off her shoes, twenty-four off her leotards, twenty-two off her panties. It was enormously dodgy work dealing with these fibres. They were so tiny, much smaller than hairs, no more than seventeen hundredths of a millimetre in size. And to add to the complexity of the job, Andrea's leotards were also made of blue material. But Crocker soon sorted out that the fibre in the leotards was wider than the other two blue fibres, that its shade of blue was brighter, and that it had more delustrant, the substance manufacturers put in materials to take the gloss off the fibres and make them appear more natural.

The two blue fibres, Crocker grew certain, the medium blue acrylic fibres and the darker blue acrylic fibres, pointed in a definite direction. He was especially persuaded by the fibres on Andrea's panties. They'd been difficult to lift, because the little girl's decomposition fluids had left the panties in such a wretched condition, slick and oily, that he couldn't use the cellulose tape to remove these fibres. He had to do it by hand, studying the panties through his microscope. But he picked off twenty-two of the fibres, on both the inside and the outside of the panties, and he told the detectives on the Atkinson case that the last contact Andrea's panties had was with clothing, pants perhaps, composed of these two blue fibres.

On the night of November 15, Johnny Terceira drank Jack Daniel's in his bedroom. He had a forty-ounce bottle of the bourbon, the good stuff, and he was sipping it, there in his own room, the Rolling Stones posters on the wall, a picture of the Virgin Mary. The Jack Daniel's was running low, not much left in the bottle.

Somebody knocked on the front door downstairs. It was the cops, the two Homicide guys, Gauthier and McNamara, and Bunting from the Forensic Unit. They had a search warrant. They wanted to look in Johnny's clothes closet. And Bunting had a camera. He started shooting pictures in the bedroom.

Johnny lost his cool.

"Get the fuck away from me!" he screamed at the cops.

Johnny's mother talked to him in Portuguese, making soothing noises. Be calm, she said, be calm.

The cops picked through Johnny's clothes. They chose a couple of underwear pants, a T-shirt, some other tops. They took away eight pieces of clothing in all. The eight included a pair of well-worn navy-blue sweatpants. They were the pants Terceira had put on at seven o'clock on the morning of the day Andrea disappeared. Bunting packed the pants in a brown bag, then put the bag in a box. The cops dropped off the box at the Centre of Forensic Sciences, attention Jim Crocker.

Crocker pulled clutches of fibres from the outer knit material of Johnny Terceira's sweatpants and put them under his microscope. As usual, the process took forever. Mounting the fibres on slides, slipping them into the microscope, looking at them, looking, eternally looking. But none of this fazed Jim Crocker, the soul of patience, and, after some time, he knew that the material in the sweatpants was made of two acrylic fibres and that the two came in different tones of blue, one slightly darker than the other.

Crocker prepared for a comparison study, placing fibres from the floors and from Andrea's clothing on one side of his double microscope and fibres from Terceira's pants on the other side.

Crocker studied each group, looking for points of similarity. He examined them for colour, for diameter, for shape, for the amount of delustrant. And he seemed to be getting matches. The fibres picked off Andrea's panties, for example, had the same dimensions, same shade of blue, same round shape, same light delustrant, as one of the two kinds of fibres taken from the sweatpants. The second sweatpants fibre had a peanut shape, and there were plenty of fibres with that shape taken from Andrea's dress. So it went, the fibres on Andrea's clothing matching up to the fibres from Terceira's blue sweatpants.

There was just one catch. The sweatpants contained a *third* blue fibre. This fibre was on the inside of the pants, threaded behind the other two fibres to make a softer fleece lining. It was an identifiably different fibre, and – here was a possible puzzle – it showed up nowhere on the floors or on Andrea's clothing.

But Crocker thought he had the answer to the puzzle. The outer two fibres would naturally shed easily. They were hanging on the outside of the pants, likely to break off, especially since the pants were well worn. The inside fibre, on the contrary, had the freedom to move around without breaking. It was soft, fleecy, yielding, unlikely to snap and fall. Still, Crocker asked himself, what would have happened in the act of rape when the sweatpants were removed? Wouldn't some inside fibre come loose and fall on the floor, on Andrea's clothing? What about that? Easily answered, Crocker thought. The sweatpants were held up with a drawstring. When the wearer took these pants off, he simply let them slide down his legs. He had no need to invert the pants, no need to expose the inner fabric to a major contact with the floor or the victim. That, Crocker thought, settled the question. He was satisfied that the fibres found in the sixth-floor rooms at Coatsworth and on Andrea's clothes were microscopically similar to the two fibres from the outside of Johnny Terceira's pants, and that the third fibre from the inside of the pants was, as an issue, a non-starter.

~

Not everything panned out for the scientists and detectives in the Atkinson case. Not every item that Sudeyko and Bunting turned up in the rooms at the top of the apartment building provided a clue of some useful sort. And not every test that the people at the CFS ran produced an evidentiary result.

Fingerprints, for example. None could be lifted from Andrea's body, because it was too decomposed. There were no identifiable prints on the cards from Andrea's New Kids on the Block collection, nor on her orange plastic bracelet, nor on any surfaces in the anteroom or boiler room.

The stream of fluid running from Andrea's body to the drain in the boiler room hadn't enough blood or anything else for testing. The two hairs in the greyish smear on the anteroom floor didn't match the hairs of anyone suspected in the case. And Keith Kelder couldn't get an ABO reading off the dried saliva on the cigarette butt from the boiler-room floor.

Still, the cops and scientists had all the other blood and semen evidence that Kelder produced, all of Jim Crocker's conclusions from the hairs and fibres. And they thought they had one more rock-solid piece of evidence, the absolute clincher, the piece of science that would point beyond reasonable doubt to the killer of Andrea Atkinson. They had the DNA results.

DNA stands for deoxyribonucleic acid, and by the late autumn of 1990, when the Atkinson case unfolded, scientists knew plenty about it.

They knew, as a beginning, that DNA is a molecule present in every cell in every person's body. That's a lot of cells, trillions of them per person, and a lot of DNA, thousands of miles of it per cell. Everybody begins life as a single cell, a cell that contains DNA. The first cell is an ovum, which gets fertilized with spermatozoa and begins dividing and dividing, almost *ad infinitum*, until it grows into a baby. Meanwhile, the DNA in the first cell remains constant, the same DNA repeated in all the subsequent cells. The cells change, but not the DNA, never the DNA.

More specifically, the DNA dwells in the nucleus of each cell, where it runs the controls of each person's genetic makeup. Scientists, describing DNA, refer to it with such phrases as "the blueprint of life." It dictates the future in so many ways. Whether a person is blue-eyed or dark-skinned or both, or has the father's nose or the mother's brains or both – that's up to a person's DNA.

There's a decided amount of organization to DNA's makeup. It's divided into forty-six entities called chromosomes. There are twenty-two pairs of chromosomes in each person, the person's father having contributed one chromosome to each pair and the mother contributing the mates. The remaining two chromosomes, to make up the forty-six, are called the sex chromosomes, the X and Y chromosomes. Women have two X chromosomes, men have an X and a Y. This means that it's the man who ultimately determines the sex of the offspring, since only he can contribute the Y chromosome that makes the offspring a male baby.

Genes are the good DNA. They're the part of the DNA that carries the blue eyes and the brains and other traits from mother and father to the offspring. Genes are, as scientists say, DNA that "makes sense." There are, as it happens, other sections of DNA, actually about half of the total in each person, that don't do any discernible job. They don't pass on blue eyes. They don't "make sense."

DNA is exceptionally narrow and exceptionally long. It's measured in a unit called basepairs, and if all the DNA in a cell was stretched out, at ten basepairs per inch, it would reach to something like 9,600 skinny miles of the stuff. Needless to say, all of this DNA is very tightly wound in order to fit inside each cell.

What is crucial in forensic terms is that each person has different DNA. Identical twins are the exception. They have identical DNA. With everybody else, although they have DNA in common, each person has DNA that is different from every other person's. It's the differences that forensic scientists look at.

They look at it by digging out the DNA from a person's blood, from semen, from saliva, from a strand of hair. It can't be just any hair strand, though; it has to be a strand with a root.

Scientists had learned all of this fascinating information about DNA by 1990, but the knowledge had been a long time, and many remarkable scientific adventures, in coming.

One of the breakthrough adventures occurred at the Cavendish Laboratory in Cambridge, England, over the course of a couple of years in the early 1950s. This was when two scientists right out of central casting – young, charming, brilliant, brash – deciphered the structure of DNA. The two were an American in his mid-twenties, Jim Watson, a fellow of such charisma that he later became known among his colleagues as "the Mick Jagger of science," and an Englishman in his mid-thirties, Francis Crick, whose reputation was as a relentless chatterbox in social settings and an audacious theorist in laboratory situations.

In their work, Watson and Crick were benefitting from almost eighty years of earlier scientific noodling with DNA. A young Swiss chemist named Frederick Miescher was the first to discover DNA, in 1869. Experimenting with white blood cells that he took from the pus on postoperative bandages, he isolated a grey precipitate that was different from all of the known organic substances. Miescher named it "nuclein," because it came out of the nucleus of the cell. It would later be renamed DNA.

It didn't take scientists too much longer to figure out that, chemically speaking, DNA was composed of four bases. Each of the four contained components of sugar and phosphate, and each was nitrogenous. But the nitrogenous part was of two kinds: a purine and a pyrimidine. The two bases with the purine were called adenine and guanine; the two with the pyrimidine were called cytosine and thymine. These four bases, adenine and

guanine, cytosine and thymine, known forever and simply by
their letters, A, G, C, T, were, scientists reasoned, strung like
beads. DNA, they thought, was like a long string of beads named
A, G, C, and T.

So far, so good. The chemistry of DNA had been deduced. But
the chemical side of DNA had to be tied into the genetic side. *Did
DNA carry genetic information?* Many scientists came at this
question from many angles. An English-born bacteriologist,
Oswald Avery, employed at the Rockefeller Institute in New
York in the 1940s, did ground-breaking work by establishing in
the laboratory that hereditary traits could be transmitted from one
cell to another by purified DNA molecules. The focus was now
undeniably on DNA as the key to genetics, as the secret substance
that passed on human traits. But in order to work with DNA, scientists needed to know everything about its structure. Which is
where Watson and Crick entered the picture.

They were two unlikely fellows to be in the DNA frame at
all. Chemical knowledge was requisite to deal with DNA, but
both Watson and Crick were in physics (a field, what's more, in
which neither had yet earned a PH.D.). But, clever and inquisitive, they got into the DNA game, keen to solve the mystery of
its structure. To add spice to the search, it happened that, in
California, the world's greatest chemist, Linus Pauling, was
embarked on the same quest at the same time, to nail down
DNA's structure.

The smart tool that Watson and Crick used was a molecular
model. Built of brass (as the foundation) and wire (for the molecules and their linkages) and held together with screws, the
model underwent all sorts of variations as the two eager beavers
fooled about with the arrangement of the four bases, A, G, C, and
T. They were partly influenced by assumptions they had picked
up from other scientists. One was that DNA must have a regular
structure, and the other was that the regular structure probably
came in the form of a helix. So Watson and Crick pressed on,

shuffling the bases around, asking themselves which ones liked to sit next to one another.

Suddenly – if a couple of years of brainstorming could be called "suddenly" – they became aware that an A-T pair was identical in overall shape and size to a G-C pair, all held together by hydrogen bonds. Now they were on to something. A could pair only with T, G could pair only with C. These were the base pairs (or, as they became identified in the DNA language, basepairs). What's more, these basepairs would be accommodated in any order of A-Ts and G-Cs in the helix form. Actually, it was a double helix that Watson and Crick came up with, something rather like a gently twisting spiral staircase, with basepairs forming the steps. The basepairs were constant, always A with T, G with C, but linearly they could proceed in any order, A-T followed by G-C, followed by another G-C, then T-A, and so on. DNA in basepairs for miles.

Here was a structure for DNA that satisfied all the chemical and other scientific requirements, everything that had been previously learned about DNA. It was the answer, and, in April 1953, Watson and Crick let the rest of the scientific world in on the discovery when they published their model in an article of only nine hundred words in *Nature* magazine.

But what of Linus Pauling in California? He had been hot on the trail of the DNA structure, with the helix form in place and everything else in proper order, until, inexplicably – at least Pauling himself could never explain in later years what happened – he made a blooper in basic chemistry, in something that a look in a textbook called *General Chemistry* would have corrected. Oh, irony, Pauling *wrote* the textbook. Nevertheless, his tiny error slowed him down long enough to allow Watson and Crick to nip ahead in uncovering DNA's structure. And it was they who went to Stockholm in 1962 to receive a Nobel Prize in chemistry for their discovery.

~

Things moved on apace in the scientific work on DNA. Its structure was known, the ways in which the basepairs lined up and
passed along genetic information within the DNA. But in order
to employ DNA for forensic purposes, in such cases as the Andrea
Atkinson murder, the world had to wait for one more large
scientific breakthrough. It ultimately came from a quite likely scientist working in a completely unlikely scientific setting.

Leicestershire, one of the smallest of the English counties, lies
about one hundred miles northwest of London. Its principal city,
Leicester, with a population of 300,000, is given over to the
making of woollens, shoes, beer, and, more recently, plastics. Just
southwest of Leicester are three picturesque villages, places of
quaint pubs and whitewashed Tudor cottages. The three, each a
few minutes apart and joined by paths and lanes, are named
Narborough, Littlethorpe, and Enderby, and it was on the Black
Pad, an isolated path running behind the Narborough church, that
someone raped and strangled bright and promising fifteen-year-
old schoolgirl Lynda Mann in the early evening of November 21,
1983. The Leicestershire constabulary put on a massive and determined investigation to catch the man responsible for the horrible crime, but, over the following couple of years, they didn't
come close to rounding up a good suspect.

Around the same time, at the University of Leicester, a smart
young geneticist named Alec Jeffreys was working on a project
that involved genes and human muscle. In style and appearance,
Jeffreys was another scientist who cut a figure of star quality. He
was thirty-four in 1984, he wore a beard, spoke with an Oxford
accent, always dressed in a turtleneck sweater, always rolled his
own Golden Virginia cigarettes.

Somehow, working on his genes-and-muscle project, Jeffreys
veered off into what he considered at first a fringe area. He began
to look for a way of developing markers that would map human

genes. By then, of course, scientists had doped out the implications of DNA, but nobody had arrived at a way of actually nailing down DNA molecules and making them sit up and be practical. This is what Jeffreys found himself getting into. He was trying to single out the areas of genetic material that seemed to vary the most from one person to the next, and, even more, to find a way to give those areas a visible identity.

Jeffreys proceeded by instinct, by his training as a geneticist, and by what he later called "a lucky streak of circumstances." And after many stops and starts, hits and misses, he arrived at a procedure that went, in condensed form, more or less as follows:

First, he extracted a DNA molecule from a sample of blood. Then, using enzymes as his cutting agent, he sliced the DNA into fragments. These fragments were stuffed into an opening at one end of a small block of gel. Then Jeffreys zapped the gel with a strong electrical current, which had the effect of spreading the fragments around the gel.

Next, Jeffreys moved the DNA fragments, intact, out of the gel and onto a nylon membrane. This was done by Southern blotting, a process named after its inventor, a certain professor Ed Southern. It was, in simplest terms, a sucking up by capillary action, which took place when Jeffreys put the membrane and the gel in contact with one another.

What also took place in and around this stage, most decisively for the whole process, was that the DNA split along its basepairs. The As divided from the Ts, the Gs from the Cs, and so on. The DNA unzipped. It became, on the membrane, single-stranded.

Now it was time for Jeffreys to incubate the membrane with probes. What exactly was a probe? It was a solution of pieces of DNA that contained repeated sequences, special sequences, ones that Jeffreys had radioactively labelled so that they would seek out and zip up with the matching sequences of DNA on the membrane. As an example, the membrane might contain a single strand with the sequence AGCCTGCTCTTA, and a probe might have the complementary single sequence TCGGACGAGAAT. If so, that probe would find the sequence on the membrane and bind with it into a double strand.

So that step proceeded, the zipping up of the single strands, and, when it was completed, X-rays came next. Jeffreys let the membrane and the radioactive probes incubate overnight. In the morning, he washed the membrane to get rid of any material that the probes didn't bind to. Then he shot the membrane on X-ray film and developed the film.

The idea that Jeffreys was operating on was that the film would show a pattern of radioactivity. The sections where the probes adhered, the probes being radioactive, would appear on the film as dark bands, and, *voilà*, a pattern. Jeffreys didn't expect much of a pattern, one dark band per X-ray maybe, or, at best, a couple of dark bands. But when the film was developed, he got a whole lot more than that. On the very first film, Jeffreys found himself staring at a wide series of bands, some black, some grey. The film looked, he thought, like a bar code on a box of cereal at the supermarket. Jeffreys, as he later said, was "stunned" at the sight of that first piece of film. He knew he'd arrived at what he'd set out to locate. He'd discovered a genetic marker, in fact numerous genetic markers, all kinds of them, clear and particular.

Jeffreys called what he'd discovered genetic fingerprints. With the bands on the X-ray, he had found a way of giving visual identity to DNA. The distribution of the bands would be unique to each person, and so Jeffreys had in front of him, on the X-ray, a DNA image that would be individually specific.

Jeffreys proceeded to do much more in his laboratory. For example, he studied family groups in DNA and showed that half the bands on the X-ray came from the mother and half from the father. All sorts of possibilities opened up with Jeffreys' basic discovery of a way to identify a person through DNA. And, as fate would have it, he was about to find out about one possibility that he hadn't counted on.

~

Meanwhile, out in the Leicestershire world beyond the laboratory, the police had still not solved the sad and shocking 1983 rape and murder of Lynda Mann. Worse, on July 31, 1986, the coppers found themselves with another, dreadfully similar, case on their hands. This one also happened in the neighbourhood of the three charming villages, Narborough, Littlethorpe, and Enderby; precisely, the crime took place just off Ten Pound Lane, a lovely footpath outside Enderby. The victim was once again a fifteen-year-old schoolgirl, Dawn Ashworth, effervescent and social. And Dawn, like Lynda Mann, had been raped, strangled, and ditched in some handy underbrush.

The good news, briefly, was that, within a couple of weeks, the police made an arrest in the case – just in the Ashworth case, not in the Mann case. The accused was a seventeen-year-old kitchen porter who had a history of sexual messing about with younger girls, activities that were probably criminal, but nothing that had led to charges. The main reason the police latched on to the boy at all was because he insisted on pushing himself forward, lurking about the Ashworth crime scene. Eventually the police thought to ask him a few questions, and the kitchen porter confessed to the murder of Dawn, though he said he had nothing to do with Lynda's death. The police decided they had half their problems solved with the confession. It didn't seem to give them second thoughts that the kid they'd arrested was, as one cop put it, "thruppence short of a pound."

Then somebody had an idea that may have changed the course of murder prosecutions forever. Who the "somebody" was remains in small doubt, although the kitchen porter's father thinks he was the one. He'd been reading somewhere, *Reader's Digest* he thought possibly, about the marvellous discovery made by the scientist just down the road at the University of Leicester, Alec Jeffreys, the DNA man, and he wondered, the father did, whether, if Jeffreys compared his son's blood and the semen in Dawn

Ashworth's vagina (in her rectum, too), it would surely prove that
the boy wasn't the guilty party. The father passed on the notion
to his solicitor for expediting. The police, for their part, said
they'd already thought of bringing Alec Jeffreys and his science
into the investigation. But they had a different slant than the father
on Jeffreys' involvement. The police idea was to provide Jeffreys
with semen taken, not from Dawn Ashworth's body, but from
Lynda Mann's, along with a sample of the kitchen porter's blood,
in the expectation that DNA science would pinpoint the porter
as a double rapist and murderer.

Whoever had the inspiration of invoking DNA, it came about
that, through the autumn months of 1986, Alec Jeffreys' lab took
delivery of semen from Lynda's body, of the porter's blood sample,
and eventually – the police dragged their feet on this one – of
semen from Dawn's body. Jeffreys went to work.

Until this point, Jeffreys hadn't used his "genetic fingerprinting"
(a system, so named, on which he took out a patent) for forensic
purposes. He'd contemplated its contribution in many areas, in
identifying whether newborn twins were fraternal or identical,
in determining if grafts had succeeded in bone transplants for
leukaemia patients. And he'd actually used genetic fingerprinting
in an immigration case that, because he and DNA resolved it,
became famous.

The facts of the case began with a boy, born in England to two
Ghanaian parents, who now was living in Ghana with his father.
The boy applied to return to England, where he planned to move
in with his mother and his siblings. The English immigration
authorities turned him down on the grounds that, according to
them, the woman whom the boy claimed to be his mother was
really his aunt.

Alec Jeffreys was summoned into the case. The boy's father,
off in Ghana, wasn't available to give a blood sample, so Jeffreys,
from his studies of family DNA, went at the matter in a round-

about-but-inevitable way. He took the genetic fingerprints of the boy, of the mother, and of the mother's other children, whom nobody disputed had been fathered by the man in Ghana. What emerged when Jeffreys compared all these genetic fingerprints was a pattern pointing to the conclusion that the same man, the fellow in Ghana, was the father, by the same mother, of all the children, including the boy who wanted into England. The immigration authorities bowed to Jeffreys' science, the boy entered the country, and the English media gave the case and genetic fingerprinting slews of adoring publicity.

"The new technique could mean a breakthrough in many areas," one journalist wrote, "including the identification of criminals from a small sample of blood at the scene of the crime."

This journalist's article appeared in 1985 in the *Leicester Mercury*. And now, in the fall of 1986, Jeffreys had the raw material for his first criminal case.

He began by analysing the semen from Lynda Mann's body. Then he did the kitchen porter's blood. And he compared the results. There was no match. The DNA in the rapist's semen and in the kitchen porter's blood came from two different men. Then Jeffreys waited a bit for the disappointed and reluctant police to deliver the semen from Dawn Ashworth's body. Jeffreys analysed it, and the result knocked everybody for a loop. The DNA in the Ashworth semen matched the DNA in the Mann semen. The same man had raped and strangled both girls, but the fellow wasn't the kitchen porter. On November 21, 1986, the kitchen porter became the first accused murderer in the world to be freed on the basis of DNA testing.

The Leicestershire police, desperate by now, came up with a scheme that seemed entirely bizarre: they asked all male residents of the three villages of Narborough, Littlethorpe, and Enderby between the ages of seventeen and thirty-four to come forward by police-arranged appointments and submit to sampling of their blood. The samples would be passed on to a government laboratory at Aldermaston that was newly equipped for DNA testing. This, the police hoped, would ultimately point to the killer. So the blooding began. From the first announcement in early January 1987 to May of that year, 3,653 men and boys had handed over their blood, with at least another two thousand males from the three villages still to come.

One fellow shied away from giving his blood. A baker in his mid-twenties, Colin Pitchfork was an artistic sort, the chap at the bakery who created the ornate designs in icing on the top of festive cakes. He was married, with kids, owned a house in Littlethorpe, and had a criminal record for flashing. It was the latter, he told a pair of lads at the bakery, that worried him. As soon as the cops spotted his flasher's background, Pitchfork said, they'd jump on him for the two murders no matter what the DNA results showed. He asked one of the bakery lads to take his blood test for him. The lad refused. Pitchfork approached the second baker. Another turndown. But a third baker, Ian Kelly, agreed to go along with the plan. Pitchfork fixed up his own passport with Kelly's photo in it. Kelly used the passport as identification at Pitchfork's scheduled blood test, took the test in Pitchfork's name, and, in due course, Pitchfork received a letter from the police advising that his test was negative. Pitchfork was in the clear.

A few months later, on a Saturday in August, over lunch at a pub in Leicester, Ian Kelly dropped his secret. He was eating and drinking with fellow workers from the bakery, and conversation got around to their mutual colleague Colin Pitchfork. A terrible womanizer Colin was, somebody said, and Kelly just blurted out that he had taken Colin's blood test. This news stuck with one of the people at the lunch, a woman, a bakery manager, and she mulled over her responsibility in the matter for six weeks before she told the police of the Kelly conversation. The cops questioned Kelly, and he owned up instantly to the deception. Late that afternoon, police descended on Pitchfork's home in Littlethorpe.

It was almost as if Pitchfork could hardly wait to confess. He revelled in the story. He seemed proud of the murders. He told the police he'd flashed hundreds of women in his career. But these two, the fifteen-year-old girls, hadn't fled like the others. Both had frozen in place, terrified. Pitchfork felt an urge to go further with them. He raped both girls, and, since he'd done that, he couldn't very well let them go, could he? They'd seen his face. He had to keep them quiet. He strangled them.

On January 22, 1988, Colin Pitchfork pleaded guilty to two charges of murder and received a double life sentence.

DNA, in an indirect way, had convicted a killer.

The forensic uses of DNA spread swiftly to North America. Police and prosecutors saw it as an infallible weapon in pinning guilt on rapists and murderers. In the United States, both government laboratories and private commercial labs set themselves up for DNA testing. In Canada, it was strictly a government affair, and the RCMP lab in Ottawa led the way. It started researching DNA as early as 1986, and, two years later, it had a small-but-fully-operational DNA setup. Canadian prosecutors began taking DNA evidence to court, and the new science seemed to inspire everybody – cops, Crown attorneys, judges, juries, even accused criminals – with awe. No one, it appeared, doubted DNA's authority.

A typical early case occurred in Ottawa in the spring of 1989, the case of John Joseph McNally, charged with rape. McNally, thirty-two years old, married, a father, was a general repairman. He had done some work on the basement floor in a home owned by a sixty-eight-year-old woman. A month later, someone broke into the woman's home and raped her. McNally was a prime suspect. He denied the crime and willingly gave the police samples of his blood, saliva, and hair. The RCMP lab compared the DNA in McNally's samples with DNA in semen recovered from the victim's nightgown and bedspread. At McNally's trial, Judge Keith Flanigan of the District Court of Ottawa-Carleton presided over a *voir dire* to determine whether DNA evidence was admissible at trial. Yes, it was, Flanigan ruled, finding DNA evidence to be no different from fingerprint, blood, or fibre evidence, which had been admissible in criminal trials for years. With that hurdle out of the way, John Waye stepped to the witness stand. He was a prepossessing young fellow with a background in medical biophysics and genetics who had helped set up the RCMP's DNA lab. He testified that the DNA from McNally's blood samples made a match to the DNA extracted from the semen at the crime scene and that the chances of anyone else leaving behind that particular semen were one in several *billion*. The statistic blew everyone away. It certainly impressed McNally, who, the moment Waye finished testifying, changed his plea from not guilty to guilty. Judge Flanigan sentenced him to seven years in prison. DNA reigned triumphant – and apparently unchallenged.

Pamela Newall is handsome and in her early fifties. She has lightly frosted hair, a great smile, and a voice that could carry across the Grand Canyon. She joined the Centre of Forensic Sciences in 1964. Both before and after that year, she made herself learned in biochemistry and embryology, in immunology and molecular biology. All of this, though she could hardly have anticipated it, was just a warm-up for DNA.

The CFS began its prep work to get into DNA testing in 1987, and Newall was front and centre from the start. She travelled to the United States and Germany in pursuit of DNA training, boned up on the literature and on techniques. But it wasn't her skill in the science that alone made Newall the logical choice as head of the centre's DNA unit. It was also the stance she took as an administrator – loyal, partisan, guardian of the gates against the hordes of doubters out there – and it was her commitment to DNA as a tool. Newall was a true believer.

"I know in my own heart," she once said, "that DNA is as close to foolproof as anything we'll ever see."

The centre's DNA unit opened for business in July 1990, and, four months later, Keith Kelder arrived in Newall's office with the samples of semen from the floor of the Coatsworth apartment building and from the clothing of Andrea Atkinson. It was the seventh case that the unit had taken on. But this was the big one, a murder case, a difficult case, a case that would focus the spotlight of justice — and the criticisms of a carping criminal lawyer — on Newall and the unit.

Newall began with the DNA from the semen stain on the anteroom floor. She didn't work alone. One of her associates in the DNA unit, Colin McAuley, ran most of the tests in the lab, while Newall looked over his shoulder, supervising, and it was Newall who made the final interpretations of the results that came off the X-ray film. These were the little bands of grey and black that Alec Jeffreys described as resembling the bar codes on a box of cereal. The bands that emerged in the CFS's lab still looked rather like bar codes. But the X-ray film they appeared on was called an autorad, and it was now a computer that helped to perform the crucial step of measuring, or, in DNA-speak, "sizing," the bands. Much had changed in the short years since Alec Jeffreys made his amazing discovery at the University of Leicester. The basic method remained the same, but, by the time Pamela Newall and Colin McAuley got down to cases in the CFS lab in November 1990, they had new techniques, more-efficient machinery, and a more-tested science at their disposal, and the technique had a name — restriction fragment length polymorphism, RFLP for short.

The first major step with the DNA from the semen stain on the anteroom floor would be to cut it into fragments and sort out the fragments that contained what are called stutters. At any point in the length of anybody's DNA, a region may be spelled out in As and Ts, in Gs and Cs, in the DNA language, but that same spelling may be repeated many times, five times, one hundred times. This is a stutter in the DNA. And it is the stutters that scientists cut out of a person's DNA. It is the length of the stutters that they measure, and it is the measurement that defines one person from another.

Initially, though, Colin McAuley gave the DNA a preliminary rough cut, using chemical scissors, the enzymes, to slice it into fragments. Then he placed these fragments in rows of holes, called wells, in something that looked like a slab of jelly, but was actually an agarose gel. Hence, in DNA-speak, which sometimes sounds like a variation on the Danny Kaye nonsense song from the 1950s movie *The Court Jester* ("The vessel with the pestle has the brew that is true"), the wells were in the gel, not the gel in the wells. And the DNA fragments were in the wells.

Next, electricity. McAuley turned on a current of electricity hooked into the gel. The electricity had the effect of drawing the DNA through the gel towards the edge of the slab, holding the fragments of DNA in their own lanes coming out of the wells and moving the fragments various distances along the lanes. In one analogy, it was like a swimming race, all the fragments splashing down their lanes, except, in this race, the fragments moved according to size, the smaller ones going faster and getting farther down their lanes than the larger fragments.

Then, click, the electricity was turned off, and the fragments were immobilized in their lanes. The very smallest had made it all the way to the edge of the gel, the very largest remained not far from the wells, and the rest were distributed in between.

All of these steps served as a sort of narrowing process, getting nearer to the measuring, getting *ready* for the measuring, and the next step involved a transference of the DNA fragments from the gel to a nylon membrane called a blot. This transference was necessary, because the gel was much more fragile than the hardy membrane that could stand up to the various manipulations that were still to come; the manipulations would be part of the search for the special fragments that held the characteristic stutters. The transference itself was carried out by something like the blotting Alec Jeffreys had done, a process that was rather similar to a sophisticated version of lifting wet ink off a page with a piece of blotting paper. The result was that the DNA fragments moved on to the blot in exactly the same positions as they'd occupied in the gel.

By this stage, the fragments had also been unzipped as they moved from the gel to the blot, the As separated from the Ts all along the strand, the Gs from the Cs. The DNA was now single-stranded and in position to be receptive to an outside probe that would provide the other half of the strand, the Ts to the As on the blot, the Cs to the Gs. The probe would zip up the unzipped strands.

Put another way, the probe would go looking for those characteristic stutters in the DNA. If the person whose DNA was under scrutiny had inherited six stutters from his mother and four from his father, which is how stutters come about, by inheritance, then that was what the probe would seek out and zip up.

The probe itself, this key little catalyst to the entire process of creating a DNA "print," was made up of other, independent, single-stranded DNA. Once let loose on the blot, the probe went searching for its other half. Not every probe found its mate, the sequence of As, Ts, Gs, and Cs that it matched. But every probe that successfully located its other half zipped up with it. It became once again double stranded.

Before the probe was launched on its mission of search and zip, it had been made radioactive. That meant it would expose X-ray film, and it was the X-ray film that made its appearance in the next step. This was a three-day step. What McAuley did was place the blot, bracketed by two sheets of X-ray film, in a cassette, so that the three items, the blot and the two films, were tightly squeezed together. The cassette went into a freezer for three days, and when it came out, McAuley developed the film.

This was the climax. On the film, now called an autorad, there was a portrait in vertical grey and black bands. The stutters in the DNA that the probe recognized had assumed a visual form in the bands, and the autorad thus offered a DNA profile of the man who left the semen on the floor of the anteroom.

But it was only a profile at *one* point, at *one* spot in the chromosome. That wasn't enough to declare a complete profile. It wasn't definitive, not anything to take to court. So McAuley pressed on. He performed the whole process all over again at another location in the DNA sample. It was the same concept, same procedure, but different location, different point, different probe. And he produced a second DNA profile, a second autorad, for the same sample from the semen on the anteroom floor. Nor did he stop there. He kept repeating the procedure until he had covered enough regions of the same sample of DNA to make a total of five autorads.

Then he stopped. Or, at any rate, he stopped this part of the long process that would lead ultimately to a comparison of the DNA from the semen on the anteroom floor to DNA from the suspects in the rape and murder of Andrea Atkinson.

Keith Kelder had delivered to the DNA unit a second sample of semen in the case, the one removed from Andrea's leotards. Newall and McAuley put the DNA from this sample through the entire procedure – gels, probes, zipping and unzipping, seeking out stutters, the whole works – and mounted *it* on autorads.

The name of the game was comparison, comparing the DNA from the semen stains on the anteroom floor and on the leotards with the DNA from the suspects in the case. That meant Newall and McAuley had to give the whole treatment to the blood or hair or saliva samples submitted by Howie Schmidt, Phil Payne, Doug Heinbuch, and Johnny Terceira. They had to mount their DNA in bands on autorads. And, for good measure, they had to do the same with DNA from Andrea's parents, Ruth Windebank and Terry Atkinson. This was because Andrea's own DNA had been destroyed during the nine days her body decomposed in the boiler room. So, for the sake of completeness in the comparison procedure, to cover all the DNA bases, the pattern of Andrea's DNA would be in effect inferred from the DNA of her parents.

Now Pamela Newall was at last prepared to take the final step, to do the comparison studies. Actually, it was a double-barrelled step: she was measuring, or "sizing," the bands of DNA from various sources and comparing them at the same time.

She began with the DNA from the semen on the anteroom floor. She placed in front of her the autorad that came out of the first probe. This was a sort of composite autorad. It held several lanes. In one lane, there was the band of DNA from the floor stain. Then, in succeeding lanes, there were the bands from Payne, from Schmidt, from Terceira, from Heinbuch, from Terry Atkinson, from Windebank, a sample of DNA from a commercial company that acted as an internal control on the technique, and, in the last lane, a molecular weight marker, or ladder.

There were two ways of sizing and comparing all these bands in all their lanes – by eye and by computer. Newall did both. To work with the computer, she placed the autorad on a light table. A fixed videocamera captured the autorad and fed it into the computer, which translated it into computer language and put it on a monitor screen. Finally, a cursor in the computer, controlled by the computer program or manipulated by Newall, moved around the screen from band to band, providing the vehicle for the sizing operation.

What Newall was comparing was the positions of the bands in their lanes. These grey and black bands, the ones that resembled the codes on the box of cereal, were frozen at varying distances down their respective lanes. The positions reflected how far they'd travelled. The distances were measured in basepairs, anywhere from 500 to 22,000 basepairs. And, to complete the circle, the distances they'd travelled determined their positions in the lanes. It was the *positions* that were being compared. If the bands in two different lanes on the autorad were in the same positions, then there was a match. They were the same DNA.

Newall was all set.

She put up the first autorad, the one that featured in lane number one the band from the first probe of the DNA taken from the semen stain on the anteroom floor. She examined the position of this band *vis-à-vis* the positions of the bands in the other lanes.

Howie Schmidt: no match.

Phil Payne: no match.

Doug Heinbuch: no match.

Johnny Terceira: a match.

Terceira's DNA, according to this first autorad, matched the DNA from the semen on the floor.

Newall put up the second autorad, from the second probe. The result was the same: a match for Johnny Terceira.

This was getting serious. It was possible to have two unrelated people match at two probes, at two locations, but such an event was very, very unusual.

Third autorad. Right away, Newall noticed a funny little quirk: the autorad showed a match between Phil Payne and Ruth Windebank. This demonstrated that, by chance, by a freak of coincidence, two unrelated people *could* show a match at one probe of their DNA. But, on more immediate business, on this third autorad, Newall once again got a match between Terceira and the semen stain. It was now a three-probe match. A three-probe match, Newall knew, had never been found in England, and, in the United States, the FBI had recorded just one three-probe match in almost eight million comparisons.

On the fourth autorad, it was more of the same, a match for Terceira. A four-probe match had *never* been heard of in North America.

With the fifth autorad, Newall decided there was no result to interpret. The fault was in the band from the semen stain. It, she thought, wasn't clear enough to read.

But there had been four matches, and Newall found that

mind-blowing. "To see that profile again," she said, "you'd have to look at 1.8 million other male Caucasians."

Newall then lined up the autorads to do the comparison featuring the DNA from the semen stains on Andrea's leotards. But this time she simplified the chore. She compared the DNA from the leotard sample only with the DNA from the stain on the anteroom floor. She knew the floor semen had matched up to Terceira and to no one else. Ergo, if the leotard semen matched the floor semen, Terceira was again on the hook.

And that was what happened. On four of the five autorads, Newall got matches. On the fifth, she declined to declare a match. But, again, four out of five was so rare that the odds were one in eight million against finding a similar DNA profile. (What made the odds higher in this match than in the tests with the semen stain on the floor was that it was more unusual to include a profile at the point where it was done in the DNA from the semen on the leotards; some places in the DNA are simply tougher to profile than others.)

The results of both tests, on both pieces of DNA, from both samples of semen, placed the conclusion seemingly beyond question. It was Johnny Terceira, according to the DNA evidence, who had left the semen on the anteroom floor and on Andrea Atkinson's leotards.

CityHome had reassigned Terceira to its housing complex on Walpole Avenue. It lay a couple of blocks south of the Coatsworth apartment building, across a line of railway tracks, and it was at Walpole that the two detectives from Homicide, Rick Gauthier and Tom McNamara, went looking for Terceira around noon on Monday, December 3. Terceira had been shovelling snow off the Walpole sidewalks, but he was taking a break, sitting in the superintendent's office, when Gauthier and McNamara arrived. Terceira looked up at the two detectives and rose slowly out of his chair. Gauthier told him he was under arrest for the murder of Andrea Atkinson.

Terceira took a small step backward, reached out his hand, pleading. "Oh, Rick, *no*, man!"

Leo Adler is a pleasantly sleek-looking man. His colouring has an olive tinge, his hair and eyes are dark, and he tends to glide when he walks. His manner of speaking, at least in private, is of the same order, unrancorous, parcelled out in long conjunctive sentences, smoothly persuasive. He seems to have been born to the courtroom.

Shortly after his call to the bar and entry into criminal law in the mid-1970s, he began developing precepts by which he would work. No plea bargaining was one. "I'm known as a defence counsel who always goes to trial," Adler says. "Every case, no matter how insignificant it may look, I'm prepared." Criminal law is no place for dabblers. That was another Adler precept. "It's very easy to be a lazy criminal lawyer," he says. "Your clients have no idea what you're doing, and if you do nothing, they don't know. My reputation – I'm sure this is true – is for digging deep into every case, learning all its parts, the technical stuff included, and going to trial."

So what happened when Adler got the most technical case of all, a DNA case, when he was retained late in 1990 to represent Johnny Terceira in the rape and murder of Andrea Atkinson?

"At first, I threw up my hands," he says. "I had the public perception that, oh boy, DNA's infallible, the odds against Johnny are one in eight million or something. I'm in deep trouble with this one."

But almost immediately he rallied, and the familiar Adler style kicked in: absorb everything about the subject, about DNA, and develop a defence. It happened that, at the same time, another DNA murder case was in the works in Canada. The accused killer was a native of New Brunswick's Miramichi River area, a man with a career of violence named Allan Legere. In a few months of rampaging through the Miramichi after his escape from prison in the spring of 1989, he was supposed to have raped, tortured, burned, and murdered four people. Semen had been left at two of the crime scenes, and the Crown expected to prove that DNA from both spots of semen matched the DNA from a sample of Legere's hair. This evidence plus ties between Legere and the other two crime scenes would, the Crown said, convict the man.

Adler phoned Legere's lawyer, Weldon Furlotte, who had an odd employment record, twenty-five years as a CNR electrician, seven years as a criminal lawyer. What do you know about DNA? Adler asked Furlotte. Nothing much, Furlotte answered. But both men had the same idea about where they might learn something.

The two criminal lawyers checked into the Barbizon Hotel in midtown New York City and sat themselves at the feet of a Manhattan attorney who had a reputation as the leading DNA sceptic at the American criminal bar. He was Peter Neufeld, one of the lawyers in the controversial Castro case. Joseph Castro, a South Bronx janitor, had been accused in February 1987 of stabbing to death two people, Vilma Ponce and her two-year-old daughter. The police detected a small bloodstain on Ponce's watch. A commercial laboratory named Lifecodes tested the blood and said it found a DNA match with Castro. But, at a pre-trial hearing, DNA experts for both the prosecution and the defence, encouraged by Neufeld, got together in private meetings and condemned the procedures that Lifecodes had followed in its DNA work as careless and inaccurate. When Neufeld announced this development to the judge hearing the pre-trial, the judge tossed out the DNA evidence.

Castro was subsequently convicted on other evidence, but DNA testing had taken a small blow. That was a lesson Neufeld taught to the two Canadian lawyers, but Adler and Furlotte were also treated to a three-day crash course in DNA and its methodology from various New York microbiologists, geneticists, and other scientists. When Adler returned home, he was launched on a study of the new science that included a solid measure of scepticism. (Weldon Furlotte carried the same attitude back to New Brunswick; nevertheless, in November 1991, his client, Legere, was convicted, largely on the DNA evidence, of four counts of first-degree murder.)

On October 23, 1992, the trial of Her Majesty The Queen against John Carlos Terceira began in the Toronto Courthouse on University Avenue. The Crown had three lawyers at its table: Paul Culver, who led the prosecution, Frank McDermott, and Cathy Finley, who had spent the previous two years getting a grip on DNA, since it was she who would conduct Pamela Newall's examination-in-chief. Leo Adler was assisted by a junior, Jacob Stillman. And the jury, composed of five men and seven women, would take their guidance on the law from the presiding judge, Mr. Justice Archie Campbell.

The trial lasted until February 4, 1993, fifty-six days in court, opening with Paul Culver's assertion to the jury that Johnny Terceira had raped and murdered Andrea Atkinson in the anteroom at 33 Coatsworth Crescent, then abandoned her body in the boiler room, and that scientific evidence would place Terceira in those rooms doing those terrible deeds. And, from the beginning, as the Crown paraded its forensic experts to the stand, Leo Adler made his strategy perfectly plain: he attacked. Gone was the private, unrancorous Adler. Now he was the sardonic, doubting, derisive Adler. He pitched into the Crown witnesses and challenged them on everything from their working techniques to their ability to tell the left hand from the right. Adler intended to show that the case against his client was built on a collection of misjudgements, goofs, and shaky scientific procedures.

Phil Sudeyko got the full Adler assault. Sudeyko was the detective from the Forensic Identification Unit who had done much of the rounding up of clues in the rooms at the top of the Coatsworth building. Adler grilled Sudeyko. Why had Sudeyko made no record of drafts and wind currents in the anteroom, breezes from open doors that might have blown around the hairs and fibres on the floor, redistributed the so-called clues, introduced different hairs and fibres to the crime scene? What about the drop of blood that spilled onto the anteroom floor from Andrea Atkinson's body bag? Couldn't that stain have become confused with the stains that found their way to the scientists at the Centre of Forensic Sciences? And hadn't Sudeyko got his directions confused in measurements of the crime scene that he recorded in his notebook? Andrea's body lay close to the west wall in the boiler room. Sudeyko wrote "east wall" in his notebook and never corrected the mistake, never realized it *was* a mistake until the trial started. Adler wondered whether there were more such errors tainting the case against his client.

To correct the confusion over east and west, Adler brought into the courtroom his own blueprint of the boiler room, complete with coloured overlays, and that led to an exchange in court right out of Abbott and Costello.

Adler (speaking to Sudeyko): "The red overlay would be the corrected location, assuming that it's the corrected location which is the correct location?"

Sudeyko: "Yes."

Judge Campbell: "Just so I get it correctly in my notes, does the red overlay show the correct location or the corrected location of the items that were incorrectly shown west/east or east/west?"

Adler to Sudeyko: "Is that correct?"

Sudeyko: "That is correct."

Campbell: "Correct. Thank you."

In the same style, sarcasm mixed with disbelief, Adler got all over Keith Kelder after Kelder testified about the connections he made between the semen stain on the anteroom floor and Johnny

Terceira's blood type. Adler spotted two incorrect dates in Kelder's records and hounded Kelder, implying the mistakes were indicative of generally sloppy lab work at the CFS.

"The wrong dates made *no* difference in the results," Kelder sniffed.

But Adler had more. He stomped on the team approach in Kelder's lab. Kelder, he said, didn't perform all the tests to which he was testifying. Others ran many of the tests. Kelder merely *oversaw* the procedures.

"In this particular case," Adler said, "you rely on a supervisor to report, you rely on somebody else to fill out the top of the report, you rely on a whole bunch of people to do a lot of things, and perhaps you do a couple of things physically yourself, but apart from that, you rely on everybody else. Isn't that correct?"

"I have supervised that area for numerous years, *sir*," Kelder answered. "I know *exactly* what is going on."

Years after this courtroom encounter, Kelder was still a trifle steamed at Adler. "Leo's philosophy is the machine-gun approach," Kelder said. "He tries to hit as many things as he can with the hope that something will fall. He hopes to create enough smoke and confusion that the jury'll get lost. That frustrates me as an expert witness. I know what he's doing, and I want to blow the smoke away and say to the court, look, here's what I've done and here are the results I found. Someone has to stop this slide into confusion."

Jim Crocker, the CFS's hair-and-fibre man, testified to the links he found between hairs at the crime scene and hairs from Terceira's body and between fibres at the crime scene and fibres from Terceira's blue sweatpants. Adler concentrated on wringing a few admissions from the witness.

Wasn't it true, Adler asked, that Crocker examined dozens of fibres from the anteroom and boiler room that didn't relate to either Terceira or Andrea?

Well, yes, Crocker answered, but that was to be expected.

Wasn't it also true that *none* of Andrea's hair and *no* fibres from her clothing turned up on the clothes, including the sweatpants, that the police removed from Terceira's bedroom?

Sure, Crocker said, but the sweatpants and other Terceira clothes were probably washed between the day of the crime and the night the police seized the garments.

And wasn't it extremely curious, Adler asked, that *none* of the third kind of fibre in Terceira's sweatpants, the inner fibre, was found at the crime scene?

Crocker didn't think it was curious. He thought that, if the pants, held up by a drawstring, were simply slid to the floor, the soft, fleecy inner fibres would remain intact and not shed.

After Adler's cross-examination, Crocker felt sanguine about his testimony. "I have great respect for Leo in terms of looking at a case," he said. "He went through my notes in minute detail, and he spread the minutiae around. But he never really pulled it together into a cohesive argument that made anyone doubt what I'd found."

Adler worked his theme – that there had been all-round bungling in the Terceira case – on all the Crown witnesses, on the scientists, on the Homicide detectives, on everyone who had a hand in the forensic work. But his longest and most concerted attack came when Pamela Newall took the witness stand. For her, and for the centre's DNA unit, Adler saved his really towering scorn.

When Newall gave evidence at the trial, both examination-in-chief and cross-examination, she concentrated on a female juror, a woman sitting in the number-three chair in the front row. This woman was in her mid-sixties, small, wore a warm knit vest to court every day, and listed her occupation as school crossing-guard.

"I always pick a juror to talk to," Newall explained some time later. "I pick the one who looks the most nervous, the person who's thinking, 'I'm not going to understand what you're telling me. I *know* I'm not.' I keep my eye on that person when I'm giving my DNA lecture, and, if the light hasn't gone on in the person, I say the same thing in a different way. If it *still* hasn't gone on, I reword it a third way. Then, when I see the person has finally grasped it, I say, 'Now let me go back and make sure I haven't left anything out.' At the Terceira trial, I made eye contact with the whole jury, but it was the school crossing-guard I kept in mind. And I think I got her to understand. I know that one time, when Leo was being very sarcastic cross-examining me, very sneering, I made a really cool remark back at him, and the crossing-guard lady just about fell out of the jury box laughing."

About thirty minutes into Adler's cross-examination of Newall, the two had this exchange:

Adler: "And what do you say your lab error rate is?"

Newall: "Our lab error rate is zero."

Adler: "We'll see about that."

This set the tone. For eight days, Adler cross-examined Newall, and for all of that immensely long time, especially long if measured in the heat and contentiousness of courtroom hours, the two debated the efficiency of Newall's DNA unit. Sloppy, Adler insisted. Darned solid work, Newall maintained.

Adler pointed out that the unit's protocols, the guide to their procedures, weren't even typed. They were *handwritten*. Awfully casual, Adler said. And Adler uncovered dating on the computer records in the Terceira tests that predated the actual work on the DNA samples. The explanation was that the clock must have broken on the computer. Careless, Adler said. He asked if, at the time the unit started on the Terceira case, they had done a dry run to ensure that all the test techniques were in place. Newall said the dry run hadn't been completed. Slipshod, Adler said. But

Newall countered that, for three years leading up to the Terceira case, the DNA unit had been in training, had been studying the techniques at other DNA labs.

Not good enough, Adler said, and he invoked an analogy to school studies to make his point. "When you were working on this case," he said to Newall, "you were still in the midst of writing your exams."

Adler and Newall were more or less agreed that sizing the bands on an autorad wasn't entirely an exact science.

Sizing, or measuring, a band is the means that determines the band's position on the autorad. The measuring is done by the computer, and it calculates the distance from the well of the autorad to the centre of the band. As mentioned, the unit of measurement is basepairs. One band, for example, might be positioned at the 900 mark in basepairs, another farther up at the 1800 mark. Those two bands would be too far apart to make a match, and it's the computer measurement that provides the information, in basepairs, about their respective positions.

But the measuring, even by computer, is never bang-on accurate.

"There's a certain amount of wobble in measuring," Newall said in her examination-in-chief. "You don't get the same measurement twice. So we allow a 2½ percent difference around the figure of measurement. That could be a difference of about sixty basepairs."

It was the 2½ percent that Adler jumped on. It was too much, he argued, this 2½ percent. It extended the match criteria too widely. A measurement of a band that would normally fall outside the range of a match with another band could suddenly be jerked within match range by calculating in the extra 2½ percent. If, for example, a band was sized at 1000 basepairs, and the 2½ percent was allowed, then the range for match purposes would become 975 to 1025, which would mean that another band sized at 980 would become a match. This whole sizing and matching process,

Adler said, was imprecise and suspect. And another thing, he went on, what if the cursor on the computer wasn't accurately placed on the band it was supposed to be measuring? Suppose the cursor added on, or subtracted, a substantial number of basepairs? Wouldn't these two factors together, the inaccurate cursor and the 2½-percent tolerance rate, combine to throw the sizing out of whack? Indeed, Adler went on, wasn't that precisely what happened in two of the five readings for Johnny Terceira in the autorads for the DNA matches with the semen on the anteroom floor? Weren't the mathematics incorrect? And wasn't Terceira actually *outside* match range on two of the bands?

No, no, and no, Pamela Newall answered. The cursor was in the right position, the 2½ percent represented perfectly legitimate procedure, and the sizings for Terceira reflected accurate numbers, which led to authentic matches.

But later, long after the trial, Newall conceded that, because of an error she made in the courtroom, it was the matter of sizing that led to her lowest moment during the eight days of cross-examination.

"It happened on the last day I was in the witness box," she explained. "I had all the sizings in court. With some of the autorads, I had sized them twice. I had the original sizings and duplicate sizings. The numbers were slightly different. When I was giving evidence, I made a mistake. I picked up the duplicate sizings instead of the originals. This was after the originals had long since gone into evidence. I read from the duplicates, and the judge got terribly upset. 'Those aren't the numbers I have in front of me,' he said. 'What are you referring to? Is there some irregularity?' Everybody was angry at me. It was all terrible. I explained I was talking about *duplicate* sizings. All it demonstrated was that if you size a second or third time, the numbers aren't going to be exactly the same. *But* it was all well within the demonstrated position of the technique."

~

Another thing that was fundamentally misleading about DNA sizing and matching, Adler contended, was the business of making tests at five locations. Only five? Were five enough to lead to definitive testing?

Adler's point centred on the enormous length of DNA, miles of it in each cell of each person's body. That added up to about six billion basepairs per person. But DNA scientists, in looking at five locations along the total length of a person's DNA, were taking into consideration only something like one-tenth of 1 percent of existing DNA or approximately six *million* basepairs. Out of the six million, the locations themselves added up to maybe a couple of hundred thousand basepairs. Adler seriously doubted whether it was reasonable, fair, or accurate to base a match on such a minuscule sampling.

"Making a judgement with those numbers," he said, "is like peeking through a knothole to get your information."

Pamela Newall thought Adler's point was in the nature of a red herring. The facts were, she said, that readings at five locations produced results. They led to matches where matches existed and demonstrated that they were absent where none existed. Five was a fair number. And five, she said, was a scientifically proper number.

Adler brought into his cross-examination of Newall a report from the National Research Council in the United States. The report had been issued in the spring of 1992, long after Newall had completed her work on the Terceira case, and it dealt with population genetics. Newall had said in her examination-in-chief that the chances of someone other than Terceira leaving the semen on the anteroom floor were one in 1.8 million and that the odds against Terceira with respect to the semen on Andrea Atkinson's leotards were one in eight million. Those numbers, Adler argued, were absurd. They were drawn from out-of-date population databases at the Centre of Forensic Sciences, and the

NRC report, Adler said, demonstrated the wrong-headedness of Newall's numbers. According to the NRC, the one in 1.8-million figure should drop to one in 74,000, and the one in eight million ought to come down to one in 214,000. The prohibitive odds that Newall had so cavalierly waved around the courtroom, Adler insisted, represented a piece of incorrect hypothesizing that prejudiced Johnny Terceira's fair trial.

Not so, Newall said. "The bottom line in terms of a four-probe match," she testified, "is that it is a very rare event. You would not expect to see two people in North America with the same four-probe profile. It doesn't matter whether the numbers are one in ten thousand or one in a billion. They're both very rare events."

That's what she said inside the courtroom. Outside the courtroom, she was even more definite.

"What's the difference if it's one in ten thousand or one in eight million?" she said. "Either way, you've gone beyond reasonable doubt. Aren't we getting wimpy about numbers?"

Pamela Newall is normally feisty, funny, exuberant, and confident. But she wasn't exactly radiating those qualities – except maybe the confidence – when Adler finally finished with her.

"Leo used all the lawyer tactics," she remembered two years after the trial. "He stood as close to me as he could get. His eyes glittered. He shouted. He whispered. He glared. On the eighth day of my testimony, he reduced me to tears. That was my last day, the day I went back into court for rebuttal after the defence witnesses had testified. That day, Leo went beyond vitriolic. He was vicious. I felt like I was getting kicked by someone wearing steel-tipped boots."

Leo Adler said, "I shouldn't have cross-examined Pamela for so long. It meant there was too much DNA information for the jury to think about."

For the defence, Adler called witnesses who fell generally into three categories. There were witnesses who offered testimony that

put Andrea and Terceira, apart, in places and at times that contradicted the Crown's placing and timing. There were scientific
witnesses who offered views on fibres, on hairs, on DNA that ran
contrary to the Crown's scientists. And there was a final witness
who fell into a category of one – the accused, the kid in the prisoner's box, Johnny Terceira himself.

Among the first group of witnesses, two tenants of the
Coatsworth apartment building swore they saw Andrea alive and
well at times long after the last reported Crown sighting at 9:15
on the Sunday morning. One, a woman in her twenties, remembered she'd been washing clothes in the building laundry room
when she noticed Andrea glide past on a tricycle. It was, the
woman thought, 10:30 A.M. A boy, eight years old in October
1990, testified that he saw Andrea in the Coatsworth playground.
When? "At lunch-time." That hour dovetailed neatly for the
defence with testimony from Terceira's mother. She said her
Johnny definitely arrived home at eleven on the long-ago Sunday
morning that meant so much.

And then there was one other defence witness who produced
evidence of a different sort that might exculpate Terceira. The
witness was a locksmith. He'd studied the lock on the boiler-room
door. "The lock has been broken into," the locksmith testified in
answer to Adler's questions. Since Terceira had a key that opened
the lock, the implication was that another person, an outsider,
someone without a key, had forced his way into the boiler room.
Was the outsider the real killer? Adler hoped the jury would at
least think the possibility of a lurking, lock-breaking stranger
raised a reasonable doubt about Johnny Terceira's guilt.

Adler had also been bothered by the Crown evidence of Dr. Noel
McAuliffe, the pathologist who performed the autopsy on Andrea
Atkinson.

"McAuliffe said she died of asphyxia," Adler explained a couple
of years after the trial. "That just meant she stopped breathing.

But why? There was no evidence she was smothered or strangled. The cause of death is still the sleeper issue in the case."

At the trial, with his first scientific witness, Adler suggested an explanation for Andrea's death. The witness was a pathologist from Vancouver with a terrific set of qualifications. James Ferris, a native of Belfast, was both professor of forensic pathology at the University of British Columbia and head of forensic pathology at Vancouver General Hospital. He had been involved over his impressive career in many difficult cases, including, most spectacularly, the famous "dingo" murder in Australia, a case that was eventually recounted in the movie *A Cry in the Dark*, starring Meryl Streep.

The case began in 1980, when the baby daughter of a couple named Chamberlain disappeared during a family camping trip near Ayers Rock in the Australian outback. The explanation of the mother, Lindy Chamberlain (the Meryl Streep character in the movie), was that, as she had witnessed with her own eyes, a wild dog or dingo had seized the child, Azaria, and carried her into the outback. Azaria's body was never found, though her bloodstained jumpsuit and underwear were recovered five kilometres from the site of the Chamberlain camp.

The Crown did not believe Lindy's tale, and put her on trial for the murder of her own child, a trial that turned into a forensic scientist's delight – or nightmare. The Crown's theory turned on a scenario that featured Lindy taking Azaria into the front seat of the family car, slitting her throat, sprinkling drops of blood around the campground to back up the story of the baby-seizing dingo, then disposing of the body and planting the jumpsuit and underwear five kilometres away. Forensic scientists testified in support of the Crown. These experts reported their finding of bloodstains under the dashboard in the Chamberlains' car, more bloodstains in the shape of human fingers on Azaria's jumpsuit, and cuts in the jumpsuit that were more likely to have been made by scissors than a dingo's teeth. The jury accepted the Crown's evidence and convicted Lindy of her daughter's murder.

But enough doubt of Lindy's guilt lingered that, in 1986, the Australian government appointed a royal commission to take another look at the case. That was when James Ferris got into the act. He was at the time president of the International Association of Forensic Scientists, and the royal commission asked him to review, at a remove of almost six years, the forensic evidence in the case. Ferris found much to criticize about the conclusions of the experts who testified at the trial. The blood under the dashboard, Ferris said, wasn't distributed in the sort of pattern that he would have expected if Lindy had slashed Azaria's throat inside the car. And anyway, Ferris went on, perhaps the spots under the dashboard weren't even blood; they could have been spots of insulating material that had been used in the manufacture of the vehicle. Nor did Ferris subscribe to the notion that the bloodstains on Azaria's jumpsuit had come from contact with bloody fingers. The stains could have resulted from contact with many other sorts of bloody surfaces.

Ferris summed up by reporting that, while he couldn't find much evidence that a dingo had carried off Azaria, he had serious doubts that the Crown's theory of Lindy's guilt was supported by the forensic testimony. When the royal commission took into consideration Ferris's report, along with all the other presentations it heard, it exonerated Lindy Chamberlain. She later collected from the government a million dollars in damages for her wrongful conviction.

As a defence witness in the Terceira case, John Ferris had a theory about the cause of death. Maybe it was more than a theory, maybe a plausible explanation. Ferris had never, of course, examined Andrea's body, but he'd read all the documents, especially

McAuliffe's autopsy report. And he thought the skull fracture held the answer.

McAuliffe had dealt with Andrea's fractured skull in his testimony, had reasoned that, after death, the pressure of interior gases had cracked the little girl's skull along its growth points.

No way, James Ferris said in his testimony.

What might have happened, he went on, what easily could have happened, was that Andrea had an epileptic fit. But even before the fit, as Ferris explained it, her skull may have been damaged; there was evidence she'd taken a tumble in the Coatsworth playground in August 1990, and the fall might have brought about an undetected skull fracture (though there was nothing about such a possibility in the report made during Andrea's brief visit to a hospital after the playground tumble). Then, according to Ferris's surmise, during the sexual assault on Andrea, she suffered an epileptic fit, her already-damaged skull flew apart, and she died. Ferris's explanation didn't point a finger at anyone, didn't identify the man who made the assault on Andrea that triggered the fit that led to her death. But that wasn't the purpose of Ferris's testimony. He was in court to present a scenario, a cause of Andrea's death, that made the Crown look bad. Adler thought Ferris succeeded.

"Our pathologist," Adler said, "did a pretty good job of discrediting their pathologist."

An American scientist named Martin King was the defence's fibre expert. King came to court equipped with a grand computerized format. It was intended to address the point that none of the third fibres from Johnny Terceira's sweatpants, the soft and fleecy inner fibres, were found on the floor of the anteroom. King's version of the fibre evidence, mounted on a computer screen, supposedly demonstrated that such a likelihood was impossible, that the inner fibres would have fallen in thick clouds if Terceira had removed his sweatpants to attack Andrea. According to King, no inner fibres on the floor meant no rape by Terceira. And as for the other two fibres from the sweatpants that *were* found on the anteroom floor, there was a ready explanation for that. They dropped off Terceira's pants during the man's many visits to the Coatsworth sixth floor to smoke his daily rations of hash and marijuana.

Adler thought King's testimony amounted to "a fairly good defence on the fibres." Jim Crocker didn't think so. Crocker, the CFS's fibre-and-hair specialist, was getting a little tired of hearing this talk of snowstorms of inner fibres hitting the floor. As he had always said, he was sure it was the *drawstring*. The drawstring that held up Terceira's sweatpants meant that he had only to slide the pants down his legs to remove them, a motion that would leave the inner fibres intact. Terceira could have raped Andrea without disturbing a single one of those soft, fleecy fibres.

Jim Crocker had already been through a small tiff with the defence's hair expert, George Neighbor, a scientist who ran a forensic consulting firm in New Jersey. Long before the trial, Neighbor visited the CFS on behalf of the defence to examine the hair evidence that Crocker had accumulated. Neighbor fixed on one of the two hairs that Crocker had discovered stuck in the greyish smear on the anteroom floor. The hair was damaged. Crocker called it larvae damage, inflicted by insects. Oh no, Neighbor said, mechanical damage, inflicted by someone's foot or something of a similar nature. And that was what Neighbor wrote in his report: hair found in greyish smear, mechanical damage.

None of this represented a really significant point. It was more like a quarrel between technicians, and nothing much turned on it except Jim Crocker's strong sense of the rightness of his own analysis. He brought George Neighbor back to the CFS for another pre-trial visit and took him once more through the evidence. This time, a light-bulb went on over Neighbor's head. He looked at the damaged hair in the greyish smear, and he changed his mind. It wasn't mechanical damage. It was insect damage, just as Crocker had been saying all along.

In Neighbor's court testimony, he didn't find a whole lot more to disagree with in Crocker's findings. Of all the hairs on the anteroom floor and on Andrea's clothing that Crocker identified as coming from Johnny Terceira, from his scalp or his groin, Neighbor challenged only two. Those two, he argued, weren't Terceira's. The rest, he conceded, were Terceira's.

Adler got stood up by his first choice as the defence's DNA expert. The man was Peter Distacchio, a New York microbiologist, a scientist vastly experienced in DNA analysis, a frequent witness for the defence in DNA cases. Adler had met Distacchio and learned much from him during the three-day crash course that Adler and Weldon Furlotte had embarked on in Manhattan at the very beginning of the Terceira case. Impressed by Distacchio, Adler lined him up for Terceira's trial. Distacchio was on side, ready to demolish the Crown's DNA evidence. But three months before the trial's opening day, Distacchio begged off. Sorry, too busy. Adler had to scramble for a new DNA witness.

He came up with Randell Libby, a molecular geneticist from the University of Washington. Adler needed an expert who would put the knock on Pamela Newall's handling of DNA, and Libby set out to deliver the goods. He pronounced Newall's work "not done as carefully as one would like to have seen." He said he had "serious problems in the degradation of the sample" of DNA taken from the semen on Andrea's leotards. He criticized Newall for running tests that matched the DNA from the semen on the leotards to the DNA from the semen on the anteroom floor, rather than matching the DNA on the leotards directly to Terceira's DNA.

And he challenged Newall on the sizing of at least one band on the autorads for the DNA from the anteroom semen.

On that last point, Libby was echoing Adler's cross-examination of Newall on the sizings. Libby got specific by calling into question Newall's reading on the fourth band. He said that, when he did his mathematics and put his cursor in the right place for the fourth band, he didn't get a match between Terceira and the semen on the floor. Terceira, he said, was outside the match range.

But, to the Crown, Libby, with all his criticisms of Newall, was vulnerable on one significant level. Libby had never done hands-on DNA testing, had never performed his own DNA sampling. He was testifying strictly as a scholar of the science. Libby insisted that this was sufficient, that DNA wasn't so esoteric that only scientists with lab experience should he listened to. But Cathy Finley for the Crown, cross-examining Libby, leaped on his supposed lack of credentials and pressed him on his real reasons for testifying in the case. Libby's motives, Finley implied, were monetary. How much had Libby been paid to appear as a witness for the defence in various DNA cases in North America between 1989 and 1992? Finley was asking the question because she knew the answer. Libby had been paid $275,000.

Adler was furious at the Crown. "I resented that whole approach," he said later. "Unless you can show a man changes his testimony according to what he is getting paid, then the point is improper and invalid."

Adler had one more DNA witness, and this fellow got similar treatment from the Crown. Lawrence Mueller was a population geneticist from California, and his role at the trial was to back up the argument about numbers that Adler had made in his cross-examination of Newall. The likelihood of finding another DNA match in the Terceira case, Mueller repeated, wasn't one in 1.8 million, as Newall had testified, or one in eight million. It was more like one in fifty thousand. When Mueller finished his examination-in-chief, the Crown took a crack at his reasons for testifying, and, as with Libby, left the impression that money explained everything. Mueller and Libby were a couple of DNA guns for hire.

Adler blew his stack. He was indignant at the treatment of his DNA witnesses, and he saw the fine hand of no less an institution than the FBI behind the Crown's tactics.

"The FBI is very active in promoting the acceptability of DNA evidence in court," Adler explained later. "So they're also active in criticizing scientists who question DNA and who testify for the defence in DNA trials. The FBI gets transcripts of testimony by these witnesses and sends them to prosecutors in later cases where the same witnesses are going to testify. My people in the Terceira case, Libby and Mueller, were cross-examined from transcripts of their American cases. The thing I learned in this trial is that the DNA community is very small. The FBI labs hire people who get hooked to the police way of operating. These people are trained to be prosecution witnesses. And they have the time to prepare and to testify. Their situation is completely different from DNA defence witnesses, who are mainly university teachers and have other responsibilities. The defence witnesses really get hit hard. Their tax returns are scrutinized, things like that. One of my DNA witnesses in the Terceira case was a British citizen teaching in the United States, and he was cross-examined on his immigration status. That kind of approach was just intended to make the jury react against my people. It wasn't dealing with DNA and its meaning in the case."

To put Johnny Terceira on the witness stand or to let him sit mute? That was the question Adler batted around as the trial neared its end. He weighed arguments on both sides. Jurors liked to hear the accused speak in court. Otherwise, they suspected the accused might be concealing a guilty secret. On the other hand, if Adler's cross-examinations had punched large holes in the Crown's case, if he'd made the scientific evidence against Terceira sound far-fetched or élitist or possibly mistaken, if his own scientists came across as delivering more user-friendly material than the Crown's gang from the CFS, then there might be no need for Terceira to testify. And what of the kid himself? Would he have a positive influence on the jurors – or at least not register with them as a sleaze and a dissembler?

On the last count, Adler had no real doubts. "Johnny was very young," he said long after the trial. "But he was always consistent in terms of his innocence. He told me right off of his concealing from the police his finding the body before the official discovery. He was the perfect client in many respects."

And Terceira looked okay, not like the foul-mouthed punk that Crown testimony often made him seem. His two years in jail awaiting trial – he'd been denied bail – helped him shake some of the ravages of bourbon and crack. He was twenty now, seemingly a gentler version of his former self. His hair was still a little weird, in cascades of black tresses. But in a suit and tie, with a soft smile, he'd more than get by.

So Adler called Terceira as a witness in his own defence.

"How do you feel taking the stand?" Adler asked.

"Nervous," Terceira answered. "I had nothing to do with her death. I don't know what else to say."

That was about all Adler really wanted of his client, just to get Terceira's denial from his own lips in front of the jury. This wasn't *Perry Mason*, and the boy wasn't a silver-tongued orator. Just a simple denial would do. Plus one other thing, perhaps, and Adler asked it: why hadn't Terceira told the police that he stumbled on Andrea's body in the boiler room?

"I just didn't want them to know what I was doing up there," Terceira said. "I was stupid. I made a mistake."

On cross-examination, Paul Culver for the Crown didn't spend much time with Terceira, either.

"It's more complicated, isn't it," he asked, "to explain how your semen got on the floor and the little girl's leotards?"

"It ain't mine."

"How did your hair and fibres get on Andrea's body?"

"I don't know."

Culver was through. It was probably going to be science, he knew, and not anybody's denials, not Johnny Terceira's plea that he'd been young and dumb, that would decide this case.

Leo Adler is in court most working days of his life. Among his cases, he averages one murder trial each year. He's intelligent, perceptive, and tenacious (just ask Pamela Newall). He's an old hand at reading the mood of judges, juries, and courtrooms, and at the end of the Terceira trial, at the very end, he said this:

"It was the DNA that did Johnny in. I had that sense in the courtroom."

After all the witnesses had finished testifying, after the Crown and Adler had delivered their closing addresses, after Judge Archie Campbell had given his final instructions, the jury had gone out on Tuesday morning, February 2, 1993, to make its decision. It had spent twenty-three hours in deliberations, and, on Thursday, it had returned to the courtroom and announced its verdict on Johnny Terceira.

Guilty of murder in the first degree.

Adler thought the DNA evidence explained the jury's verdict, and though he disagreed with that rationale – "DNA wasn't worthy of swinging the case because you can play games with numbers" – he understood why DNA would motivate the jury. And it didn't, in Adler's view, have anything to do with science.

"This jury," he said, "was susceptible to ignoring the quarrel in the DNA community, the differences between Pamela Newall's view and the views I brought out in my cross-examination and in my witnesses' testimony. The jury was susceptible to ignoring the alibi that Johnny's mother gave him. It was susceptible to ignoring the absence of the third fibres from Johnny's sweatpants on the floor. It was susceptible to ignoring the possibility that another person broke into the locked boiler room. It was sus-ceptible to ignoring all of those possibilities. Why? Because they wanted to avenge this sweet little girl, and DNA was a way of doing it. DNA, this wonderful, perfect new science, gave the jury a way to convict a man for this terrible crime."

Adler paused.

"When you have the death of a child, the jury wants *someone* to go down for it. DNA showed how."

DNA,
The Future of Forensics?

On a sunny late-May morning in 1995, sitting behind a desk on the fourth floor, the biology floor, at the Centre of Forensic Sciences, Wayne Murray was calculating where the Johnny Terceira case should be positioned as a piece of DNA history.

"Probably in the Dark Ages," Murray said. "In terms of how far we've come in the science, in terms of how many people around here work on DNA now, what's happened since Terceira is that DNA analysis itself has got a ton more sophisticated, and the whole field of forensic biology is turning into a DNA-specific deal."

Wayne Murray is the Keanu Reeves of DNA, tall, dark, drop-dead handsome, a speedy talker, and – and this sets him apart from some of the characters Keanu Reeves plays in the movies – smart as a whip. Murray came out of McMaster University in Hamilton, Ontario, with a PH.D. in molecular biology in the spring of 1991. "I didn't know a thing about forensics," he says, "but I knew a lot about DNA." That spring, the DNA unit at the CFS comprised one scientist, Pamela Newall, and one technician, Colin McAuley, and both were prepping furiously for the preliminary hearing in the

Terceira case. This was the time and situation when Wayne Murray signed on as the unit's third member.

"Compare that with the way things are now," Murray said from his desk, waving a hand to encompass the labs on the biology floor. "We're in the process of converting this whole place, thirty-five people, into one massive DNA unit."

Murray ticked off the numbers as of May 1995: five scientists who take DNA cases to court, six technicians who perform DNA analysis in the lab, eleven technicians and scientists who are in training to handle DNA testing and testifying.

"These eleven people are forensic biologists who are being turned over from other kinds of testing to DNA," Murray said. "We're getting out of the conventional systems like ABO blood typing. The RCMP lab hasn't done ABO in a year, and soon we won't either. It's because DNA has greater discriminating power than the old systems. DNA's more stable. It's more certain in the result."

Much of the certainty springs from the improvement in existing DNA techniques. For example, where scientists were once limited to five probes or tests in a single piece of DNA, now they go for seven probes. "A seven-probe match," Murray says, "is the same as saying there isn't another person in the whole population of the entire world who matches that sample."

And even more of the certainty is the result of new techniques and sciences. Mitochondrial DNA, for instance. At first, scientists worked only with DNA that came from one place in a cell – from the cell's nucleus. Now they've found another kind of DNA that exists in different locations in the same cell. This is mitochondrial DNA, and there's more of it than of nucleid DNA, from one hundred to a thousand times more per cell. What this means is that scientists can work, for example, on the mitochondrial DNA in a shaft of hair. With nucleid DNA, scientists need a shaft with a root to get a result. With mitochondrial DNA, just a couple of stray rootless hairs will do. If a sexual assailant leaves a hair on his victim's sweater or pillow or skin, chances are strong that DNA scientists can type him in a flash.

Then there is, most compellingly, PCR. It's the second and most recent of the DNA techniques. First came RFLP, for restriction fragment length polymorphism, the technique that Pam Newall used in the Terceira case. And now there is also PCR, for polymerase chain reaction. (The CFS had acquired three PCR systems by mid-1995.)

One of two tremendous benefits of PCR is that, unlike RFLP, it can operate with tiny samples of DNA. Extremely tiny. Minuscule. Not just the size of the head of a pin, but the size of the *tip* of the pin. In one 1994 case in the United States, the FBI lab identified a kidnapper when forensic scientists, using PCR, got a DNA reading off the faint and fading traces of saliva on the licked flap of an envelope containing a ransom note.

The second advantage of PCR lies in its ability to read DNA that comes to the scientists in terrible condition – degraded DNA, abused DNA, DNA that has been left out in the rain for weeks. This is because PCR can work with such small amounts. Where RFLP might need fifty miles of DNA to draw a result, PCR can do the job with a half mile, a length that's much easier to pick out of a degraded segment.

"The DNA has to be in really bad shape for PCR not to work," Wayne Murray says. "So PCR gives us an increased span of cases we can look at and get a result from, and that means, down the road, when we come into court, we're getting a bunch more guilty pleas. Criminals realize they're not going to beat the new DNA."

Allan Rock has looked at crime solving's future, and, like Wayne Murray, he sees DNA. Rock agrees it is perhaps the most productive tool that criminal-justice people in Canada have ever acquired, and he wants to put in place legislation to make it easier for the police and the forensic laboratories to work with this marvellous piece of anti-crime science. As Canada's minister of justice and attorney-general, Allan Rock is just the man to get the job done.

Rock brought to the House of Commons in the summer of 1995 a piece of legislation that will affect DNA and its use on one profound level: it will allow police, in the course of an investigation into a violent offence, to take biological samples – blood, hair, saliva, mouth swabs – from a suspect without the suspect's consent.

As forensic scientists will tell you, the problem in DNA cases in the early 1990s was in obtaining "comparison samples." These were samples of any fluid from a suspect, a fluid from which they could extract DNA to compare with the DNA they took from semen or blood recovered at the crime scene. There was no shortage of the latter; the comparison samples presented the tougher proposition.

In some cases, Johnny Terceira's for one, the suspect solved the problem by handing over a blood sample, a hair sample, saliva, without question or resistance, without consulting a lawyer.

In other cases, the scientists resorted, successfully, to capitalizing on fluids that a suspect discarded in some manner, usually casual; one sexual offender was nailed when scientists extracted his DNA from the nasal mucus on a Kleenex he'd tossed away.

And in the mid-1990s, police were obtaining comparison samples from suspects under the authority of a section 487.01(1) general warrant. This section of the Criminal Code authorizes a judge to issue a warrant allowing the police to use techniques that would ordinarily fall into the category of "an unreasonable search or seizure in respect of a person or a person's property." To get such a warrant in a DNA case, the cops must satisfy the judge on many points: that the forensic lab requires certain samples; that the process of taking the samples will be painless for the suspect; that the suspect can choose which sample he'll give, a prick of blood, a hank of hair, just a messy old goober of spit; that the police will be so open and public about taking the sample that they'll videotape the blood pricking or hair pulling, even the one-man spitting contest.

At trial, lawyers for people accused in DNA cases now routinely raise objections to the ways police take comparison samples, especially the ones the cops get under general warrants. The sample taking, counsel argue, is a violation of the accused's various rights to privacy under the Charter of Rights. So far, these challenges haven't much impressed judges, and the courts have mainly placed a stamp of approval on general warrants as a means of obtaining comparison samples. Significantly, though, by mid-1995, no case involving section 487.01(1) and DNA had yet reached the Court of Appeal level, where a more scholarly examination of the whole issue might result in a finding that taking fluids from an accused under the general warrant provision did indeed violate that person's Charter rights.

At which point Allan Rock's legislation enters the picture. Under it, in an attempt to head off the courts, Parliament will legislate a specific procedure for seizing biological samples during the investigation into a crime. The legislation will cover all the bases, designating what degree of justification the police need to demonstrate in order to obtain the sample, which samples – blood, hair, saliva – may be taken, what medical and scientific conditions need to be observed during the sampling. The point of this part of Rock's legislation is this: if DNA is going to solve crimes that would otherwise remain a mystery, let Parliament lay down a process that gets the DNA and gets it right.

In the autumn of 1995, Allan Rock plans to introduce two more parts to his DNA legislation. The first of these is to create a national DNA data-banking system. The Identification of Criminals Act already allows for a reference bank of fingerprints from people convicted of crimes. Now the same principle, on a more sophisticated level, will be applied to DNA. People convicted of certain kinds of offences – murder and sexual crimes for sure, and possibly other violent crimes – will be required to give samples of fluid that generate DNA profiles. The profiles go into a computer system for possible future reference. Then, when the police have a mysterious murder or sex crime on their hands, with semen or blood left behind at the crime scene, but with no suspect, a swift run through the database of past violent offenders might yield a suspect. In the same way, the bank of profiles could revive and solve old cases that have wasted away in the files, baffling investigators for years. The overall idea is that, by profiling present offenders, the DNA will lead to the solution of future and past offences.

The second part of Rock's additional legislation will establish a series of controls over laboratories that carry out DNA testing. This is a step that looks mainly to the future, when private labs get into DNA in a big way. As of 1995, Canada's DNA work took place almost exclusively in three public labs: the RCMP lab in Ottawa, the CFS in Toronto, and Direction des expertises judiciares in Montreal. By contrast, the United States boasts hundreds of private labs – in the O. J. Simpson case, the prosecution assigned one government lab and one private lab to handle its DNA analysis. Canada is only beginning to see private labs edge into the field.

Vancouver biologist Terry Owen was a trail-blazer in this area, establishing in the mid-1990s a lab called Helix Biotech, which performs DNA work in paternity disputes and immigration cases and does some independent testing in criminal matters. Many more of this sort of DNA lab are coming on stream, including one in Hamilton, Ontario, run by John Waye, the whiz in medical biophysics and genetics who played a large part in setting up the RCMP's DNA lab. Indeed, Hamilton may be busting out as a DNA headquarters. Brad White, the chair of the biology department at Hamilton's McMaster University, runs a new DNA lab. But White isn't analysing human DNA. His subject is the DNA from

black bears, from moose. White is in the business of forensic
identification of game that hunters and trophy collectors may
have illegally poached.

"DNA," as the CFS's Wayne Murray says, "is exploding."

Jim Lockyer brings a touch of scepticism to his view of DNA.
Lockyer is a Toronto criminal lawyer, and he frequently defends
clients in cases where DNA results make up the most damning evidence against the accused. In style and personality, Lockyer is an
attractive mix of the academic and the advocate. Toss in some
humour, too. There's nothing Lockyer enjoys more than a good
argument, unless it's a good laugh. With these qualities, he'd
make an effective classroom lecturer or platform politician (as a
matter of fact, he ran for public office, both times unsuccessfully,
as an NDP candidate in Ontario ridings in the 1980s). As for DNA,
Lockyer respects the science, but, in his professional capacity, his
counsel's role, he questions the bias of forensic scientists who
perform DNA analysis on behalf of the Crown. "I think it's often
the fact," Lockyer says, "that scientists read the results they *want*
to read. They find the numbers that match the accused person
because that's what they *want* to find."

And then Jim Lockyer acquired as a client a beleaguered young
man named Guy Paul Morin.

Sometime close to 4:30 on the afternoon of Wednesday,
October 3, 1984, Guy Paul Morin's neighbour vanished. Morin,
who was twenty-four at the time, a short, solidly built man, with
pale skin, jet-black hair, and a perpetually composed air, lived with
his parents in the small village of Queensville, about sixty kilometres northeast of Toronto. The Morin property existed in a
constant state of chaos, the house in an on-going renovation
mode (Guy Paul doing much of the fine refinishing work) and
the yard strewn with automobiles in various stages of recovery
(Guy Paul handling the tinkering under the hoods).

The neighbours to the immediate south, the Jessops, didn't

much object to the disrepair on the Morin home front, mostly because the Jessop place wasn't itself a candidate for *House Beautiful*. The Jessop family consisted of parents Bob and Janet and two children, teenage Ken and nine-year-old Christine. Christine was a tiny thing, four-foot-five, forty pounds, with an overbite and freckles that gave her an appealing resemblance to Howdy Doody. It was Christine who vanished. One moment, she was buying bubblegum in the Queensville General Store; the next, she was stepping out of the store and, without a single witness, disappearing into what might as well have been thin air.

The police, mounting a search for Christine, almost immediately focussed on Guy Paul Morin as a suspect in whatever crime had been committed. It wasn't because Morin had a criminal record or seemed a shady character. Just the opposite. He had never broken a law, and he was entirely normal in an old-fashioned way. He was polite, private, thoughtful. He played the clarinet in three community bands, was a featured performer on tunes from the Tommy Dorsey and Benny Goodman songbooks. Guy Paul had no time for rock 'n' roll. That kind of taste in a young guy disturbed the cops. Three investigating officers wrote the same word in their notebooks to describe Morin: "weird."

Christine's body was found on December 31, 1984, partially concealed by brush in a field about fifty kilometres east of Queensville. The body, lying on its back, badly decomposed, had been beaten and stabbed. Christine's ripped shirt, the splayed position of her legs, the location of her pants and underpants to the side of her body indicated that she had been raped where she lay. Her panties, as it turned out, contained traces of semen.

Now the police fixed on Guy Paul Morin as the rapist and murderer almost to the exclusion of other possibilities. They built a case against him on fragments, supposition, and a set of anti-Morin feelings. They reasoned that Morin had had the opportunity to abduct and murder Christine, since he seemed to have arrived home shortly before the little girl was last seen.

(Morin insisted it must have been shortly *after*.) They thought it suspicious that Guy Paul didn't take part in the neighbourhood search for Christine immediately following her disappearance. They received a preliminary report from a CFS hair-and-fibre analyst named Stephanie Nyznyk that a hair found on Christine's necklace might be similar to Morin's scalp hair. And they figured Morin was just the sort of wacko, from a family of oddballs in a house that was never finished, who would commit a horrible sex crime. The cops charged Guy Paul Morin with first-degree murder on April 22, 1985.

Awaiting trial in the jail at nearby Whitby, the guileless Morin struck up acquaintance with a couple of fellow inmates. One was Robert May, doing time for fraud, cheque-forging, attempting to escape, and assaulting a guard. The other was a man identified on all court records as Mr. X, a criminal convicted of several sexual assaults. Both May and Mr. X rushed to the police with the revelation that Guy Paul had confessed the killing of Christine to them. The cops put May and X on their list of witnesses.

Meanwhile, Stephanie Nyznyk, the CFS analyst, perusing thousands of hairs and fibres from Morin's Honda, reported that five of the car fibres were similar to fibres found on Christine and that three hairs in the Honda were similar to Christine's scalp hair. None of the five fibres came from seat covers, blankets, or anything else in the Honda that was made of material. Nor did the fibres on Christine originate from her clothing. In short, there had been no transfer of fibres from the Honda to Christine, or the other way around. It seemed to have happened, no more and no less, that both the car and Christine had come in contact with an unknown material made of similar fibres. That didn't appear to be an oddity, not when the two people in question lived next door to one another and could be exposed to similar materials. Nevertheless, the police were happy to take Nyznyk's fibre analysis to court as possible evidence that Christine had been in Morin's Honda. And they likewise welcomed the evidence of the three hairs, even though Nyznyk had been able to work with only the middle sections of each hair, the roots and ends being damaged beyond analysis.

In early 1986, Morin stood trial for five weeks before Mr. Justice Mac Craig and a jury in London, a neutral site removed from the passions the case had whipped up in York and Durham regions where the abduction and murder took place. Clay Ruby, a counsel of massive self-assurance, an intense man, media hip and generally loathed by Crown attorneys, represented Morin, and he offered the jury a risky and perplexing double defence. He insisted that Morin did not commit the crime, but if he did, he was not guilty because he was mentally ill. Ruby summoned to the witness stand a clinical psychologist and a psychiatrist who testified that, based on interviews with Morin, it was their view he suffered from simple schizophrenia. Guy Paul was crazy, and if he murdered Christine Jessop, he should be found not guilty because he was crazy.

Guy Paul didn't think he was crazy. Neither did anyone who knew him. Mildly eccentric, perhaps. But crazy? Never. The jury, having seen and heard Morin testify at length in his own defence, earnest, rather sweet, and apparently normal, agreed with Guy Paul on the state of his mind. The jury had a choice of three verdicts: guilty, not guilty, not guilty by reason of insanity. They voted not guilty.

The Crown appealed. On June 5, 1987, three judges of the Ontario Court of Appeal handed down a split decision, two to one in favour of overturning the first trial and directing a second trial. One of the two judges in the majority wrote that Judge Craig's errors in his instructions to the jury on the issue of reasonable doubt necessitated a retrial. The other majority judge jumped on Ruby's double defence as grounds for a new trial. He wrote that Ruby shouldn't have been permitted to have it both ways, to say that Morin didn't murder Christine Jessop, but, if he did, he was mentally ill.

The second trial also took place in London, but with two crucial changes in the cast of characters: this time around, the judge was James Donnelly (son of Frank Donnelly, who defended Steven Truscott in 1959), and Morin's principal defence lawyer was Jack Pinkovsky. These two made a large difference in the length and nature of the trial – Pinkovsky because he was a passionate, intensely partisan, painstakingly thorough counsel, given to marathon cross-examinations and endless motions on minute legal points, and Donnelly because he came to look with clear disdain on Pinkovsky's courtroom tactics. The result was that preliminary motions in the second trial consumed the best part of a year and a half, and the trial proper, before the jury, began in November 1991 and lasted until the dying days of the following summer. It was the longest, most costly trial in the history of Canadian jurisprudence.

And it ended with a verdict of guilty. The jury heard essentially the same evidence that the first jury had heard: the timing of Morin's arrival home *vis-à-vis* Christine Jessop's disappearance, the CFS hair-and-fibre analysis, the tales of Morin's confession to Robert May and Mr. X. The case against Morin seemed neither stronger nor weaker the second time. And yet the second jury convicted. Why? Perhaps because the jurors resented the nine unexpected months in the courtroom and, blaming Pinkovsky, took out their resentment on Morin. Or perhaps because Morin, rehearsed to a fine tuning for his testimony – as he had not been in the first trial – came across to the jurors as less natural, less open, less innocent. Or perhaps because the jurors interpreted Judge Donnelly's charge to them, coming from a judge whom they plainly admired for his strength and patience, as an invitation to convict. Whatever the reason for the verdict, the last act was Donnelly's. He sentenced Morin to twenty-five years in prison.

At this point, through two trials, DNA had not entered the picture officially, as evidence. This was the DNA from the semen on Christine's panties, the panties that placed Christine's rapist and killer in the field where her body lay, the tattered panties that had been exposed to weeks of wind, rain, and snow. In August 1989, by court order, the small supply of semen from the panties was divided between the Crown and the defence for testing. The Crown immediately submitted their share to two American forensic groups, to the Cellmark Lab in Maryland and to Dr. Edward Blake's lab in California. Both used an RFLP technique, and neither could pull a DNA reading from the semen. The technology, they said, wasn't yet accomplished enough to work with DNA in semen from clothing that had been so abused.

The defence came closer to producing a DNA result. This was in 1991, before the end of the second trial, when David Bing of the Centre for Blood Research in Boston tried a PCR technique on the semen. In the system Bing used, the DNA appeared on a small strip of nylon. The nylon was marked off by numbers, each number signifying a type of DNA. Small lights acted as indicators for each particular DNA type; if the DNA of the person whose blood or semen was being analysed was, for example, 1.2 in the numerical language of the system, then the 1.2 light came on. Bing got a reading for the DNA in the semen on the panties. But there was a catch. The system he was using included a "C-dot." The "C" stood for control. It was a minimum-intensity dot, and it regulated the test. If the light for the C-dot didn't come on, then Bing wasn't free to interpret the nylon strip. So, although Bing had a reading, he was disqualified from using it because the C-dot light remained dark. The reading, he later confided, ruled out Morin as the man responsible for the semen in the panties.

Three years later, in the late summer of 1994, DNA again surfaced as an issue in the Morin case. By this time, Jim Lockyer was calling the shots for Guy Paul. Lockyer was Jack Pinkovsky's partner, and he took charge of the appeal of Morin's conviction to the Ontario Court of Appeal. Lockyer felt confident about his chances on the appeal, and the confidence had nothing to do with DNA.

"It was the fresh evidence," Lockyer says, glee in his voice. "We had fresh evidence to present to the Court of Appeal that would knock everybody's socks off."

One piece of fresh evidence came from the fibre specialist who worked for the Metropolitan London Police in England. It was this expert's fibre study that Stephanie Nyznyk and the other CFS people had used as their basis in doing the fibre work on the Morin case, and the London man swore in an affidavit that the CFS had got his study all wrong, that the fibres did *not* establish Christine Jessop's presence at any time in Morin's Honda.

Even better in the fresh-evidence department, Robert May, the jailhouse tattletale, admitted that he had lied at both trials, that Morin had never confessed Christine's killing to either May or Mr. X in the Whitby jail.

Shortly after May dropped his bombshell, the Crown, in the person of its lead counsel on the appeal, Ken Campbell, began discussions with Lockyer about taking one more crack at getting a DNA reading from the semen in the panties. It may have been that Campbell, seeing his case headed down the tubes on appeal, looked on the possibility of a DNA test as the last best chance to nail Morin forever. But his situation was tricky. It's the appellant on an appeal who is most entitled to introduce fresh evidence. Lockyer represented the appellant, Morin, and he wasn't wildly enthusiastic about going for another DNA test. The Crown, who was the respondent, not the appellant, and therefore not so entitled to introduce fresh evidence, appeared to want the DNA test desperately. Lockyer played it cool. He agreed that, okay, the defence and Crown would work together in ordering up yet another DNA analysis, but Lockyer tacked on a proviso: the scientists who conducted the test would have to guarantee that there was a strong likelihood of at last achieving a result from the test.

Lockyer and Campbell cooperated in choosing a team of three DNA experts. The Crown named John Waye of Hamilton as its representative. The defence picked Edward Blake, the California forensic scientist. And Campbell and Lockyer agreed on David Bing as the neutral third party. The tests would take place at Bing's lab in Boston, and, in preparation, all the scraps and pieces of panties and DNA were shipped to Boston: the bit that Blake had retained in California from his 1989 test, some stored at the CFS labs in Toronto, some that the police still held at their offices in Whitby, and the remains of the DNA left over in Boston from Bing's 1991 testing.

The three scientists got together in Boston in mid-December of 1994, and two key findings emerged from the meeting.

First, they determined that there was indeed enough DNA, when all the bits and pieces from near and far were collected in one spot, to justify another attempt at a test.

And, second, Edward Blake came up with a solution to what might have become an insurmountable testing obstacle. The problem began with the limited amount of DNA available to the scientists; there was little to start with when the panties were found, and the earlier tests had further eaten into the supply. In addition, the semen on the panties was riddled with what scientists call inhibitors and what laypeople call pollutants. These inhibitors or pollutants made it difficult to extract the DNA from the semen, and the process of extraction threatened to eat up the dwindling quantity of DNA.

That was when Blake came up with his brainstorm. He reasoned that there was semen on the panties that contained no human DNA, but was subject to the same inhibitors as the semen that did contain DNA. So, Blake suggested, why not inject anonymous DNA into the non-DNA samples and then develop the cleanest, least-wasteful technique for extracting the DNA? Once that technique was mastered, the scientists could use it to remove the target DNA from the semen, past the inhibitors, with zero or minimal damage to the DNA. John Waye and David Bing agreed that, eureka, Blake had it.

The three scientists broke for the Christmas holidays and

reassembled in Boston on Tuesday, January 17, 1995, to commence their testing. This was cutting it fine, since the appeal in the Morin case was scheduled for the following Monday, January 23. The scientists bent to the task, and late on the evening of January 18, Blake telephoned Lockyer. His message was that the three men had developed a system for getting around the inhibitors, that they were in possession of samples of DNA from the semen, and that they thought there was a strong likelihood, as Lockyer had stipulated, of at last getting a result. What they needed now, from Lockyer, speaking for the appellant, was authorization to proceed.

Lockyer put Blake on hold and telephoned Guy Paul Morin. "Go for it," Morin said.

Speaking to Blake, Lockyer added one more condition. He had earlier insisted that the tests on the semen be done blind. That is, he wanted the three scientists to get a reading from the semen *before* they tested, for comparison, the DNA in the blood sample that Morin had given them. First, the semen from the panties; second, Guy Paul's blood. The scientists had agreed to that, and then, on the telephone, Lockyer had another request. He asked that, once the three men began the testing process, they stay at it until they had a result. There should be no starting the tests on one day, then taking a break until the next. Nobody's nerves, Lockyer thought, could stand the tension of delay. Keep on testing, Lockyer asked Blake, until you're finished. Understood, Blake answered.

The testing, using a system within the PCR technique, began on the morning of January 19. At the lab in Boston, besides the three scientists and their technicians, were a couple of lawyers from Toronto. One represented the Crown's office, and the other, Michelle Levy, was an associate of Lockyer on the appeal.

Shortly before seven o'clock that evening, Levy phoned Lockyer at his office. "They've got a result on the semen," she said. "They've got a reading. Now they're starting on Guy Paul's blood."

Lockyer left the office and, with another lawyer on the case,

Joanne McLean, he drove to his house in the Beaches neigh-bourhood of Toronto.

"By this time, we were completely freaked out," Lockyer says. "There was nothing funny about it. We were *terrified*. Sure, we knew Guy Paul was innocent, but the testing had us on edge. Actually, the only person who wasn't scared was Jack Pinkovsky. When I told him about the testing, he said, 'Good, good. Now everybody will understand that Guy Paul is an innocent man.'"

At 10:33 that night, the phone rang in Lockyer's house. Joanne McLean got to it first. It was Michelle Levy on the other end. She spoke two words.

"He's excluded!"

"It was instant party time at my house," Lockyer remembers. "I made phone calls, and by 12:30, a hundred people connected to the case had come over to drink champagne. And the guests of honour drove down from Queensville, Guy Paul and his parents."

On the following Monday, January 23, Ken Campbell for the Crown stood in the Court of Appeal before a panel of judges presided over by Chief Justice Charles Dubin. Campbell said it was the Crown's position that, since Morin was not the donor of the semen on the panties, as established by the DNA tests in Boston, he could not have been at the scene where Christine Jessop's body was found. He could not have been the rapist and murderer. Campbell asked the court to quash Morin's conviction and enter an acquittal. Judge Dubin said the court would comply with the Crown's request. And then, in a gesture that Lockyer describes as "all class," Ken Campbell turned to Morin in the courtroom and shook his hand in apology from the Crown.

Next morning, Lockyer and Morin called a press conference in a large boardroom at the offices of the Canadian Bar Association in downtown Toronto. Dozens of reporters turned out, press, radio, and television, men and women with notebooks, tape recorders, and cameras.

"Guy Paul," one reporter asked, "how come, after all you've been through, you seem so relaxed and don't appear to have any bitterness or anger in you?"

Morin took a second, this man who, more than any Canadian, owed his freedom, owed proof of his innocence, owed a large piece of his life, to a powerful new crime-solving science that dealt in cells and basepairs, in DNA molecules, in genetic material of all sorts, and then, wearing the poker-faced expression of an expert standup comedian, he got off the perfectly appropriate one-liner.

"I guess," Guy Paul Morin said, "it must be in the genes."